LAUGHING AND CRYING ABOUT ANESTHESIA

A memoir of Risk and Safety

Gerald L. Zeitlin, M.D.

ISBN: 1463798067
ISBN-13: 9781463798062
Library of Congress Control Number: 2011914031
CreateSpace, North Charleston, SC

For Aideen

Allandale Publishers,
Chestnut Hill, MA and London England

Contents

Foreword

We wish to commend Gerald L. Zeitlin, MD, FRCA, for his generosity in assigning to the Foundation for Anesthesia Education and Research (F.A.E.R.) one half of all the royalties from the publication of his creative and entertaining memoirs entitled, "Laughing and Crying About Anesthesia, A Memoir of Risk and Safety". Dr. Zeitlin has made this gift as a tribute to honor the work of the foundation.

Denham S. Ward, M.D., Ph.D.,
President

Alan D. Sessler, M.D.,
President Emeritus

Foundation for Anesthesia Education and Research (FAER)
Rochester, MN 55905
July 2011

Preface

At least 40,000 people undergo general anesthesia each working day in the United States. Most patients accept the safety and efficacy of anesthesia. Fifty years ago when I began my career as an anesthesiologist neither of these attributes could be taken for granted. In the 1950s one in every fifteen hundred patients died or was permanently injured by the anesthesia *itself, irrespective of the surgery or the illness that brought the patient to surgery.* Today, what we so blithely label mortality or morbidity is too low to measure.

My professional lifetime coincided with this dramatic change – something for which I and my contemporaries will always be grateful. Nevertheless, much of what we still do is so frightening that I reflect this in the title of the book – Laughing and Crying about Anesthesia.

Doctors trained as specialists in anesthesia are called anaesthetists in the United Kingdom and anesthesiologists in the United States. In the United Kingdom surgeons are addressed as 'Mr.'. This is an historical hangover not worth explaining.

The word anesthesia applies to two different methods of obliterating the pain of surgery. Regional anesthesia means numbing the part of the body that the surgeon cuts or manipulates. General anesthesia means providing the patient with oblivion. When I discuss anesthesia I mean general anesthesia.

The book is intended for the interested non-medical reader – the person, if I may use the conceit, who enjoys the brilliant work of Drs. Atul Gawande, Jerome Groopman and Oliver Sacks: that is not to forbid anesthesiologists and other medical persons from 'LOOKING INSIDE' as Mr. Bezos and his Merry Amazons would have us do on his website.

Sensitive readers should omit Chapter 26 in which I relate instances of surgery before anesthesia.

Much of this book makes for nervy reading and so, just as in a Wagnerian opera you will find respite in the three Intermissions. Shorter versions of the first and second of these Intermissions were previously published in the journal 'Anesthesiology' and are reproduced here with permission.

We anesthesiologists should never forget that it is our privilege to have been invited in by our courageous, skilful and thoughtful surgical colleagues. Nor should we forget all those millions of people we call patients who trust their surgeons, and us.

Chapter 1 FIRST RUNG

My troubles began with ophthalmology but diminished when I discovered anesthesiology.

My father, a family doctor, wanted me to become a full-fledged eye surgeon, the cutting sort. Before I went to college and then medical school he sometimes talked to me about cataracts, glaucomas and a new operation, blepharoplasty. I faked interest and remained doubtful – until circumstance intervened.

At the Oxford Medical School I attended, starting in October 1954, we spent most of our time studying medicine, surgery and obstetrics but we did rotate for short periods through as many subspecialties as could be crammed in. In England medical education relies on a combination of lectures and reading and later, 'hands on' involvement in patient examination and care. Like most medical students I loved helping the sick when that was possible – the perfect answer to the old question 'Do you enjoy what you do for a living'? One meaning of Buddhist Nirvana is an enduring and transcendental happiness though I cannot truthfully say that's how I felt testing urine specimens from 28 patients for protein and sugar at 6.30 each morning.

The time came for the sixteen students in my class to rotate to the Oxford Eye Hospital for a month. The first lecture, quite logically, concerned the anatomy of the eye. The lecturer was on time, bald and stern. I sat in the front row, perhaps as a gesture to my father.

Dr. Dome pulled on a pair of rubber gloves and picked out an eye from several floating in a bottle of formalin standing on the lectern. They could have been expensive hybrid Spanish olives.

"Now boys," (we had one lady in our class but that was no impediment to most of our lecturers), he said, holding the glutinous sphere so that the pupil faced us,

"The best way to understand the structure of the eye is to look at a sagittal section. I'm going to cut it fore and aft for you."

Holding the eye in the rag duster from the blackboard so that it did not squidge out of his hand, he picked up a scalpel with a hooked blade and sliced it like cutting an apple from the top and then examining its seed case as seen from the side. He began to draw on the blackboard. Colors must have pleased him because he used purple for the lens, in reality a transparent sliver - except when it is affected by cataract and turns a cloudy yellow.

Before going to the Eye Hospital I had taken the precaution of buying some childrens' colored pencils from Woolworths. I copied the lecturer's drawings. He began at the front with the cornea and moved back through the eyeball with the lens, the iris, the vitreous, the retina and the optic nerve, each in a vivid color. The actual colors of living flesh are rather muted.

As I drew the optic nerve disappearing sideways off the edge of my notebook page and through a hole in the base of the skull on its way to the brain, a red splodge appeared on my page. For a moment this puzzled me. There may be better words to describe the appearance of a nosebleed dripping on white paper but I favor 'splodge'. I stole my handkerchief out of my trouser pocket and squeezed my nose in the approved manner. As soon as I put it away to start writing notes about the rods and cones, those important little sparklers in the retina that send messages about color and shape to the brain, my hemorrhage worsened: splash, wipe, squeeze, scribble.

The lecturer halted his declamation, carefully selected a piece of red chalk, broke it in two and threw one half at me accurately, scoring a bull's eye on my chest.

"If you insist on having the menopause in my class, please go to the back," he said.

My fifteen colleagues laughed out loud. I found nothing to laugh at. My morale was so badly damaged I never went back to the Eye Hospital, not once. I hoped would be no ocular questions in the Surgery Final examination. To this day I don't really understand the difference between myopia, presbyopia and hypermetropia, such elitist words. I kept this incident hidden from my father.

There remained many specialties for me to choose from other than eyes.

After graduation as a doctor each of us had to do a six-month internship in a medical specialty and then the same in a surgical specialty. The purpose of an internship is to isolate you from normal life by confining you in the hospital buildings with its patients for six months: the nights you were not on call were spent catching up with lost sleep. A hermit's life is easier.

I was fortunate to get the desirable post of House Officer to the Senior Consultant Physician, Dr. Alec Cooke.

Many of the patients I admitted when Dr. Cooke's team was 'on call' for emergencies were elderly men who had smoked all of their adult lives, many starting during the First War when cigarettes were handed out freely to the men in the trenches. When I met them in Casualty (Emergency Room in the USA) they were so short of breath that three or four words at a time was all they could manage. In between they struggled for breath and tried to cough up the sputum drowning them.

On one of my early on call nights Charlie M. appeared in the Emergency Room.. I had seen him in the Out-Patient Clinic a week earlier. Now, his respiratory distress was so severe his wife had to take over the conversation.

"Doc. Charlie knew he should not smoke again, but when he came home from the pub last night he was coughing so bad I knew he was in trouble. The last time here you gave him a lecture about the ciggies. He took no notice. I don't know what to do with him," she said.

I found Charlie M. struggling in the late stages of cor pulmonale; heart failure due to lung disease. His lips and fingernails showed a dusky blue color called cyanosis, the result of inadequate amounts of oxygen clinging to his red blood cells. I started an intravenous infusion containing digoxin, a heart stimulant, a large dose of Penicillin to treat the infection and a diuretic to reduce the fluid accumulated in his lungs that prevented the oxygen in air from entering his circulation. The nurse placed a mask over Charlie's face to supplement the oxygen he breathed.

Before he was sent to the ward I saw his neck muscles, normally quiescent, working to lift his exhausted ribs. I wrote up his history and the orders for the night and went to bed at 1 a.m.

That was Charlie's last night. His wife and a nurse sat with his body until the men came from the mortuary to fetch him. At the bedside early next morning Charlie's wife thanked me for trying. She held my hand and comforted *me*, by repeating,

"Doc. He would not listen to you about giving up those ciggies."

My fascination with how the lungs function began with these dying men. I still have the autopsy schedule for the day after a particular night when I was on call and admitted four men in their sixties and seventies, each of them with cor pulmonale. When I went down for breakfast I found two of the four names on that morning's pathologist's post-mortem list.

In those days we called their disease chronic bronchitis with emphysema - their lungs so damaged that the heart no longer had the strength to force the blood through them. We could not interrupt a vicious circle: the heart muscle struggling for oxygen and damaged lungs unable to supply sufficient amounts of that life-supporting and invisible gas. Their hearts failed in the night. They died peacefully because the gas we breathe out and which they were accumulating, carbon dioxide, was a mild anesthetic agent and they slipped into oblivion before their hearts gave up.

Sometimes the nurses phoned me at night to formally certify death. I listened to the heart and checked the pupils. Death is not a difficult diagnosis and young doctors soon become expert. I went back to bed on those nights because I was allowed to complete the death certificate before my early morning round of the patients.

Derek also had respiratory failure but his pathology, the cause, was different. It was his tragedy that indirectly led me to anesthesiology. He was twenty-three years old, tall and muscular and told me he hoped for a career as a professional golfer. He told an unusual story the afternoon I first saw him in Casualty.

"Each successive day out at practice I become more and more tired." He said.

Remember, in those days in England golfers walked between shots.

"No. The word 'tired' is incorrect. The further I go the weaker I get," Derek went on.

He explained that his daily routine of eighteen holes was now down to three or four when his weakness stopped him

His clear statement suggested the diagnosis. I asked him to look at the finger I held at his waist level and follow as I moved it up in front of his face and then higher. He could not. The muscles that lift the upper lids were too weak. That suggested myasthenia gravis, a failure of the chemical acetylcholine released from the nerve ending to stimulate its muscle to contract. The treatment seems simple, a drug called neostigmine that stimulates the release of extra acetylcholine. I gave him a dose by injection and in ten minutes he regained his strength. His anxious parents wanted to take him home. By then I knew enough that things were not that straightforward.

When I think of Derek I remember Jackie Kennedy's second husband Aristotle Onassis, the Greek tycoon. If you look at the photos taken late in his life and published in magazines such as Life you will see that the muscles of his forehead, the ones that lift the upper eyelids are contracted and the skin of his forehead is wrinkled. Weakness of the upper lids is called ptosis and is a hallmark of myasthenia gravis, although there are other causes. Two weeks before his death Aristotle underwent surgery for gall bladder disease. Doubtless he received a general anesthetic. The only description of his last days I have been able to find describes him as struggling with weakness until he died. One wonders if his surgeon or anesthesiologist recognized the cause, myasthenia gravis.

Derek came into and out of my ward for the six months that coincided almost exactly with my period as a medical house officer.

Myasthenia presents us with two main problems. The junctions between nerve and muscle become increasingly resistant to the neostigmine. If you reduce the dose they become more sensitive to it but that is a dangerous maneuver. He had to be admitted to the hospital for observation each time we tried it – his breathing might have failed completely when at home unobserved. Derek had a life-threatening form of myasthenia because it affected the muscles with which he breathed, coughed and swallowed. Twice he came in with pneumonia because of his inability to cough out his own secretions.

I happened to sit next to one of the anesthesia residents at lunch one day. I told him about Derek because I knew that anesthesia as much as anything concerned itself with lung function.

"Why don't you let us put him on a respirator machine up at our new centre, at the Churchill Hospital up the hill from the centre of Oxford and take him off the drug completely for a while. One of our machines will breathe for him. Dr. Crampton-Smith the head of the Respiratory Unit told us that 'resting' the neuromuscular junction this way sometimes allows it to become more sensitive to the neostigmine. It may save his life." He said.

Next day at ward rounds I mentioned this to Dr. Cooke. Dr. Cooke often guided his juniors with mantra.

"Be not the first to try the new nor the last to try the old," he said. At that time in medicine one did not contradict the boss. So, that was that.

On the last day of my medical rotation the hospital provided a free lunch for the house officers. Dr. Honey, my Registrar (Senior Resident in the USA) walked out of the cafeteria with me.

6

"I'm sorry, Gerald," he said, "Do you know that Derek died last night at home? Overwhelming pneumonia."

I went to my room to pack. I sat on my bed and cried. I am not sure why: perhaps frustration, more likely fatigue and sorrow. Derek had been denied a chance, perhaps only a very small one. I also thought that the anesthesiologists must be doing something remarkably powerful for patients with respiratory failure, the end stage of a number of completely different illnesses and injuries.

On my way to the station for a couple of days off, I stopped at the Medical School office. I had hoped to also get one of the top surgical house officer jobs. Instead I had been appointed as House Officer to the Ear, Nose and Throat (ENT) department.

"Ugh." I thought. "Tonsillectomies, myringotomies, sticking a tiny knife through the eardrum to release pus, and straightening broken noses in huge but terrified rugby players."

As it turned out the E.N.T. rotation led me further into anesthesiology.

After a few weeks on the ENT team my Senior Registrar, Dr. Roland Macbeth, caught me one evening as I tried to complete the day's paperwork.

"Get your coat and meet me at the front entrance. We're off up Headington Hill to where the gasmen are doing respiratory machine stuff. They have a crushed chest they're putting on one of their machines and you and I are going to do the tracheostomy for them. They'll pass their breathing tube through the opening we make." He told me.

What was a gasman? Then I realized he had used a vulgar appellation for anesthesiologists!

"I think I have done more tracheotomies than any other E.N.T Registrar in the country simply because the gasmen here have started what is probably the first ever Respiration Unit in this country. I think those chaps are really onto something," he said as his ancient Morris convertible struggled up Headington Hill into a wet headwind.

"The last time I went they told me the Danes started doing this new stuff for bulbar polio and then the Americans started a respiratory support unit. *They do the breathing for the patient until the cause of the respiratory failure resolves either by itself or with other treatments. It buys the time that is needed,"* I heard something in Dr. Macbeth's voice that suggested he was talking in italics. His words have stayed with me my whole life.

The patient was a young man who had crashed his car into a tree. He had few injuries other than to his rib cage. His chest had been thrown onto the steering wheel that cracked the five or six ribs on each side of his sternum, the breastbone.

Understanding the act of breathing is not as intuitive as you might think. Please imagine you are holding a closed set of fire bellows with the nozzle pointing up instead of down, the way you would if your grate fire is weakening. The two sides of the bellows are close to each other. This is similar to our lungs at the end of expiration, breathing out. Using the handles slowly separate the halves. Air rushes in through the nozzle to fill the space between them. This resembles inspiration, breathing in. The two halves of the bellows are stand-ins for our intercostal muscles, the muscle sheets between our ribs, and the diaphragm, the great domed muscle that separates the lungs from the contents of the abdomen.

Now imagine that one of the hard sides is broken and separated from its handle. It would 'flail' around and suck the air in ineffectively. This image explains why our young driver would die of respiratory failure without appropriate treatment.

There is nothing new about this. The English physiologist John Mayow described the idea three hundred and forty years ago:

"... *it is quite clear that animals in breathing draw from the air certain vital particles which are also elastic. So that there should be no doubt at all now that an aerial something absolutely necessary to life enters the blood of animals by means of respiration.*"

Our young man had a 'flail' chest. In the past, surgeons would have tried to stabilize the fractures with wires and splints but that was ineffective. That brings me to the dramatic history of artificial ventilation - a subject central to the growth of modern anesthesiology, and in which I and my colleagues became involved.

One way to understand this is to look at the effects of poliomyelitis before the vaccines were developed. The vestiges of polio epidemics that haunted us when I was a young man remain with us. Last winter in Florida, Yitzhak Perlman played the Beethoven Violin Concerto at the Van Wezel Hall in Sarasota, Florida. As a boy growing up in Israel he lost the use of most of his leg muscles to poliomyelitis. Now he lumbers on stage with crutches. The orchestra's concertmaster hands him his violin after he is seated.

As the last chords of the concerto crashed to an end the applause started vigorously but stopped completely as Perlman struggled to his feet and nearly lost his balance. I saw our neighbors hold their breath in fright. He made it finally, and taking his bows from his crutches responded to the applause. Those who *died* of polio cannot tell us their stories.

When the polio virus affects the breathing and swallowing muscles it is called 'bulbar polio'. I still have my 1956 copy of Price's Practice of Medicine, the standard textbook for medical students of my era. Here is a sentence from the section on bulbar polio:

"...respiratory embarrassment makes its appearance early and in the absence of artificial respiration in some form it may lead to a fatal outcome within a few hours of the onset of paralysis."

Embarrassment in this context is an evasive word. Try holding your breath until you feel in extremis – it's a horrible sensation.

If the handles of your bellows have broken off, that is, the muscles of breathing are paralyzed, there are only two remedies. Either, place the bellows inside an airtight box with only the nozzle protruding into the atmosphere and arrange for a pump to cyclically suck the air out of the box. That, in turn sucks air through the nozzle *into* the bellows. That method is negative-pressure ventilation as in the 'iron lung'.

Or, do the alternative: drill a small hole into one of the sides of the bellows, make a tight fitting connection to the same pump and inflate it with positive-pressure ventilation. That is what Dr. Macbeth and I were about to do.

Dr. Crampton Smith the anesthesiologist, wheeled the patient into a small operating room. He was breathing *for* the patient by squeezing the rubber bag on an anesthetic machine with only the oxygen turned on. The gas flowing into the rubber bag was attached to an endotracheal tube, a rubber tube passed through the mouth, through the pharynx, which is what you see in the mirror if you open wide and stick your tongue out; then on into the trachea, the main conduit from the exterior into the lungs. Anesthesiologists first started this procedure when caring for surgical patients in the late Victorian era but it only came into general use in the 1920s.

"If I stop breathing for him he goes blue in about four minutes. We have to sedate him heavily so he can tolerate the tube. If you chaps do the tracheostomy we'll hook him up to our new breathing machine and I'll be able to go home and get some sleep. The police estimate this bloody fool was doing nearly one hundred when he hit that tree," Dr. Crampton Smith told us.

Dr. Macbeth made a tracheostomy dexterously. It's a simple operation – a horizontal cut through the skin in the midline below the Adam's Apple and the surgeon fashions a hole in the front of the trachea where it runs near the surface. We passed a tube into the trachea through this hole that is called a stoma, inflated a balloon so it fits the interior of the trachea snugly and connected the outer end to Dr. Crampton Smith's tubing. Dr, Macbeth let me put in couple of sutures to fix it to the skin and then we were off. I remember thinking we two surgeons were the technicians in this situation and the anesthesiologist was the physician. Anesthesiologists are sometimes accused of the opposite.

As we left a memory returned to me. Two years earlier when we students were rotating through obstetrics (we had to 'perform' twenty deliveries for graduation) we were exempt from most lectures for two months because we lost so much sleep. One night, Terence and Alasdair and Jeremy, my three fellow students and I were hoiked out of bed and put on the hospital bus and sent to the Respiration Unit.

"I need you boys to squeeze this bag. The patient is a girl with polyneuritis. She cannot breathe on her own. She'll recover if we can breathe for her for a few more days. Our machine has broken down and I'll need you to do two hour shifts until we can repair it," Dr. Crampton Smith told us.

And that is what we did. Two hours on, squeezing the bag, one man standing by and the other two asleep for four hours. It was tedious and its significance did not sink in. My mind was on the baby business at that time. I had thoughts of becoming an obstetrician because I like little babies.

Years later I discovered the drama of the Danish polio epidemic of 1952. We students in Oxford were without realizing it re-enacting that drama. We were the repertory players stumbling through 'Hamlet' and all the while the audience was thinking of Olivier's performance they had seen in London five years earlier.

Nevertheless whether it was Terence or Jeremy or Alasdair or Gerald, we were all in at the beginning of a major change in medicine, the beginnings of Respiratory Intensive Care. That is partly why I became an anesthesiologist and is also why, you should hear about the polio epidemic in Denmark in 1952 and Drs. Lassen and Ibsen.

Imagine you are a 12 year old girl living in Copenhagen in 1952, late summer. You are getting ready to go back to school, excited with anticipation. One day you feel unwell and feverish and in a few days you struggle to breathe. Your parents are in a panic because they know of others who have suffered polio and take you to see Dr. Lassen the Chief Doctor at the Blegdam Hospital for Infectious Diseases. The nurses put you into an iron tank from Germany with only your head protruding at the top end. It is hot and most uncomfortable and makes sucking noises and machine noises that disturb your sleep. The windows down the sides open to allow the nurses to clean you and see to your needs and stick needles into your veins. You cry a lot no matter how kind they are. But the struggle to breathe is less because the machine is helping you.

One time after a few days when your exhausted parents think you are asleep Dr. Lassen comes in with another doctor. You listen.

"This is Dr. Ibsen. He is an anesthesiologist and he has an idea from what he does in the operating room. You should listen carefully to him," Dr. Lassen says.

"Dr. Lassen has shown me the blood tests that show the iron lung is not strong enough for your child. She has too much carbon dioxide, the waste gas from her lungs, even though the iron lung is working at maximum. We are losing the battle," Dr. Ibsen said.

You do not mind hearing this news except for how your parents will feel after you have gone away. They will be sad forever. But you are in a dreamy state and do not mind dying.

"Just by looking at her I can tell that she is floating away on a tide of carbon dioxide," Dr Ibsen continued. "I have a simple but radical method to save her life if you let me."

You see your parents look at each other. Then you remember nothing until you wake up suddenly. The front of your neck is sore and you are no longer in the iron box, just in an ordinary hospital bed and by turning your head you see a handsome young man with brown eyes, wearing a mask and rhythmically squeezing a rubber bag that seems to be connected to a tube attached to the front of your neck.

He smiles at you and says,

"I am Hans. I am a medical student and Dr. Ibsen taught me how to do the breathing for you by squeezing this rubber bag with my hands. When one hand gets tired I change to the other. You no longer need to be in the iron lung. As soon as the polio virus goes away in a week or two you will be able to write messages to us," he smiled.

"As long as the tube is in your neck you cannot talk to us. Soon after, you will be able to breathe on your own and we can take the tube out of your throat. You may have a little scar but a necklace will hide it and you will be well and as pretty as ever."

You have never fallen in love but you wonder if it is like what you feel now in your heart.

"I will be with you for four hours. Then I will sleep for the next four hours and my friend Alexander will take over the squeezing. The hardest part for you is to relax your need to try and breathe by yourself and let me squeeze the air into your lungs."

You feel completely secure now and when you wake next it is daylight and a man with a huge red beard, a modern Viking, is squeezing the bag and your parents are sitting there – smiling and not crying. Your life is in his hands is what your English teacher said was a metaphor. When you are dying of bulbar polio it is literally true.

In short you have a tracheostomy and you are receiving positive pressure breathing, the very opposite of the ineffective negative pressure that the 'iron lung' uses. The iron lung tries but does not succeed very well in mimicking the way we all breathe.

Years later you read what happened.

Dr. Lassen wrote,

"Although we thought we knew something about the management of bulbar and respiratory poliomyelitis, it soon became clear that only very little of what we did know at the beginning of the epidemic was worth knowing."

Dr. Lassen had been advised to consult Dr. Bjorn Ibsen, a freelance anesthesiologist at Copenhagen's university hospital. Lassen was genuinely skeptical about the contribution that Ibsen could make. Anesthesia was just emerging as a medical specialty and was held in low regard. Moreover, its activities were confined to the operating room. Here are the words of Dr. John Severinghaus one of our specialty's greatest scientists and also an historian.

'Lassen allowed Ibsen to go ahead because of the first 31 patients he had admitted with bulbar polio 27 had died despite the use of the 'iron lung' and similar 'negative pressure' devices. Nearly all the patient were young. Dr. Ibsen used the method already in daily use for the anesthetized and deliberately paralyzed patient on the operating table; in essence by passing a tube into the trachea and using 'positive pressure' breathing. The only difference with the polio patients was that they would not tolerate a tube through the mouth and thus received a tube via a tracheotomy, surprisingly much more comfortable for the weeks during which the 'bag squeezers' did their work.'

I and my student colleagues did just that for a few days in 1955 without realizing the importance of what we were doing. By the time I passed the final exams and became a doctor the directness and power of anesthesiology predominated in my thoughts.

Chapter 2 DECISIONS

In order to advance in a medical specialty in England in the late 1950s a young doctor had to climb up an ever-narrowing pyramid: similar to the steps of the Mayan temples in Mexico each stride required strength and endurance. The steps were named Senior House Officer, Registrar, Senior Registrar. Then came the 'Hillary Step' (now we're in the Himalayas on Mount Everest!) the hardest of all, to Consultant, with freedom to choose how much work you wanted to do for the National Health Service and how much private work. To climb this pyramid the junior doctor had to build a reputation for reliability and obedience and get good recommendations.

The hope was to crawl out of an unglamorous peripheral hospital and struggle, carrying a heavy banner with the words, 'Yes, Sir, No Sir; Whatever You Say, Sir' in large letters, across a muddy moat surrounding and then into the enemy's headquarters, a fashionable teaching hospital such as St. Bartholomew's Hospital, or Barts, as it was called by hospital gourmets. I struggled for six and a half years – until we came to America in 1965. The only excuse I can give for the above metaphorical mess is that they still, fifty years later, inform my nightmares and influence my waking emotional state.

I had two choices after I completed my obligatory House Officer year: either apply for the most junior position in the anesthesia department of my teaching hospital, the Radcliffe Infirmary in Oxford, where for better or worse I was known, or apply elsewhere for 'locum tenens' work at a peripheral hospital near London to fill in for vacation or sickness. These vacancies could be found advertised each week in the 'Help Wanted' section at the back of the British Medical Journal (BMJ). My more cynical colleagues said that each week they only read the BMJ from the back.

At this point in my career I had almost no money. I had once owned a 1936 Austin convertible, an automobile with a windshield wiper held onto the glass by a weak magnetic device and a length of wire connected to the battery. The canvas hood pivoted up at the back and was held onto the top of the windshield by two wing nuts. Once, driving two of my heftier colleagues sitting in the back seat to London to play in a rugby match against one of the London medical school teams, I had forgotten to tighten the wing nuts. As we reached the top of Headington Hill a gust of wind got under the hood and, acting like a horizontal parachute, lifted the front wheels of the car right off the road. As I slowed and it slumped down I looked in my rear view mirror. My two muscular buddies may have been heroes in the blood-streaked, ear-wrenching scrum in the mud on the rugby field but horizontal flight in a 1936 Austin convertible terrified them.

The car then slept quietly in the rain near the hospital incinerator, unstarted for my whole internship year. At the end of that year it did not, indeed, would not, start. I looked under the hood. The engine block was coated in rust. I sold it without guilt to a new medical student for sixty Pounds. He was a mechanical type.

Years later I learned the phrase 'net worth'. A medical diploma, a few clothes and 27 Pounds in the bank was all I had in the world. At that moment I owned about a dozen pairs of socks. All except two had holes at the heels and the toes. I had no one to darn them.

My mother said "Send them home and I'll do them".

But I was too worried the parcel would break in the mail and then everyone would know about my vices. So I went to Marks and Spencer and bought new ones. One of my fellow House Officers had told me,

"Never accept a nurse's offer to darn your socks. You might as well be proposing marriage."

At least I had no debts, thanks to generous Governmental payment for medical education. No one offered me career advice.

Aptitude testing had not even entered the language. You had to make your own mind up about what you wanted to do and find your own way.

I knew that the anesthesia department at Oxford was the only academic department of anesthesia in the United Kingdom and that Dr. Robert Macintosh, its professor was a leader in the specialty. Macintosh had come from New Zealand to London before the First World War. In 1917 he joined the Royal Flying Corps. The Germans shot him down and imprisoned him later that year. He was not injured. He spent the rest of the war escaping and being recaptured. That alone was enough to attract me to him.

Years later I discovered that H.E. Hervey a fellow prisoner and escaper, had written a book published by Penguin in 1940 that recounts their dangerous and sometimes hilarious attempts to escape back to England to try to fight again. Its title was 'Cage Birds'. Dr. Macintosh wrote the preface.

I found my precious copy on EBay and it's a great read, similar to a Boy Scout adventure, but real and true. It showed the mettle of these two men. I don't know what happened to Hervey but Macintosh became an iconic figure to the whole of our generation of anesthesiologists. We still use some of the equipment he invented.

After his professorial appointment Macintosh again displayed his adventurous spirit. He accepted the invitation to provide anesthesia for the American plastic surgeon Eastman Sheehan, who was volunteering his services to rebuild the mutilated faces of soldiers from the terrible but now forgotten Spanish Civil War of the late 1930s.

As I neared the end of my year as a house officer in the autumn of 1958, I made an appointment to see Dr. (later, Sir) Robert Macintosh. His secretary told me to go to his office at 5 p.m., the end of the working day.

I knocked on the closed door.

"Come in. Sit down," came a muffled shout. I walked into his narrow office and at the far end saw a thin naked figure standing outside a shower in a steamy cloud.

"Where the devil is my towel?" the figure said.

"On the towel hook behind you, Sir," I answered even though the question was rhetorical.

The towel said, 'Hospital Property. Do Not Remove'.

"I have to dine in my College Hall tonight," Professor Macintosh said as he put on his underwear. "But that won't hinder us. You will do the talking. I will listen. Why do you want to become an anesthesiologist?"

I was young and reasonably fit. I was twenty seven and he was sixty one but I could barely keep up with Dr. Macintosh as he marched into town. I told him about my contacts with the members of his department particularly those in the respiratory unit. It was the immediacy, the direct impact of anesthesia drugs and maneuvers on the patient's physiology (how it works) that fascinated me. He listened carefully.

"I hope you realize most of your life will be spent in the operating theatre, (operating room in the United States), taking care of surgical patients. Even there the need for and opportunities for improvement are vast. Things are not yet as safe as they can be and will be," he said. That sentence confirmed my intuitions and observations about the potential of anesthesiology as my life's work.

"Let me talk to Dr. Badenoch (the Dean of the Medical School) and if you are not one of the usual layabouts at the Royal Oak, I'll give you a try."

The Royal Oak was the pub directly across the road from the main gates of the Radcliffe Infirmary. They made an excellent shandy – a mixture of light ale and lemonade – a substance unknown in the United States. It kept many students in 1950s England afloat.

"Thank you very much indeed, Sir," I said, trying to keep my voice steady.

"Is my bow tie straight?" he asked in front of the main door of Merton College and marched off to the dining hall saying,

"My secretary will phone you tomorrow and let you know what vacancies we have. Good night, Zeitlin."

No application forms, no interview committee, no credentialing. Just a walk and a talk. Years later I discovered I had spent time with a great man and a clear original thinker who with a few others took us in the 1940s to 1960s from the lowlands of anesthesiology up onto the first plateau. I and all the others of my generation of anesthesiologists had the privilege of climbing the next hill.

The next morning when I phoned his secretary she said,

"Dr. Macintosh has an opening for you a year from now. He would welcome you. He said you should go to London and find a good teacher and gain some experience."

Off I went to London with my socks to undertake the 'breaking-in' route until I returned to Oxford a year hence.

Years later, after we came to America a certain Professor Epstein in writing an encomium to another famous anesthesiologist, Dr. Ray Fink, misspelled Macintosh's name thus - MacIntosh. Because of this accidental slight to my hero, I wrote a corrective poem. I hope that Professor Macintosh's shade looks at it as my tribute to his kindness when he interviewed me

Sir Robert Macintosh – not MacIntosh
To the Editor of 'Anesthesiology'.
> *Doc EpsteIn's eloquent Ink*
> *Lauds outstanding Ray FInk*
> *With praise and with prose*
> *That reminds us of those*
> *Like Sir Rob and Ralph Waters*
> *Who in laryngeal quarters*
> *Were joined by Doc Ray*
> *To make an airway.*
> *But Sir Robert might spy*
> *With perceptive i (eye)*
> *An upper case I*
> *Where a lower should lie*

The conflict between love and duty is one that has intrigued poets and philosophers since men first put their ideas down on paper. In London I was introduced to a beautiful, joyous young violinist with the slightest of Irish accents. I fell in love with her and never went back to the Oxford Anesthesia Department. Soon it became apparent she found me acceptable.

What's a fellow to do under these circumstances? Particularly as our two respective mothers had between them arranged the meeting. In those days one was to an extent obedient even though we were in our mid-20s. How things have changed in that regard in the last 50 years! But for me it was the least difficult and the best of all the choices that life so generously provides.

Aideen's career in classical music was blooming but the concert work either took place in London or was organized from London. Had we moved to Oxford it would have blunted her progress. In the world of freelance classical music, availability, often at short notice was all-important. In that way lay a similarity between our careers.

As for me: at that time London had thirteen medical schools and although none of the anesthesia departments were led by a great man like Macintosh they offered the possibility of experience, prestige and advancement, or so I believed at the time.

I proposed marriage to Aideen on the front (the promenade) of her home town, Westcliffe, on the Thames Estuary, after buying her a Rossi's Soft-Serve ice-cream, and she said "Yes".

Ten years ago, that is, 40 years after that affirmative moment we flew over the Atlantic to attend the annual meeting of the British History of Anaesthesia Society held in Westcliffe. During a break between lectures we walked on the front. They were still selling Rossi's Softserve.

Chapter 3 IN AT THE DEEP END

On a Sunday evening in early October 1958 I drove my Lambretta motor scooter to the North Middlesex Hospital in the outer London suburb of Edmonton. It was raining the usual English rain, persistent and confident. As I entered a roundabout on the North Circular Road I did the proper mild centrifugal lean but this time, skidded and fell. As I lay there in the wet gloom, briefly stunned, yet intrigued by the iridescent colors in the oil slick on the road that had spilt me, unseeing cars nearly ran me over. If they had succeeded it would have spared me a year of apprehension and sleeplessness, my first year as an anesthesiologist. With the insouciance of youth I recovered quickly, picked up the bike and drove on.

Six white columns, perfectly symmetrical supported the entrance portico of the hospital. On each side of the driveway I saw grimy brick buildings that had once been a poorhouse, like so many other hospitals in England.

"Sir. Good evening."

A tall thin man in a formal but undistinguished cap and a raincoat appeared, helped me off the machine and took my bag. He had been waiting for me just inside the main door.

"Come inside. You look a right mess. Did you skid on that thing? You're all scratched up and bloody. And your bike's all mucked up," he said.

Then he gave me an editorial that I learned during the coming weeks was his particular way.

"We get lots of messed-up knees and ankles in Casualty from these two-wheelers. They should be banned. And the National Health should pay you young docs enough so you can buy a car."

He guided me inside with a firm grip on my elbow.

"I'll park it for you as soon as I've settled you in. I'll take it round the back of the hospital so no one pinches it."

Did he treat all new young doctors this fatherly way or did I look particularly frail?

"Name's Charles MacIntyre. With a capital 'I'. I'm a London lad with a Scots name. I'm the Night Porter but I start my shift early on a Sunday 'cause it's the missus's night out. So I eat with the docs in their dining room and they don't mind at all."

There seemed no suitable rejoinder. I realized, as the American jargon we all admired in England had it, I was being 'put in the picture.'

"Pardon me for asking but … , " he hesitated a moment, "Mavis at the switchboard says you must be the new anesthetic doc and that your name is Doc Zeppelin. I told her to shut her lip, that it ain't funny. There's just Mavis and me and a few nurses here on a Sunday evening after visiting hours is over."

He paused and asked,

" Do you mind spelling your name for me?"

I did, while Mr. MacIntyre steered me down a long corridor. In some areas I could see two prior coats of paint in shades of yellow under the current peeling buff.

"It's Zeitlin isn't it?" He had pronounced it correctly the first time, an unusual event.

"Yes," I said.

At last I had been able to enter the conversation. We turned into a side annex.

"This is the resident docs' quarters."

He opened the door carefully, leaned in and gave me a glimpse of a small but well-furnished dining room. Two armchairs at the far end contained recumbent figures. They could have been Henry Moores they were so still. I knew enough about weekend call for house doctors to know they were either asleep or dead. Upon examination it would have been hard to tell the difference. As an anesthesiologist I would have to learn how. We turned back.

"Here's your room, Doc," MacIntyre said. "No telephone here, I'm afraid. They only just installed them in all the wards. Until then us porters had to run around the hospital carrying messages. Apart from that kind of thing the National Health is good, especially for us working people."

Charles MacIntyre had turned the absence of a communication device into a political statement.

"If they need you at night I'll come for you. The bathroom and toilet are round the corner. Please get yourself cleaned up. You got some blood behind your right ear. You don't want to frighten the patients come tomorrow morning. I'll put some supper together for you. How about a cheese and pickle sandwich on brown bread? There might be some Guinness left in the cupboard in your dining room."

He left. As I unpacked he returned with an envelope for me.

"This was in your letter cubby." Charles was more like a personal valet for confused house officers than a hospital porter. Later I realized we were his substitute children now that his had left home.

The note read, 'Zeitlin. Gyne. list. Mr. Harmsworth. Room 4. 8.30 a.m.' I peered at the scribbled signature and saw 'A.W. Mountford'. He was the senior Consultant Anesthesiologist at the North Middlesex.

I slept irregularly that night and in the waking intervals read "*Aids to Anaesthesia*" by Dr. Victor Goldman. I had finished medical school and my two internships at the Oxford Medical School a month earlier. I had passed my Final exams, so I should have known everything about everything. The Consultant in Anesthesiology at the Radcliffe Infirmary in Oxford, Dr. Joe Alsop, had given me his old copy of '*Aids*', published in 1946. I still have that slender volume, six and a half inches by four, less than half an inch thick with a dusky red cover, just right for any pocket. A few months ago I found a first edition on EBay, published in 1941 the second year of World War 2. On the title page the author's name is displayed as *Major* Victor Goldman. The text is printed on paper that looks and feels like an old newspaper, yellow and fragile.

Before the war Dr. Alsop had been a general practitioner in Burford, a comfortable village west of Oxford. When he was called up in 1943 the army had almost no anesthesiologists, so they told him he should become one. He taught himself by reading Dr. Goldman's handbook.

"You'll get by with this until you get some experiences under your belt," Dr. Alsop had told me. "When you've read this buy the latest edition. Just came out. Not much seems to have changed these last fifteen years."

From then on I obsessed about his 's' at the end of 'experience'. The book contained two-dimensional drawings of three-dimensional pieces of equipment that I had never seen, let alone touched. I was not too worried about that because as a child I had loved building cranes, tractors and long-range guns with my Meccano set.

When I reached Chapter XV my worries began. I never thought of it as Chapter 15. The martial-looking Roman numeral XV, seemed more appropriate to its content.

Chapter XV was titled *COMPLICATIONS OF ANÆSTHESIA* in upper case. I noticed that the letters 'A' and 'E' in *anæsthesia* leaned into each other. The 'A' leaned to the right, intimate with the upright of the 'E'. It reminded me of the teenage English girls I had seen leaning into the tall American soldiers in 1944. I used to see them in the corners behind the pubs when I walked home from Hebrew School in the blackout. Then but not later, I thought the girls were begging for sticks of chewing gum, like the ones the soldiers threw us as they drove by in their trucks, in response to our chants of "Any gum, chum?"

Dr. Goldman's book had 235 pages. It was not clear why he waited until page 127 for Chapter XV. It should have been the Prologue. Under XV he listed ten subheadings each with two or three pages of text: Anaesthetic Eyes, Cardiac Failure, Convulsions under Anaesthesia, Explosion Risk, Postoperative

Pneumonia, Postoperative Vomiting, Pulmonary Collapse, Pulmonary Oedema (the 'o' and the 'e' were also glued to each other but it's hard to think of this as anything salacious in the presence of fluid in the lungs due to a failing heart), Respiratory Arrest and lastly, Shock.

I knew a little about shock. As a medical intern I had taken care of patients suffering heart attacks and in shock. It took me a while to realize his list was not in order of frequency. It was simply Dr. Goldman's tidy alphabetical mind.

'Respiratory Arrest' disturbed me the most. All the other complications could be blamed on the patient's general condition, but not 'respiratory arrest'. I knew that respiratory arrest under anesthesia would be my fault and frankly, I had no idea what to do about it. Calling for help was the obvious answer; but would anyone respond? After all, I was a doctor. No one had even mentioned respiratory arrest in medical school other than that it was an accompaniment to and a criterion of death. I had the diploma that gave me the right to place M.B., B.Chir. after my name and my mother was paying to have it framed. This acronym came from Latin and alleged I was both a physician and a surgeon. When you become responsible for a patient's cure or at least her survival, the great puzzle is to fit the book learning with the symptoms of the live patient sitting in front of you. It just would not do to hear rales (bubbles of fluid in the chest) through your stethoscope and then say to the patient,

"Hold on a mo', while I look at my Texbook of Medicine."

I had read my diploma with its gobbledygook, that word another brilliant American invention on the diploma and it said nothing about the management of respiratory arrest during general anesthesia. A useful diploma would tell the general public what a doctor is good at and also the parts of the body he or she should never touch. Look round the walls of your own doctor's waiting room at the framed diplomas: lots of elegant script, some incomprehensible Latin, seven or eight signatures of famous doctors – all very impressive but completely uninformative. Such a diploma is of no use to an ophthalmologist trying to deal with the agony of gout in your big toe.

The medical diploma is analogous to the Ketubah, the Jewish marriage document. They both make you promise to be a good conscientious chap and provider but avoid practical details like who will feed the baby at 4 a.m. or how to deal with respiratory arrest in the operating theatre.

Let's return to 1958, the North Middlesex Hospital and my first breakfast as an anesthetist. I had little appetite but I made some human contact. The two bodies in the doctors' dining room had gone away or had been removed. A chunky chap in a short white coat came in,

"Good morning. Try the bacon. It's really crisp."

He stared at me. "You must new the new gasman. I am Jamison Ryan. I'm the Surgical Registrar. If you're still in Room 4 this afternoon we've got two stomachs. Both peptic ulcer. If things go well we'll be out in time for tea and if you haven't got a girlfriend we'll go to the pub later."

"Thanks. Nice to meet you," I was becoming more voluble. More articulate.

At the entrance to the operating theatre suite a masked and gowned figure met me. The figure lacked shape but had long eyelashes, an uncreased forehead and a feminine voice, somewhere between strictness and kindness.

"Is this the Theatre Sister (Head Nurse)?" I wondered. She did not introduce herself by name; I suspected that was reserved for more important doctors. Becoming more astute by the moment I decided this one had to be treated with respect.

Once when we four were brand-new medical students our Ward Sister was demonstrating bedmaking to us – with the patient *in the bed*. She tucked the sheets in so tight I whispered to my three colleagues,

"She must think the patients are two-dimensional."

She overheard me. She would not talk to me directly for the next three years.

The ice was broken when as a House Officer and being the only Jewish one, I covered for all the other chaps over Christmas. I was invited to the Sisters' (maidens; in those days Sisters – Head Nurses in the USA, had to be unmarried) Christmas dinner. Sister Crockett could not have been more friendly. I do believe it was not the brandy on the Christmas pudding. In her eyes I had popped out of my medical student pupa and transmogrified into a real butterfly and become something tolerable – a real doctor.

"Put your name on a locker, lock it and take the key after you've changed. There should be plenty of clean theatre suits. The laundry came on Friday and we had only a couple of emergencies over the weekend. Sometimes when it's busy at the weekend I have to launder the bloody things and we can't start the operating lists until they're dry. I think Dr. Mountford has complained to the Minister of Health about these shortages." She said.

I was unsure whether 'bloody' was literal or epithetical.

She pointed at a row of rubber boots.

"Be sure not to wear any of the surgeons' boots. They have their names on them. The anaesthetists don't seem to care what they wear."

Since I knew no one's name I searched for a nameless pair. I picked them up and sampled the smell of stale sweat and rotting foot debris. I'm quite sure this is where I picked up my lifelong case of Athlete's Foot, a disease for which there is no cure because it's never fatal. Some people brush their teeth before bed. I apply fungicide, to my toes of course.

"They all stink. You'll get used to it," said a voice behind me. "I'm Mountford. Nice to meet you."

I turned and found a gentleman in operating clothes, medium in all aspects, standing and wearing a smile. He shook my hand. The hair on his forearms looked orange and I saw some orange freckles on his nose.

"I got good recommendations from your Oxford chiefs. I'm sure you'll do well here," he said.

He led me to his tiny office next to the Induction Room for Theatre 4. In England the patients are prepared for surgery and anesthetized in an Induction Room, not in the sanctus sanctorum of the operating room. They are moved in after being anesthetized.

In the United States, either the patients are less emotionally fragile or the attendants are less feeling but in either case the patient is usually wheeled into the operating room wide awake, these days often to the accompaniment of raucous rock music. In my view that is a despicable indulgence to some surgeons and the more jiggly scrub nurses. Surgery is a serious matter. If a surgeon's nerves need soothing, let alone the patient's, let us at least have a slow movement of a Mozart Piano Concerto and not the Force 7 earthquakes produced by George Clinton and his Parliamentary Psychedelics.

"The patient will be here any moment now," Dr. Mountford said, "and that's the difficulty. You're not a Catholic, I hope?"

I am what I like to think of as a Festival Jew. I go to synagogue for as long as I can bear it once or twice a year and for Barmitzvahs and weddings. But those are for dancing and eating. On the other hand, I had tried hard that morning but could not get the bacon down, no matter how crisp.

"No Sir. I'm not.'

"Well, this poor girl has to have an abortion. Rape. There's two letters from the psychiatrists saying it's legal. The trouble is, I am Catholic. So I'll help you put in the Gordh needle and I'll stand at the theatre door and advise you. The priest said that's fine as long as I don't touch her skin. Go in and fiddle with the knobs on the Boyle machine. Be sure there's enough ether in the vaporizer."

I knew enough from my required ten anesthetic experiences at medical school that the Boyle machine consisted of a frame on wheels from which hung cylinders of oxygen and nitrous oxide - laughing gas. Actually, nitrous oxide is not at all amusing – as we'll see. On its own without added oxygen it is very good at asphyxiating a patient. A cynic might say asphyxia and death resemble Laurel and Hardy - the first prepares the joke for the second to crack.

The two gases are highly compressed in the cylinders but when you open a valve they turn into gases at atmospheric pressure and flow though tubes for the patient to breathe. On the way they can be diverted over a more potent liquid in a glass bottle, usually ether in those days. This resembles a driver stopping briefly and picking up a hitchhiker. Ether is flammable but very rarely explosive. If you spill some on an impervious surface and apply a lighted match it will burn with a rapidly spreading blue flame: it's quite a party trick.

Ether is a forgiving and effective anesthetic vapor. It depresses the breathing before it depresses the heart's function and therein lies its safety; the volume of the patient's breath is *the* guidepost to its safety. As I write this in 2011 I have heard of shortages of the modern intravenous anesthetic agent, Propofol. This makes me chuckle. I and perhaps a few hundred other living fossils like me would be the only anesthesiologists in the United States with any experience of using ether! Would the regulatory authorities re-license us on this basis? Who would pay our malpractice insurance premiums?

Within a few months of my early involvement in anesthesia, a new, powerful, non-flammable and non-explosive agent appeared. It was a British invention. It was named halothane and in a few years was used all over the Western world..

When I returned to the Induction Room I found a young woman on an operating table covered in a lasagna of blankets with her left arm exposed. I had thought she would be tearful but she smiled at me.

"Dr. Mountford and Mr. Harmsworth said you were giving me the anesthetic and that you are very good. Thank you, Doctor."

Doctors rarely talk about this amongst themselves but the courage of so many patients is a daily reward for us.

"Veins are often the problem," Mountford said. "Here's the most important thing I'm going to teach you today. A warm patient is a patient with big veins. All this young lady will need is a shot of Pentothal. Harmsworth's really quick."

No physiology, no pharmacology, no neurocellular membrane ion transfer, no intrapulmonary gas pressure gradients. Just 'lots of blankets to get a warm patient with big veins'.

And to my pleasure, after gently tightening a rubber tourniquet on her upper arm I found a fine fat vein near the crook of the elbow and the Gordh slid in smoothly. This young woman did not even flinch or bite her lip as I jabbed her.

"Always use lots of sticky tape. Nothing worse than a Gordh coming out in the middle," Mountford said.

A Gordh is steel needle that protrudes through the skin with a rubber diaphragm at the outer end, that protrudes through the skin. Any syringe with any needle containing any drug can be injected through the diaphragm and the drug enters the circulation almost instantly. If it is an anesthetic agent like Sodium Pentothal it reaches the brain in thirty seconds. And then, 'blam', the patient's asleep; to be more precise, anesthetized. Or, to be even more precise, oblivious.

Dr. Alsop had once told me about Dr. Gordh. He was the first and only medically trained anesthesiologist in Sweden in the 1930s; a reflection of the unpopularity and lowly status of anesthesia as a specialty only twenty five years before I began. Dr. Gordh died just a few months ago at 104, defying the common belief that anesthesiologists die young as a result of stress.

"Just give her half a syringe of Pentothal. That should do it." Dr. Mountford said.

It did not quite 'do it'.

I obeyed Dr. Mountford's instructions. To my pleasure, the patient's eyes closed, her body relaxed and her pulse that I could feel beating at her temple with my fingertip, slowed somewhat but felt regular and distinct and, most exciting for me, when I placed the mask on her face out of which flowed a mix of nitrous oxide and oxygen with a soupcon of added ether, she breathed quietly and freely. With relief I watched the rubber bag on the inflow tube deflating as she breathed in and inflating again as the fresh gas refilled it. I pushed the table into the operating room and connected her to the gas flow from another Boyle machine already standing there.

The nurse raised the young woman's legs, suspended them from stirrups and painted her with a pink antiseptic solution. Mr. Harmsworth sat on a stool facing the relevant part and inclined his head like a biologist seeing a new microbe through his microscope for the first time. He did certain things that clinked but that I could not see because of the sterile drapes. Then he mumbled through his mask,

"Dilating."

What happened next is educational. The patient's legs freed themselves from the stirrups, curled round the back of Mr. Harmsworth neck and crushed his head against her, like the German Army's Schlieffen Plan to envelop Paris in one gigantic pincer movement in 1914.

His next words were louder but more muffled.

"She's asphyxiating me. Where's Mountford?"

Please note he blamed the patient for his discomfort and not me. It took Dr. Mountford about five seconds to break a lifetime of devotion to Catholicism.

"Didn't you hear Harmy say 'dilating'? Didn't they teach you about the pain of cervical dilatation at your fancy Oxford medical school?" Dr. Mountford did not raise his voice but the words themselves hurt. He was not really angry, just chagrined. His judgment in allowing a neophyte to anesthetize had been challenged. He emptied the rest of the syringe into the Gordh and relaxation and serenity returned.

"Happens to the best of us," was all Dr. Mountford said as we lifted the patient onto her hospital bed.

We rolled her on her side so that if she vomited on emerging from the anesthetic the ejecta would trickle out of the corner of her mouth. If that should happen while she was lying on her back and was not under observation in her bed on the ward it was quite possible that the vomitus would sit in her pharynx, her throat, and obstruct her breathing and she would be deprived of oxygen.

Also, if the lingering effect of the anesthetic blunted her protective reflexes, the jaw and tongue might fall back into the pharynx and obstruct her breathing channel.

In those days recovery rooms were almost unheard of in Great Britain. Patients were taken directly from the operating room back to their own beds - as though nothing had happened. An anesthetic does not switch off like a toaster when it pops up. The drugs we use are either breathed out or broken apart by the liver, slowly. If you put a patient into a non-stimulating environment, for example a cozy, warm bed they can easily become re-anaesthetized by these residues and their reflexes once again become obtunded.

In 1975, ten years after we settled in America we returned to London for a visit. I dropped in to see old friends at the Middlesex Hospital, the teaching hospital where I had last worked in London. Except for the few patients who had undergone open-heart surgery none of the other surgical patients enjoyed the benefit of a recovery room where specialized nurses watched them until they were awake and stable. As early as 1975 that situation would have been unthinkable in an American hospital. I suspect this was the result of chronic underfunding of the National Health Service in Britain.

An incident in British political history illustrates the need for the above simple but vital maneuver. In March, 1963 at the height of the Cold War, Sir John Profumo the British Minister for War developed a relationship with a lady by name of Christine Keeler who was in the business of renting her body by the hour, just like Elsie in the show 'Cabaret'. Keeler had a similar and more or less coincident relationship with Yevgeni Evanoff a senior naval attaché at the Soviet Embassy in London. I believe this situation is called a 'security risk'. Profumo's initial denial in Parliament and subsequent public admission led indirectly to the fall of the Conservative government.

An osteopath, Dr. Stephen Ward, who treated members of British high society introduced Keeler to her future visitors. As the scandal broke the police prosecuted Ward for living off immoral earnings. In the USA he'd be called a pimp.

He attempted suicide with an overdose of sleeping pills. A cynical anesthesiologist might call this unmonitored anesthesia.

The next morning all the London newspapers displayed a picture of ambulance men carrying him out of his apartment on a stretcher. It can be clearly seen he is lying on his back with his chin down on his chest – the hallmark of what we anesthesiologists call "upper airway obstruction" due to the tongue falling back and closing off the pharynx. Ward remained unconscious for several days, undoubtedly the result of insufficient oxygen-containing blood reaching his brain. We call this hypoxic injury. He died a few days later.

Poor Michael Jackson: it is likely he died from the same, easily preventable cause. As I write this, the full facts have not appeared but enough is known to allow the asking of questions. Was the cardiologist Dr. Murray who dosed Jackson each night with Propofol, one might say a most unusual use of the drug, a Board-Eligible anesthesiologist? There are several ways to define an anesthesiologist: one might be a physician who will not leave his patient for even one moment, something Dr. Murray is alleged to have done.

Dr. Mountford patted me on the back in an encouraging sort of way,

"Keep up the good work. Got to run and do some private cases at the London Clinic," he said.

Now I was on my own. I had heard this was a possibility but I found the reality both stark and frightening.

Mr. Harmsworth's morning's list of operations consisted of three more ladies who required D and C's – dilatation and curettage, a supposedly minor procedure in which the gynecologist obtains samples of the lining of the uterus to diagnose whether the patient has cancer or some other dysfunction of the reproductive system. I had learned my lesson: lots of blankets and a Gordh needle. But my genius was to strap a syringe full of Pentothal to the arm with its needle embedded in the diaphragm of the Gordh. I also took an extra syringe of Pentothal into the theatre with me.

"Dr. Mountford never does that," the smooth nurse said.

"I am not Dr. Mountford. Don't you know this is the first time I've ever given an anesthetic all by myself, with no direction, no supervision, no advice. Just Dr. Goldman's little book," I muttered, feeling sorry for myself.

The big challenge came after the mid-morning cup of tea in Sister's office: a hysterectomy, for which procedure the surgeon needs relaxation of the abdominal muscles. Even though a patient may be unconscious from an anesthetic, subconscious reflex activity continues and when the skin is cut the abdominal muscles tighten in response, makings things difficult for the surgeon.

Please note how freely I use the words 'unconscious' and 'subconscious' in the context of anesthesia, as though they bear a relationship to the behavior of our brains when *no* drugs are involved, the drugs we anesthesiologists use every day. We are sloppy in our terminology. Anesthesiologists and other medical types should only use words like 'anesthetized' or, 'continuing reflex activity although the patient is chemically unaware', or, 'chemical oblivion'.

I gulped my cup of tea and rushed off to the lavatory hoping no one would peer under the door and see that my trousers were up. I urgently consulted Dr. Goldman. I found the heading "Surgical Anesthesia" on page 34. I skipped the Light Anesthesia section: that would not do for a hysterectomy. I read the next heading:

Signs of Deep Surgical Anesthesia:

1. Automatic respiration solely abdominal in character. "What's so special about that?" I wondered.
2. Fixed eyeballs, the pupils dilated. During my rotation through neurology at medical school the professor emphasized that these signs were indicative of approaching death.
3. Absence of reflex action.
4. Complete insensibility to pain.
5. Muscular relaxation.

3, 4 and 5 cheered me up. All I would have to do is add more ether to the gas reaching the patient through the mask until the surgeon stopped complaining about the patient's muscles being tight. The next sentence lowered my spirits again.

'It is this stage of deep surgical anesthesia that must be maintained for the majority of abdominal operations. If more anesthetic is given to the patient, the breathing will become shallower and shallower until it finally ceases, when we have reached the stage of:

Respiratory Paralysis.

I heard the orderly calling me, "Dr. Zed, they are ready for you."

I had read a lot about both World Wars. Now I knew what it must have been like for the men going 'over the top' on the Somme in July 1916 straight into the German machine guns. The difference was that their purpose, to kill, was much easier than mine. Mine was to keep the patient alive.

As it turned out, help appeared. Mr. Harmsworth the surgeon, stood by my side as I put the patient to sleep with Pentothal and said,

"Now just ease the ether into the circuit very gradually and you'll get the hang of it very quickly. If she coughs, back off for 20 seconds. I will let you know well in time when I need more relaxation and also when I'm starting to close so you can ease off. So far as I can tell she has huge fibroids but I'll shell those out one by one so the actual hysterectomy will be as easy as pie."

He bent his head and whispered,

"To tell the truth I wanted to be a gas man. Less bloody. But there was no money in it in those days. I already had three children."

All those years ago I was less emotional than I am now, but I almost cried with relief. Dr Alsop, my medical school teacher had somehow, intentionally or unintentionally left me with the impression that surgeons were the enemy. Now I knew differently - only some were.

Dr. Goldman and I alternatively blundered and recovered from the blunders the rest of the day. I did not seem to have harmed a patient so I was able to eat my supper. Jamison Ryan sat next to me.

"You did a pretty good job your first day. The boss doesn't say very much but if he doesn't complain it means you and I are doing alright. But ... no pub for us tonight,"

It was then I discovered I was on call. He was also on call, for surgery. After giving anesthetics for five minor and three major operations I had visited all the patients on the ward and except for pain and nausea they were all intact. Two of them had visitors who thanked me profusely.

I should have said, "Well I'm only the anesthesiologist," but I just mumbled,

"It all went well," and escaped.

After supper I had to visit nine patients who were to be operated the next day. I had to take a brief medical history, listen to their lungs, reassure them of the safety of the anesthesia and the incredible skill of their surgeons and how well we could treat postoperative pain and nausea and would not dislodge any of their teeth. On some of these preoperative visits the patient would ask, tentatively,

"Doc, do you know what operation Mr. Thompson (or whatever the surgeon's name) will be doing on me tomorrow morning?'

When I became more senior I would ask the surgeon whether he or she had properly explained the operation and its risks to the patient. They always replied they had explained things in detail at the preoperative consultation. It was then I realized that as soon as the patient heard the word 'surgery' or 'operation' their minds 'switched off'. They retained very little of the surgeon's subsequent explanation.

Chapter 4 DOCTORS AT NIGHT

It was 3 a.m. when Charles MacIntyre the hospital porter shook me awake. His hand felt cold on my shoulder. I remembered my situation: on call for emergencies requiring anesthesia at a hospital in the outer London slums. I felt like a man who expected to step into a warm shower but found the mixer jammed at 'cold'.

"Doc, they need you over at St. Mary's. You know, where they do the mums and babies. Just your bad luck. Usually they never bother us. Seems the O.B. Registrar over there is in a spot of bother. I brought your Lambretta round the front. I'll cycle with you so you don't get lost. Here's a cup of tea while you're getting dressed. I put two lumps of sugar in and stirred it. You'll need the energy," Charles always spoke in paragraphs.

The cup of tea was appealing but I could not get it down. I still do not understand why being called to an emergency in the middle of the night made me nauseated.

"That's where we had our kids, me and the missus. The wife got gas and air and she told me it took most of the hurt away. Why they should want you now I can't imagine," Charles said as he pedaled beside me through streets of sleeping houses.

Despite the fatigue I felt elated for a moment. What heroic feat would I accomplish? Would it help me get a good recommendation for a teaching hospital post, the road to a Consultancy?

The delivery room resembled those I had seen in medical school, green tiles on the walls with a jellyfish-shaped lamp fixed to the ceiling, focused like a stage spotlight. Pink tiles would have been more useful. One of the key criteria of Dr. Virginia Apgar's score of newborn health is skin color. The light reflecting off a pink wall would have made us more optimistic about the baby's condition. It probably would have saved me from passing breathing tubes with all their attendant dangers into a few babies' lungs. In those days we had no objective method to measure oxygenation. We looked at the color of the skin and estimated: that is, we guessed, and then we spoke, with unwarranted conviction.

The mother lay on her back affixed to a sparse steel table, her legs hanging from stirrups. In those days babies were never born in bathtubs or with the mother in a squatting position in a rice field a la Sylvana Mangano in Bitter Rice or with a reluctant husband rubbing the small of her back. Husbands were strictly excluded from delivery rooms in 1958. After they *were* admitted I had to resuscitate more fainting husbands than babies who did not breathe. My, and my anesthesiological colleagues' hostile attitude to husbands' presence at that time was misbegotten. We did not believe they could handle the sight of an epidural or spinal needle being pushed into their squirming wives' backs. Most of the time we were wrong.

A sour smell hung in the air in the delivery room, the smell of congealed blood.

"I've got a retained placenta. You're Zeitlin the new anesthesiologist aren't you?" said a female voice through a mask hanging below her nose. The voice came with authority. She, the obstetrician, sat facing the exit for babies. I saw only one other person in the room, the nurse-midwife.

"I'm Trish Bonnington-Smith. I'm the OB Registrar. I need some general anesthesia for this lady. The trilene isn't strong enough for a manual exploration of the uterus. I have to get my whole hand in," the obstetrician said.

Trilene is trichloroethylene, a volatile blue liquid once used by dry cleaners. It's particularly good for removing borscht stains from white tuxedo shirts. In a low concentration breathed in from an inhaler held by the laboring mother it is a moderately effective painkiller but useless as a general anesthetic agent. It is no longer used for either purpose; among other disadvantages it promotes cancers in animals.

"Everything will be fine," I told the mother. "Congratulations on your new baby." I had seen a small person snoozing in a bassinet near the door.

"He's beautiful," she replied. She looked white.

"I'm sorry to get you up so late, Doctor."

I took a quick look at her hospital chart. Her name: Jane Buswell. A multip; that is, pregnant with her second or subsequent baby. Dr. Bonnington-Smith had noted in the chart that Jane's general health was good. In an ideal world all anesthesiologists would be given the opportunity to go into the details of a patient's medical history. In an emergency like this you have to make do with the minimum and make your own observations on the fly.

"Is the anesthesia machine nearby?" I asked the midwife who was helping the obstetrician. "If you tell me where to find it, if you're too busy helping Doctor, I'll get it myself."

"There's your equipment Sir," I liked the 'Sir' but did not like what I saw on a small table near the patient's head.

"That's what the anaesthetists use here, Sir."

On the table I saw a bottle of ether, a bottle made of dark glass because light disintegrates the chemistry of the ether, with a dripping tube protruding through the cork; also a Schimmelbusch mask, a device used by German doctors to anesthetize the injured during the First World War. It has the shape of a small turtle shell and consists of two hemispherical wire meshes hinged together at one end, that when locked together hold a surgical sponge in place. We drip ether onto the sponge, where it disperses. The ether vaporizes as the patient's warm breath ebbs and flows though the sponge. The patient inhales the vapor. This is the principle behind many of the earliest ether inhalers dating back to October 1846 when William Morton gave the first useful anesthetic in Boston. One hundred and twelve years later there I was, obliged to use the same primitive technique.

I held the mask in my left hand using the first three fingers. I hooked my fourth and fifth finger behind the angle of her jaw.

Protracting the jaw, that is, pulling it forward lifts the tongue away from the back wall of the pharynx, the throat. That way one keeps the breathing channel open. An important side effect of general anesthesia is loss of muscle tone, that constant slight contraction that maintains our shape and posture when awake. I dripped the ether from the bottle in my right hand, slowly at first, until she lost consciousness - because ether is noxious and makes the patient gag.

She went 'to sleep' very quickly, too quickly I thought. I knew there was something bad about that but at that fraught moment could not remember what. I put the bottle down and felt for the temporal pulse in front of her right ear. Nothing. Her blood pressure must be low or absent.

I believed and I hoped the patient was alive despite the absent temporal pulse. I pulled an eyelid up; the pupil contracted as the light hit it. That is a clear signal the brain is receiving sufficient oxygen-containing blood. When I pressed an area of skin on her forehead to blanch it, it refilled slowly.

The question was: how alive was she? Looked at the other way - how depressed was her circulation? Feeling the pulse in the carotid artery, the artery that carries the main blood supply to the brain is more difficult. Put your second and third fingers on the larynx, the Adam's Apple, move them sideway and press back steadily. If you do that correctly, and fortunately Dr. Alsop in Oxford had taught me how, you feel the pulse beat in the carotid artery, itself directly connected to the aorta and thus to the heart: usually, it is easily palpable. Palpable is another of those words medical people use to distinguish themselves from the laity. What is wrong with 'easy to feel'? Hers was feeble and difficult to identify.

I happened to look down. A slow tide of dark blood had crept up to my shoes. Blood is liquid when it's in the circulation. Spilt blood has the consistency of cheap jam.

"She is exsanguinating. She is bleeding out," I said, loudly. My anxiety made me repeat myself.

"Nurse, please get me a blood pressure cuff, an intravenous needle, a drip with some saline and an oxygen cylinder," I spoke as calmly as I was able.

"*Don't panic,*" I told myself.

"I've already telephoned for Dr. Harmsworth," came her reply.

By now I was in turmoil. She did not seem to understand the urgency of the situation. This was not the time to wait for Dr. Harmsworth to get in his car and drive 20 miles to St. Mary's. Then I remembered Dr. Alsop's words.

"When things go badly in theatre, *you*," and he had underlined the word 'you' with his voice, "you are responsible."

"Nurse! Now! Immediately please. A blood pressure machine, an intravenous bottle of saline and an oxygen cylinder. And then you will come and hold the mask on her face. I will need both my hands free."

It was my tone of voice, not my actual words that made her jump into action and find what I needed.

The obstetrician had her right hand inside, peeling the placenta off the uterine wall like scooping a ripe avocado from its shell. Her left hand vigorously massaged the uterus through the abdominal wall to stimulate it to contract and slow the bleeding. None of these maneuvers would have been possible without the anesthesia.

Dr. Bonnington-Smith looked up,

"I simply could not leave this end to start an intravenous," she said.

In a frantic way I found a vein in the patient's neck and got a needle into it. You find a vein by obstructing the flow of blood returning to the heart with your fingertips at a point beyond the intended puncture site. Three or four hands would have been useful in this situation but I had to make do with two. I had no time for niceties like a swipe of antiseptic to the skin or to scrub my hands and put on sterile surgical gloves. I could not see any veins in her arms. The nurse had finally 'got it'. She assembled the intravenous drip with a bottle of saline quickly and adeptly. She applied the blood pressure cuff to the other arm and gave me bad news.

"It's very hard to hear, but I think it's sixty over thirty."

She held the Schimmelbusch mask correctly while I urged the saline to flow rapidly into her vein. I did this by standing on a stool and lifting the bottle high. Gravity was all we had in 1958. There were no pumps for rapid infusion. I complimented the midwife on the way she held the mask.

"I always watch what Dr. Mountford does when he comes over here," she said.

"The most experienced anesthesiologist, the one who knows how to deal with desperate situations like this, is snoozing in bed. The ignorant neophyte, me, is trying to save the patient's life." So ran my thoughts.

I felt bitter but also a little proud. I had dealt with one of the worst emergencies that can face an anesthesiologist.

The next blood pressure reading was slightly higher. I asked the nurse to telephone Dr. Mountford again. There was no need for him to come in. I had things under control. Anesthesiologists called to emergencies in the middle of the night just pull a sweater and a pair of trousers over their pajamas. He would get back into bed in a jiffy.

At Dr. Bonnington-Smith's request I gave Jane a drug into the intravenous line to help stimulate the uterine muscle to contract and thus slow the bleeding. Ergotamine is an extract of a toxic fungus called ergot that grows on rye. The obstetrician excavated the placenta. She checked there was none of it left behind and the bleeding stopped.

The patient woke slowly after I stopped the ether.

Jane survived, barely. She developed kidney failure as a result of the prolonged low blood pressure. No one had recorded her blood pressure *before* I arrived. There was no way to know how long she had been as we call it, hypotensive. In 1958 we had no kidney dialysis, only a low protein diet and prayer. I used to wonder if she and her husband got much pleasure from the new baby in those early critical weeks.

How could this have happened? In the middle of the last century it was less than usual to regard obstetric practice as anything requiring what we now call intensive care – care given by an anesthesiologist, care that the obstetrician is unable to provide because he or she is concentrating on the delivery and *its* potential complications. Mothers and babies died and although leaders in both obstetrics and anesthesiology organized commissions of study to make recommendations for improvement, change came slowly. In the last 50 years we have seen a swing from general anesthesia for delivery to the use of regional anesthesia; that is, numbing the part of the body where the pain comes from – the dilating cervix, by using epidural and spinal injections of local anesthetics and narcotics.

This is not the place to discuss the dangers of general anesthesia for childbirth nor indeed the fascinating and far wider topic of pain relief for childbirth all mixed up with religion and the feminist movement. I recommend a book by my friend Dr. Don Caton. It has a paradoxical but significant title "What a Blessing She Had Chloroform". These words were uttered by Queen Victoria about her daughter in labor. The Queen herself loathed pregnancy and particularly childbirth until the one great anesthesiologist-scientist in England Dr. John Snow, gave her chloroform for her third baby. She had four more before her beloved Albert died.

Do not believe the statistics screamed from newspaper headlines that maternal mortality in the USA is disgracefully high. In well-regulated obstetric centers with first-class and specialized obstetric and anesthesiology services it is extraordinarily low. Poverty in certain populations and the accompanying lack of health insurance in the U.S.A. give rise to no or poor care during pregnancy. These women are often ill when they come in to deliver: it is they who distort the numbers. This is a social and hardly a medical problem.

I arrived back at the North Middlesex at 7 a.m. just in time for breakfast. I am no different from most other doctors who have to

43

work at night. It must be the adrenaline flowing. Now I was hungry. I ate the bacon. It was crisp and delicious.

I had a quick bath and changed into clean theatre clothes. Dr. Mountford had arrived ahead of me.

"Heard you had fun last night at St. Mary's. Good on you, as the Aussies say," he said.

I felt like a stray dog that has found a kind and loving home.

"Cheswick's got a couple of old ladies this morning with hip fractures to pin. I was going to show you my spinal technique. Maybe even let you do one. But ... ," he pondered.

"There'll be other days. Go and get some sleep."

Chapter 5 EXAMINATIONS

Why did I choose a medical specialty at a time when its status in the medical hierarchy was low, in which patients sometimes hovered between life and death and whose hours were irregular, unpredictable and often at night? Anesthesiologists cannot regulate their own working hours. They have to respond to the needs of surgeons and obstetricians and their patients. The only way to deal with this is for anesthesiologists to work in groups in order to develop a shift system. I remember that I and my colleagues at medical school felt that anesthesiologists did mysterious and extraordinary things for and to patients yet were almost invisible on the hospital scene; either they were to be found in the operating suite or were off-duty and at home.

In addition to my fascination with respiratory intensive care I also think my interest paradoxically grew after another conversation with my father. He graduated from the London Hospital Medical School in 1918, late enough in the year of the Armistice to avoid being slaughtered on the Western Front in France. Go to any medical library and get a bound volume of the British Medical Journal for 1916 off the stacks. Each week the obituary column reported the death of three or four *doctors* in the trenches in Northern France.

Like the majority of newly graduated doctors at that time my father became a general practitioner. In the United States he would have been a family doctor. Before establishing his own practice in the East End of London where many immigrants lived, he did locum tenens work for country doctors to gain experience.

"Why on earth do you want to do that?" he said, when I first mentioned anesthesia as a possibility.

"When I did my first locum for a country doctor near Sheffield he did tonsillectomies on farmhouse kitchen tables. He took me with and he had me spray ethyl chloride onto a rag covering the kiddies' faces. In the months I was with him two of the children's hearts stopped suddenly and that was that."

'That was that' rang something in my mind. I had no good answer for him other than,

"I just want to give it a try."

That was double-speak. I was already intrigued. The seed had been planted. The moisture and nourishment came later. Perhaps the tragedy in his story was one reason *why* I wanted to do anesthesia. I have an element of rebelliousness in me and a desire for risk-taking. I must have felt that a specialty as primitive as anesthesia was at that time could only be a source of excitement and intellectual challenge.

I am no longer sure what I thought fifty years ago but the few clues I had then about anesthesia suggested that the specialty was about to change from a primitive and empirical (if it works and does not seem to harm too many patients, use it) non-science to something at the forefront of surgical care. One proof of this lies in the difference between the two specialist exams I took, the first in the United Kingdom and the second in the United States seven years later.

If you passed the examination in the United Kingdom you received a degree with the clumsy title of F.F.A.R.C.S., the Fellowship in the Faculty of Anaesthetists of the Royal College of Surgeons. This illustrates the subservience of anesthesia to surgery in those days. The exam had two parts and it had much more to do with general medicine than anesthesia – for the reason that not enough was known about the latter to make up a whole and thorough examination. Like an amoeba, we British anesthesiologists finally budded off from the surgeons into the independent Royal College of Anaesthetists 20 years after I took the exam. Now I am F.R.C.A. Makes me feel special although I'm not sure where the Queen comes into it.

Seven years later, after we settled in the U.S.A., I sat the written and oral parts of the American Boards in Anesthesiology. The American exam tested one's knowledge of drug action, the physiology of the circulation and the respiratory system and the practical details and decisions that go into the correct way to handle very sick patients with complicated diseases in the operating room and the intensive care unit.

I got lucky in both exams. In the oral part of the British exam (called *viva voce* which, when translated means "by word of mouth") you were given a patient, usually someone with a number of conditions diagnosable by physical examination, listening with a stethoscope, tapping and probing. Each of us candidates faced three 'short' cases, more or less related to problems in anesthesia. For example, a patient with protruding eyeballs. This allowed the examiner to question you about thyrotoxicosis - often a challenging problem for the anesthesiologist during thyroid surgery because of the overactive heart action and unstable blood pressure that accompanies the condition.

The 'long' cases were more fun because you were given half an hour with the patient. This allowed you to take a history and to perform a full examination. The patients were volunteers and received a modest honorarium, their bus fares and afternoon tea with McVitie's Wholemeal biscuits. For many of them, retired, it was exciting to see young doctors jumping through hoops: something new to talk about in the pub that night.

My gentleman was in his late fifties. You always start with 'social history': What is or was your job? What is your favorite food? Do you smoke? How much do you drink? Are you married? What did your parents die of?

His name was Gibson. He had completely white hair. This intrigued me. He saw me looking,

"You know why my hair's white, doc? Well, I'll tell you why. I went down with my ship in the North Atlantic twice when we were torpedoed. And I survived. Once on the Murmansk run. Water temperature always at freezing."

I had grown up in and around London during the war and I retained a morbid interest in what war is, and what it means. I was moved by the idea of a man facing almost certain death from hypothermia and surviving twice.

"I have read about those convoys. I saw the film 'The Cruel Sea'. But I still cannot imagine what it was really like," I said.

He took a shine to me.

"Pull up a chair, doc. I don't often do this but I can tell you're going to be a good doc. You listen to me carefully," he said. He started to whisper.

"I got aorta stenosis with a neck murmur. I got Buerger's disease in my toes. Some docs say that's from being in the water; others say it's the fags (cigarettes). I got a bloody great inguinal hernia on the right hidden beneath this sheet. I also got a fused knee from a crane dumping a tank on my leg. And I got high blood-pressure."

I listened to his heart and looked at his other handicaps. I made notes. The examiner approached, questioned me and seemed satisfied with my findings.

"And what was his blood pressure?"

"Oh my God," I said aloud, "I forgot to take it."

I passed, but I'm absolutely sure that without the other information that Mr. Gibson had revealed to me, I would have failed.

The American Board exam in Anesthesiology eight years later differed in many ways. The written part was tolerable and was all about the new discoveries in the physiology and pharmacology of anesthesia. The oral exam was held in a motel in Phoenix, Arizona, in the late Spring.

Each candidate met two examiners who were tucked behind a table in a standard motel room. One was the Junior Examiner, usually a young academic and the other was the Senior, often a well-known Professor or Chairman.

"We are here to find out what you *do* know? Not what you don't know," the younger man said.

That was a comfort until I looked at the Senior Examiner. It was Dr. William Hamilton. I had heard he was tough. These rumors flit around nervous candidates like an ocean foghorn that comes and goes in a thick fog. Things went along fairly well until Dr. Hamilton said (in my paranoid state his voice had the snarl of the hunting dog),

"Tell me what little you know about 'apneic oxygenation'."

The 'little' stung, but, Aha! I knew I had him. By sheer luck I knew all about apneic oxygenation. This phenomenon is related to how patients pick up oxygen when the surgeon is performing a bronchoscopy and we have to paralyze the breathing. I had done some research on these patients and published a paper based on work I had done at the London Chest Hospital, so, of course I knew most of literature. I fed him little bits of information just as one would when confronted with a lion and has a shopping basket to hand with 2 pounds of fresh hamburger.

The date I took the American oral boards became a much more terrifying one that evening, but for a different reason. It was June 5 1968, the day Robert Kennedy was assassinated. There was something horrible about being in the brilliant sunshine of the late Arizona spring and trying to come to terms with an aspect of American life that we had not nor could have foreseen: the ease with which citizens can carry concealed guns. How many times since have I been called to the Emergency Room by the E.R. doctor to pass a breathing tube (intubate) and ventilate (breathe for) a young man molested or destroyed by a bullet?

I well remember American and British soldiers getting into arguments and fights when the pubs closed in London in 1944. But they fought with fists, sticks and broken bottles until the Military Police arrived and hauled off the drunkest. But it was non-lethal fighting. No guns. No one died or was paralyzed. Their brains *were* saturated but only with alcohol and started functioning again the next morning unlike the poor sods in the American emergency rooms with a bullet that had tumbled in and mashed their brain tissues; as had happened to Robert Kennedy's brother five years earlier.

My intuition about the potential inherent in anesthesiology turned out to be correct, as we'll see. I realized that it was the relevance of what one knows and the immediacy in applying it for the patient's benefit that had appealed to me. We know how the body works in real time.

Chapter 6 TAKE-OFFS AND LANDINGS

Let us go then, you and I to Operating Theatre Number 4 at the Whittington Hospital situated on the high hills of North London. The Whittington is pressed against the perimeter of the Highgate Cemetery where Karl Marx is buried.

After my brief engagement at the North Middlesex Hospital in late 1958 I spent the next two years doing locums tenens jobs of varying length, that is, covering absences by the permanent staff due to illness or vacation. Sometimes, later, driving round London I felt I could give a visitor a Cook's Tour of the many hospitals where I had spent a week or two. The Whittington gave me my first permanent job - with a one year tenure. I had been promoted from Senior House Officer to Registrar. Inflation swallowed the salary increment.

One of the first patients I anaesthetized there was called Mr. Ian McKendrick. Most nights for the previous five or six years Mr. Ian McKendrick had slept poorly. Burning upper abdominal pain woke him frequently and by trial and error he found that drinking a bottle of cream settled the pain. Mr. and Mrs. McKendrick had five children and they wanted all of them to go to University. Even though it was heavily subsidized by the government University cost much more than Mr.McKendrick could earn as a Police Sergeant in the East End of London. After coming off duty he bolted the bacon sandwich Mrs. McKendrick had made for him and drove to his second job: his own business of fitting central heating systems to some of the thousands of houses in London that relied on single gas fires in the main rooms and hot water bottles and each other in the bedroom. The demand was large and recently he had taken to adding weekends. When I visited him the previous night he told me that Mr. Savage (it's true!), his surgeon, planned to cut out the part of his stomach that made too much acid. The acid had ulcerated his stomach.

I examined Mr. McKendrick and heard wheezy noises all over his lungs. Some sounded high and brief; others had a lower note and did not end before he had to take another breath. Those noises called rhonchi told me that mucus narrowed the tubes in his lungs that carried air in and out. He confessed that even though Mr. Savage had told him to stop smoking, he could not. He had also put on a lot of weight recently.

That night I also slept poorly. What if, when I put him to sleep he regurgitated acidic fluid from his stomach and inhaled it into his lungs? With his already clogged lungs he would likely get aspiration pneumonia after the operation and I would be blamed.

What if, because his lungs were full of secretions he did not breathe adequately during the operation; or, even if I assisted his breathing he did not get enough oxygen. This was particularly likely because the surgeon packed the intestines out of his field of action with large cotton pads. These would push the contents of the abdomen upwards and compress Mr. McKendrick's lungs. For a junior anesthesiologist to tell a senior surgeon his patient was in trouble was humiliating. Even today it is not uncommon for a patient to suffer because of poor relationships between doctors. If I was lucky one of the Consultant anesthesiologists might be free between his or her cases to advise me.

Humans short of oxygen become cyanotic, a blueish discoloration of the skin. I had read the work of Dr. Julius Comroe, an American physiologist who had demonstrated that even for experienced observers cyanosis was a poor indicator of *the degree* of oxygen lack. We guessed a lot about the patient's condition in those days.

Before starting my stint at the Whittington I phoned my predecessor, Dr. Donald Short. I had met Donald at an educational meeting for residents at the Association of Anaesthetists. He told me about the equipment I would find, the quirks of the Consultants, both the surgeons and the anesthesiologists and before we hung up he said,

"Stick to Embry and you'll do well."

I wondered who or what an Embry was. I had learned to arrive at a new post a day early whenever that was possible. I would check my bedroom. Did the phone work? Were there any mouse droppings?

I went to the operating theatre suite and checked on the equipment. In those days the operating rooms were never locked up. I do not remember any difficulty with the theft of drugs, a problem these days. Last, and most important I checked the rota, which is the English for call schedule. It was not too bad at the Whittington. A full five day week, two weekday nights and every second weekend on call, which meant I had every second weekend off.

Mr. McKendrick, arrived in the Induction Room at the same moment I did. An orderly wheeled him in on a stretcher and dexterously helped him climb onto the operating table.

I looked round. Someone had drawn the drugs I would need into syringes: sodium pentothal, succinylcholine, curare, atropine, ephedrine all neatly arranged on a table. Sodium Pentothal was the modern equivalent of the *intravenous* induction agents discovered by German scientists in the 1920s. Remember how I anaesthetized the obstetric patient who was bleeding two years earlier; she had to breathe ether in, a slow and noxious process.

Succinylcholine is also given intravenously, a powerful but short-acting paralyzing agent that allows one to insert the endotracheal (breathing) tube quickly and easily. Curare is a long-lasting paralyzing agent. Atropine speeds up the heart if it slows too much and ephedrine raises the blood pressure of it falls too much.

We kept the patient asleep, better, *oblivious* by allowing them to breathe a mixture of nitrous oxide, ether and oxygen supplied from the machine and that flows into the endotracheal tube.

On the Boyle machine itself I saw three different sized endotracheal tubes, airways, which are props between the teeth so the patient, if 'lightly' anesthetized cannot bite the endotracheal tube, a roll of adhesive tape and a Gordh needle. Everything I could possibly need. Who had prepared all this for me? I knew that only the Consultant anesthesiologists had nurses to prepare their drugs and equipment. The lower grades to which I belonged were expected to prepare their own.

The orderly stood still watching me with his hands on his hips and leaning to the left. His arms made a neat parallelogram.

Was he appraising me? His only remarkable feature were the waxed points of a moustache sticking out at the sides of his face-mask.

"I wonder who got all this ready for me?" I mumbled to myself more than to Mr. McKendrick and the orderly.

"Mr. Embry did," said the orderly.

"I'd like to meet him and thank him."

"You have and you are," came the reply.

The moustachioed orderly was the Embry that Donald Short had mentioned.

"There's a nice fat one on the back of the left hand," Mr. Embry said as he handed me a rubber tourniquet and a Gordh needle. The 'nice fat one' of course, was a vein. He was correct and as I tested the patency of the Gordh with the syringe of saline he also handed me I felt calmer, more confident.

"I'm sure you'll be wanting to measure the blood pressure on this one. Also, I can smell the smoke on his breath, so you'll want a precordial," Mr. Embry was a talking book of helpful hints. I didn't have to read Dr. Goldman this time.

A precordial is not the opposite of a whisky chaser. It's a long stethoscope you tape onto the front of the chest, in front of the heart, therefore precordial, so you can listen to the heart and lungs during surgery.

Mr. Embry seemed to demand more of my attention. He had an interesting way of doing this; he would stare at me, pull his mask down and open his mouth open as though to say 'Doc' – but no sound actually came out. His left index finger (pointer, in the

USA) rested on the patient's lower lip and his thumb on the point of the chin.

"I've laid out several different sizes of Mac blades for you," he said.

A Mac is anesthesiologists' slang for the laryngoscope with a curved blade invented by Dr. Macintosh in 1940, the naked Professor in Oxford for whom, regrettably, I never worked. It is still used all over the world in every operating room seventy years later. A laryngoscope is a device for exposing the larynx (the voice box with the vocal cords vibrating to produce intelligible speech) through which the anesthesiologist can slide an endotracheal tube. Of course only after the patient is asleep and usually paralyzed.

Yes, that's right: paralyzed. Paralyzed simply means that the muscles all over the body are flaccid. Paralysis is needed both by anesthesiologists and surgeons. Without paralyzing agents anesthesiologists would either need to saturate the patient with lots and lots of vaporous general anesthetic agents that are breathed in, or give large amounts of chemicals such as Pentothal that are injected into a vein. But lots and lots was never such a good idea because lots and lots depress the activity of the heart. Therefore we give a little of the lots so that the patient is just unaware, or as we say, *deep enough*, and then paralyze the patient so that we can pass an endotracheal tube.

The surgeon needs paralysis to abolish the body's reflex response to a scalpel blade, a tightening of the abdominal muscles that would impede his or her access to the contents of the belly, his work site. These below-consciousness reflexes continue to operate even though the patient may be profoundly anesthetized.

If you like carpentry, or even if you do not, please imagine trying to make a mortise joint through a rip, torn in the National Enquirer: very difficult. That is what most surgeons do. That is why they need assistants. All that assistants really do is to mop up unsightly amounts of blood, small amounts being socially acceptable, and retract.

The act of retraction is similar to joining a tug-or-war team, with the difference that you cannot see the opposition. For the assistants this is a not desirable situation because, at least in teaching hospitals, the assistants are often surgical residents in training. The surgeon positions a sort of curved steel egg spatula called a retractor so that the assistant by pulling like H-ll separates the abdominal or thoracic (chest) muscles to give the surgeon a nice clear field of vision. The assistants' arms penetrate the little gap between the surgeon and the scrub nurse but he is behind them and cannot really see what is going on. He can study the scrub nurse's coiffure and the pimples on the surgeon's neck but little else.

This oddity may in part explain the high mortality rate during surgery before we anesthesiologists took over. In those days surgical residents were required to give the ether or chloroform and leaning over the so-called, 'ether screen' (a draped bar that separates the 'dirty' anesthesiologist from the sterile surgical field; it is still called that in 2011) *they watched the surgery instead of the patient* from the vantage point at the head of the table.

My colleague Dr. Rafael Ortega recently developed a transparent drape over the ether screen that reduces or even eliminates the physical and psychological barrier that often seems to separate surgeons from anesthesiologists. Along with this is the observation I have often expressed, that until about fifty years ago anesthesiologists published their discoveries in surgical journals and vice versa. Now we have our own, exclusive to anesthesia. Sometimes when I'm reading one of ours I wonder if I am anesthetizing a different patient from the one the surgeon is operating on even though we each are working on the same body as the other.

At the time of Mr. McKendrick's operation the most used paralyzing agent, or to give it it's more dignified, for-public-consumption name, muscle relaxant, was curare. This is a purified extract of Indian Arrow Poison. The extraordinary story of how the fluid toxin in a weapon of war became a modern pharmacological agent in the operating room is fascinating but is much too large to tell here.

"No jaw. Difficult intubation," Mr. Embry's finger-caliper told me. This is one of the most frightening situations for any anesthesiologist. The patient is paralyzed, that is, not breathing and during the time you insert the laryngoscope blade into the mouth trying to see the larynx, his body continues to use its supply of oxygen with no possibility of replenishment until the tube is in the correct place, the trachea leading to the lungs. During these critical minutes one or more exciting possibilities might become realities. Acid may reflux up the esophagus (the gullet) from the stomach and trickle down into the lungs, the patient may regain consciousness because the original intravenous dose of Pentothal leaves the brain, or the heart may slow dramatically and frighteningly because if you take too long getting the tube through the larynx the patient can run out of oxygen.

Or, you may never see the larynx at all for a number of reasons, mostly to do with the anatomy of the mouth and jaw. Sometimes, these days during a cocktail party I find myself studying the guests and estimating their thyro-mental distances. Could I successfully intubate that chap with a receding jaw smirking over his Scotch and soda?

Back in the late 1950s and early 1960s when I began, patients would come to the operating room as we say 'poorly prepared'. An example might be a child with abdominal pain and all the signs of acute appendicitis. When the patient has an inflammation somewhere in the gut, the stomach no longer empties its contents into the duodenum, the next bit of bowel. That is why one of my chiefs at the Middlesex Hospital, in central London where I worked later on, Dr. Brian Sellick, invented what we now call the Sellick Maneuver – also used to this day. In a patient such as the one I have just described an assistant presses hard and backwards on the cricoid cartilage, the horizontal spar just below the Adam's Apple. This compresses the top end of the esophagus and stops the pints, yes, sometimes pints of acid gastric (stomach) juice from running up the esophagus and then down into the larynx while you are struggling to pass the endotracheal tube, and drowning the patient as it floods into the lungs.

If this happens it results in what is called Mendelsohn's Syndrome named after the doctor who first described it. It is a devastating complication. Acid burning the delicate lung tissues is potentially a bad thing. That is why in awake life even the tiniest amount of foreign material touching the vocal cords in the larynx causes explosive coughing – what we call "it's gone down the wrong way".

Although the main responsibility of the anesthesiologist is to render the patient oblivious to the pain of surgery we also have the responsibility of protecting the whole patient. We must tape the eyes shut so they do not dry out, we must pad all the places where nerves run near the body's surface to prevent pressure damage, we have to prevent cooling or over-heating, we must treat abnormal heart rhythms, keep them properly hydrated and so on. By abolishing the reflex response to surgery we abolish all our patients' other protective reflexes that normally keep them out of harm when they are awake. We do this in addition to responding to the often drastic changes that result from surgery. An example or two would be the sudden huge blood losses that sometimes accompany a radical prostatectomy or, the effect on the patient's oxygen uptake when the surgeon has to collapse a lung to get at a cancer.

If there is a risk that after the patient has been anesthetized you will not be able to see the larynx, is there no way of avoiding this perilous situation? This is a large and complicated subject that can mesmerize a group of anesthesiologists for hours and hours. When I returned to the Brigham and Womens Hospital in Boston in my latter years I shared an office with Dr. Rao Mallampatti, the inventor of the Mallampatti classification of assessing intubation difficulty *before* the patient is anesthetized. I don't know how many specialist anesthesiologists there are in the world, perhaps 150,000. I can warrant they all know the Mallampatti classification.

Is it better to be famous than to have befriended the famous? I have no idea. In England schools have mottos. Mine was 'Rather Use Than Fame'. I'm not so sure I still believe that.

Mr. Embry attached the largest Mac blade I had ever seen and I got a quick clear view of the larynx. To an anesthesiologist nothing is as beautiful as the letter 'A' made by the vocal cords and the tip of the breathing tube sliding between them.

All went smoothly after that. Well, more or less.

"I'm losing more than I expected. There's two pints cross-matched," said Mr. Savage.

By then I knew enough to know that it was not Mr. Savage who was bleeding but Mr. McKendrick. Patients before surgery, even in those less litigious days, signed a piece of paper with the title Informed Consent. I very much doubt that the nurse who got him to sign it explained that he might lose more blood than Mr. Savage's average for a gastrectomy, removing part of the stomach.

Today when all the potential risks are minutely explained I doubt that most patients are really *informed*. I have undergone a lot of surgery and invasive cardiological interventions in the last 25 years. I sign the permit only because if I did not the nurse would be disciplined. The permit in no way comforts me. If I do not trust my doctors what use are written permits? As you will see later they are the invention of that devil, the hospital's lawyer.

Consider that even surgeons and anesthesiologists are not truly informed. There is no way we can remember the details of the innumerable published studies of risk attached to surgery and anesthesia, let alone be able to explain them to the patient before surgery. If a patient asked me, and this happened only rarely,

"Doc, what's the chance of my dying from the anesthetic?" In 1961 I would have said,

"About 1 in 1500 to 1 in 3,000."

Today I could honestly reply, "Much less than 1 in 150,000."

Those statistics come from large scale demographic studies that include all sorts and conditions of patients having all sorts of surgery by surgeons of differing aptitudes and anesthetized by anesthesiologists with widely varying skill and training: including me, the beginner, in 1961.

Each surgeon is allowed a ration of two nurses. The scrub nurse is sterile, if you catch my meaning and the circulating nurse does not actually circulate. She hangs around and fetches and carries. This one brought me two bottles of blood in a picnic cooler containing bags of ice.

One of the worst possible disasters is to give the wrong blood. The anesthetized patient cannot speak up for himself so you have to be very careful checking the compatibility of the donor blood with that of the patient. That day the blood was hunky-dory when I checked it against the information in Mr. McKendrick's chart. But I had a little problem. It would not drip when I plugged it into to Dr. Gordh's needle. I had to crawl under the sterile sheet to try and flush the Gordh with sterile saline. That sheet not only covered Mr. McKendrick's's body but also his arms.

"Don't do that," said Mr. Savage, "you're making a difficult situation worse. Bloody fat patients. I hate them."

There you can see another benefit of general anesthesia. The surgeon can curse uninhibited by the patient hearing him. Or maybe so, as we'll see later. Until now, I have never heard a lady surgeon curse.

I spoke up. "Sir. Mr Savage. Sir."

Because I was still so junior it took courage to speak up.

"Yes, what is it now?"

I had not said a word other than those four. I had tried to erase any hostility from my tone of voice, despite what I felt.

"Sir, Mr Savage, Sir. The Gordh needle is blocked and I need to flush it so the blood will drip."

"Did I say you couldn't flush it?"

To this day I do not know whether or not that question deserved an answer. All went well for a while.

"His blood is blue. Are you giving him enough oxygen?" came the next snappy enquiry from the scene of action.

"Sir, is it venous or arterial?

The blood in arteries is supposed to be red at all times because it has been through the lungs to pick up oxygen before being pushed out into the arteries by the left side of the heart. The blood in veins is supposed to be blue because it is returning from the tissues that have extracted the oxygen to keep their chemical machinery going. It's difficult for the anesthesiologist to look into the wound and ascertain whether he is seeing arterial or venous bleeding. Arteries are supposed to spurt and veins ooze but frequently even the surgeon cannot tell the difference. The red meniscus simply creeps up into his field of view and either he sucks it out or dabs it up with a cotton pad. If the surgeon is aspirating, that is, sucking the blood out instead of mopping with sponges, then the anesthesiologist can watch the amount of blood accumulating in a graduated drainage bottle.

"Are you bloody well insinuating that I don't know the difference between arterial and venous blood?'

Mr. Savage seemed fixated on blood and its angry derivatives but again I thought it wiser not to answer. Then I noticed Mr. Embry standing by my side proffering me a stethoscope.

"Here you are," he said.

Once again I cottoned on. Sometimes the breathing tube is inserted too far down the trachea, the main channel made with scaffolding of cartilage (gristle) that carries air, oxygen, atmospheric pollution; or coal gas if you are trying to end it all but which is now all but unobtainable; and in the operating theatre, anesthetic agents, into the lungs. If the endotracheal tube slips into one side of the division of the trachea into two bronchi, only one lung will get oxygen and the other will allow blood to pass though it, unimproved. There is no coming back for a patient that suffers cyanosis from persistent one-lung ventilation and the damage it may cause in the brain.

I took the stethoscope from Mr. Embry. I carefully slid it under the sheets and listened. The left lung was silent. The tube had slipped into the right bronchus. I undid the tape, pulled the tube back about an inch and re-taped it securely at the mouth using a roll of fresh adhesive tape that Mr. Embry produced from his back pocket.

"He's gone pink. Bloody good work. I'll tell Belam," said Mr. Savage.

Another lesson for me. No matter how angry you are with a surgeon, listen to him. Particularly if he is going to tell Dr. Belam your boss, that you did something correctly. That day began my suspicion that a raging surgeon is not being personal. He is raging because his operation is such a risky struggle or even, as Dylan Thomas said, (a struggle), "… against the dying of the light." He just seems to rage against you the anesthesiologist. To him you are just the closest piece of human furniture.

Mr. McKendrick did well, healed and went home swearing he would never touch another cigarette. He remained unaware of the drama during his surgery.

Mr. Savage's second patient's operation that day had been cancelled and I had a gap until lunch. When I visited that patient the previous night, he, also up for a gastrectomy, told me he suffered from two kinds of pain: one was the burning pain relieved by antacids and milk, typical of peptic ulcer.

"Tell the doctor what happens when you walk the dog or dig in the allotment," his wife had interrupted.

In the 1960s in England, growing your own vegetables in an allotment of land was widespread, a residue of thrift that began twenty years earlier, during the war.

He described pressure under his sternum (breastbone) and into the left side of his jaw. The second symptom sounded like angina pectoris. Translated from the Latin that literally means 'strangling of the heart'. That is correct; the blood supply carrying oxygen through its own narrowed (coronary) arteries to the muscle of the heart is inadequate as soon as the body demands the heart pump a little harder.

I ordered an electrocardiogram for early the next morning and asked the nurse to arrange for a cardiologist to visit him before the surgery. Also, he was quite anemic, bleeding from the peptic ulcer - altogether a much riskier proposition for surgery with general anesthesia. A heart attack at the same time as surgery is often fatal. The cardiologist had postponed the surgery.

With his facemask removed I could see the reason for Mr. Embry's carefully waxed pointy moustache. It turned a pinched Cockney face into something glamorous and dashing.

"I bet you can't guess what my hobby is," he said.

Try as I might I could not guess Mr. Embry's hobby. I ranged from a supporter of the Arsenal Football Club to making his own brand of mustache wax to collecting matchbox labels.

With a proud smile he said,

"I go to Heathrow and watch the planes take off and land. I'm a bit like the chaps who spot trains. Only I'm waiting for one to crash. I feel guilty about thinking that but it's like fishing for the big one."

"And, if you don't mind me being personal that's why you have that wonderful moustache?" I asked. He grinned and twiddled the points to smooth them.

"How did you guess? I always wanted to be a pilot but they wouldn't take me on account of my bad eyesight."

"How did you get into anesthesia, Mr. Embry?" I asked.

"Don't you see? Starting and ending an anesthetic is like taking a plane up and landing it. It's the beginning and the end that are most dangerous."

I could not contradict Mr. Embry.

Four consultant anesthesiologists staffed the Whittington Hospital. Whenever my lists finished earlier than one of theirs I would present myself to one of them hoping to pan some grains of golden knowledge. I did not expect nuggets. They were not paid by the National Health Service to teach; they were paid to do. They were paid by the session. Half a day defined a session, more specifically 3 ½ hours. Most of them undertook to do seven sessions a week, in effect three and a half days. The other day and a half was reserved for private work. This was the result of the bargain struck by the Consultants with the Minister of Health Aneurin Bevan, in the late 1940s when the National Health Service was founded.

No surgeon can guarantee that his operating list will only last exactly three and a half hours and it would it have been unseemly when the clock reached 5.30 p.m. for the Consultant Anesthesiologist to abandon the patient to his or her own devices. It's not easy for an *unconscious* patient to watch his or her own breathing, take his own blood pressure, set up his own blood transfusion when the surgeon did a "dammit, a bloody great vein where it shouldn't have been", or wake himself up as the last suture went in and the dressings were glued on and walk by himself to the recovery room.

This uneasy set of circumstances frequently led to conversations like the following.

A TINY FLAKE OF GOLD IN THEATRE NO. 2

SCENE: Operating Theatre No. 2 at the Whittington Hospital, London:

Consultant Surgeon (C.S.), peering into pelvic cavity through a lower abdominal incision:

"I can't see anything down here. The light's all wrong."

Consultant Anesthesiologist (C.A.), climbing onto a stool at the head of the table and teetering perilously over the sterile surgical site:

"I'll see what I can do with the light, Fred. And I really *will* have to transfuse this lady."

ENTER: Registrar in Anaesthetics, Zeitlin (R.I.A.Z.).

C.A: "Aah! Very good, Zeitlin. How did your list go? All well I'm sure. Now, be a good chap and climb up on these steps and move the light for Fred. He's got a little venous bleeding and I'll hang the blood. Your legs are steadier than mine. Ever since I fell off that horse last weekend. Not so good in the shanks."

R.I.A.Z: " I'll do my best, Sir."

R.I.A.Z. adjusts lamp with the full knowledge that light travels in straight lines and surgeons' heads are opaque.

C.S. "Bloody good show, Roger. Where do you get all these intelligent young chaps? Why isn't he doing surgery is what I'd like to know?"

C.A: (ignoring C.S.) "Well, Zeitlin I suppose you've had your tea."

R.I.A.Z: (feeling for an appropriate response). "Yes, Sir. And Mrs. Embry sent in some home-made scones. With the kind of currants you like, Sir."

C.A: (feeling for an even more appropriate response). "Good show. You do know why the nitrous cylinder gets covered in frost in a long case, don't you?"

R.I.A.Z: "Yes Sir. Latent heat of vaporization needed as the liquid nitrous oxide evaporates."

C.A: (with pleasant smile, feeling his one question suffices as a day's worth of teaching, *his* nugget of gold): "Good show." A pause. "I understand you're on call and there's no hot cases in Casualty."

R.I.A.Z: (reluctantly, but realizing that C.A. has antennae that reach all parts of the hospital) "Yes, Sir."

C.A: "Well then I'll be off. Fred you're in good hands now. (Note: he said the surgeon was now in good hands, not the patient). I'll see you at the R.S.M. (Royal Society of Medicine, a dining club for medical intellectuals and similar types in London's fancy West End) for dinner at 7. You know, the parking in the West End is getting awfully difficult. Try Selfridge's garage."

C.S: "I'll try to get a move on. I wonder if they'll have that halibut in lemon sauce on the menu again. I think theirs is even better than the way Monica does hers"

C.A hands proximal end of precordial stethoscope to R.I.A.Z. with no attempt to remove earwax, and departs, quietly.

The curtain does not come down. The aspiring young actor, me, is not unionized and the play goes on longer than his contracted work hours, but he cannot go on strike. If he went on strike he might just as well emigrate to the Marshall Islands and pick coconuts.

Chapter 7 VIOLENCE

Giving anesthesia can be quite boring, except when it is exciting, too exciting. We live with that paradox.

I had thought of representing the life of an anesthesiologist in this chapter in the following way. I would describe some dramatic life-saving or even a horrifying incident over two or three pages. Then I would leave a couple of hundred pages completely blank to represent the daily routine and the efficacy and safety of what we do. But that would be a waste of paper and would not do in these days of tree-hugging particularly when such influential and substantial figures as Mr. Gore might read this book and get upset.

Anesthesia can also become involved in violence: against others and against yourself.

On the night of Thursday July 1, 1965 I was the on-call Senior Registrar in Anaesthetics at the Middlesex Hospital in Central London. It was late evening and I was still visiting patients who were to undergo surgery the next day. I had phoned Aideen that I would spend the night in the hospital. I was too tired to risk being called back in the middle of the night from our home in the outer London suburb of Wembley. I had not had my supper but the kind-hearted ladies in the cafeteria told me they would leave me a sandwich. I had just said goodnight to the last patient when I was paged. In those days all pages were 'overhead': no portable pagers and no cell-phones. Dr. Hobbiger, the Senior Registrar in the Professorial Medical Unit spoke.

"I have a man here bleeding to death from esophageal varices. None of us can get the Sengstaken tube down him."

Esophageal varices are the result nearly always of cirrhosis of the liver. They are what they sound like: varicose veins *inside* the esophagus and fragile ones at that. Cirrhosis of the liver is the result of widespread death of liver cells and their replacement by fibrous tissue, a sort of gristle, often but not always the result of alcoholism. This gristle blocks the flow of blood into the liver (portal) vein and the pressure in that vein rises. This is like turning the garden hose on and then stepping on it. In turn the veins that feed the portal vein become engorged or varicose and then they burst and bleed.

"We have lots of blood typed and cross-matched but we cannot catch up with him. D'you mind coming over to our ward with your equipment?" Hobbiger continued.

"Not at all," I said. "But I would much prefer to try to get the Sengstaken down on an operating table than in a bed."

Two New York surgeons in the 1920s developed the Sengstaken-Blakemore tube. The idea was to slide a tube down the esophagus and inflate a cylindrical balloon at its lower end to tamponade, that is, compress, the bleeding varices and hope that the bleeding would be controlled. It works about half the time it is used.

"We'll bring him right over," Hobbiger said.

The esophagus is the muscular self-propelled but flexible tube that conducts oysters and champagne down into the stomach. If you could remove an esophagus and put it on show in a funfair it would look like a snake swallowing a salt shaker.

The man's blood pressure, as best the medical registrar could get it, was about 70 over 30, about half of normal. He counted a pulse rate of 120 beats per minute. I saw blood all over the patient's pillow and mustache. He barely responded when I told him I would spray his throat with something to numb it.

"We have given him quite a bit of Nembutal and Pethidine (Demerol). He seems to need a lot of the stuff," Hobbiger told me. Even though alcohol differs in chemical structure from standard sedating agents, alcoholics need more of the latter than a healthy person for sedation or anesthesia.

As we moved the patient onto the operating table in order to have his head in the best position for me to look down his throat he vomited gouts of blood, a mixture of clots and liquid blood. I sucked all this away and saw at least a pint of blood in the suction bottle, some of it gastric juice. That combination has a disquieting smell.

I used a Macintosh laryngoscope to look into his throat to numb it by spraying a 4 percent solution of cocaine. He struggled less than I thought he would when I slid the Sengstaken tube into the upper end of his esophagus and when we estimated the balloon was up against the varices Dr. Hobbiger inflated the balloon.

There followed a period of quiet and a feeling of relief. But the medical registrar reported no improvement in his blood pressure. The Registrar went to the phone. When he came back he said,

"The lab is running out of his blood type. They might be able to get some O Negative blood over from St. Thomas's."

The patient vomited more blood. After more suctioning I saw that the Sengstaken Tube balloon had been regurgitated up into his mouth. Hobbiger asked me to insert it again. I did. This time the patient did not resist at all. The Registrar could not get a blood pressure but could hear a faint heart beat with his stethoscope.

I took Hobbiger to the corner of the operating theatre.

"Seems to me this chap's only hope is to get one of the chest surgeons to open him up. I've heard they can sometimes get at the veins and tie them off via the mediastinum," I told him.

"I had the same idea Gerald. I phoned the boss. He does not want surgeons messing with his patients. I don't argue with him any longer."

In this situation it's hard to know the precise moment of death. It's a progressive matter. But you can be certain it's all over that when you shine a light into the patient's pupils and you see them widely dilated and unresponsive to the light. Their normal response to bright light is to contract. If you are ever unsure how alive you are stand in front of a mirror and do just that.

The face of a man dying of blood loss looks grey. Rather, it looks grey until you place a sample of fine grey English wool suit cloth from Saville Row next to it. Then you see it lacks all color. It

69

looks just like the skin of the cadavers I had worked on in the dissecting room twelve years earlier. Not surprising.

By this time an operating theatre nurse and my anesthesia nurse had arrived. Gently, carefully and respectfully they washed the whole body with its distended belly quite clean. They covered him with a sheet and two hospital porters arrived with a morgue trolley.

"Thank you, Gerald. Don't feel bad," Hobbiger was senior to me. "We all tried hard."

"Who was he?" I asked.

"Some American novelist. Name of Ruark. Quite successful I believe. But a drinker," he replied.

Robert Ruark was born in 1915 in Wilmington, North Carolina, the son of Robert and Charlotte Ruark. Between the end of World War 2 and his death in 1965 he became one of the best-known syndicated columnists and book authors in the United States. He corresponded and was friendly with the likes of Richard Nixon, Bernard Baruch and, most significantly, Ernest Hemingway. Today he is largely forgotten although there is a society devoted to his memory. I recently joined that society although I'm not sure why I did.

Ruark's father also Robert, was a successful accountant until he was ruined financially in the Great Depression. Both parents became alcoholics. Robert was more or less abandoned by his parents and spent more time with his maternal grandfather Captain Edward Adkins, a retired Cape Fear river pilot. One of Ruark's most successful novels is based on this relationship.

Ruark started to drink and on his doctor's orders to try to distract him from the addiction he fulfilled a boyhood dream and went big-game hunting in Africa together with his wife. This led to more successful books including one on the bloody Mau Mau uprising in Kenya. In the 1960s he settled in Spain but remained restless and unhappy particularly when his wife divorced him in 1963. They had no children. In a review of Hugh Foster's 1991 biography of Ruark we find the following: 'His (Ruark's) greatest pleasures in life were drinking and making love and he could not give up drinking.' I call this violence against self.

Two years before this incident I held the post of Registrar at the Middlesex Hospital with Dr. Michael Rickerts as my Senior Registrar. He spent a good deal of his time teaching us juniors. He was thin, good-looking and single. I heard the gossip he never had fewer than two girlfriends at any one time among the nursing and other female staff.

I happened to be in Casualty (E.R.) one morning talking to a patient with acute appendicitis due for surgery later that day when things quieted down in the main operating theatre. The main door opened. Rickerts ran in, grabbed a wheeled stretcher and, saying nothing, still running, disappeared into the street.

"Has there been a car accident on Mortimer Street?" I asked the Casualty Department Sister.

"If there has been I think I would have had a phone call from the Police by now. To get ready," she replied.

"Do you think I should run after him to see if I can help?"

"I think Dr. Rickerts knows what he's up to. If he needed help, he would have said." She was quite correct.

Yet I hung around the Casualty Department just in case. Also, one of the surgeons was forever bringing boxes of Fortnum and Mason's chocolates for the nurses who worked there. I worked my way through the hard centers; I hated the creams and when I ate one by accident I had to counteract it with a nut centre. This took 25 minutes and the nurses insisted I wash them down with a cup of tea.

The street door nudged open. I observed Michael Rickerts doing mouth-to-mouth respiration on a young woman on the stretcher. He stopped for a moment, short of breath. He smiled at me.

"Gerald. Be a good chap and run upstairs and bring me what I need to intubate her."

The truth came out later. This particular nurse had received the impression that Dr. Rickerts was at least as interested in her soul as her body. When he told her he was marrying no one until he was a full Professor, which eventually he became, she phoned him from his flat behind the Middlesex and told him she was about to put her head in the gas oven. In those days heating gas was called coal gas and contained carbon monoxide. Carbon monoxide has a huge affinity for hemoglobin, the pigment in the red blood cells that carries oxygen round our bodies to where it is needed – all over. If the oxygen is replaced by carbon monoxide, and despite the fact that it turns you a bright pink color, little or no oxygen gets to your tissues. That is a bad thing.

Michael had arrived at his apartment on the fourth floor (no lift of course, they were what we called 'cold-water flats') and found his front door bolted from the inside. He ran down to the basement, found a ladder and a hammer. He ran up, broke through the ceiling of the landing, crawled across the joists and broke though the ceiling of his own kitchen. She was not pretending. She had indeed put her head in the gas oven.

He started mouth to mouth respiration, not with much affection I imagine. Morning suicide is quite inconvenient. It's the busiest time in the operating rooms. He carried her downstairs, laid her on the wheeled stretcher and ran back to the Middlesex pausing to do mouth-to-mouth every 20 seconds. She did well. I do not remember whom he married.

The only reason I tell this one anecdote instead of dozens of others is that it illustrates how knowledgeable anesthesiologists are about respiratory physiology and how one's emotional state can lead to violence – against oneself.

My last example is what might be called hierarchical violence. To an unquantifiable extent I was at fault.

My chief at the Middlesex sent me to The London Chest Hospital for a year.

"It will broaden your experience," he said. He was right.

There I learned to care for the very sickest patients with lung and heart diseases, in the operating theatre and in what passed in 1962 for an intensive care unit. Many of the patients suffered from advanced lung cancer and one surgeon in particular, Mr. Jack Belcher approached these unfortunates in a radical way. He was able to completely resect the cancer in a few and they lived out their God-given years. He justified the many failures by giving the patients some hope, instead of saying,

"Go away and die."

In the early sixties surgeons began operating on the heart with greater confidence, in particular on the valves of the heart. These delicate integrated flaps have a tendency to calcify and narrow as we age. One such patient was called, let us say, Sir Arbuthnot Lanes or perhaps Sir Montgomery Abergevenny. It does not matter which – I invented the names to suggest their social and political importance. Belcher cracked his narrowed aortic valve open. Unfortunately Sir X.X., as I'll now call him, also had severe coronary artery disease, which at that time was surgically irremediable. The day after surgery we found him suffering from low cardiac output syndrome, our fancy name for a heart failing as a pump. Thus, he was dying. But he was too important to just let die and extreme measures were judged in order.

Sir X.X. and I, the Registrar in Anaesthetics were packed into a London County Council ambulance and sent westward across London to the Brompton Hospital where they had a hyperbaric oxygen chamber. The theory of this, put crudely, is that high pressure oxygen will penetrate the cells of the heart and thus allow them to contract and pump normally. When the ambulance men lifted him and me into their vehicle I judged that Sir X.X. was certifiably dead. I asked the ambulance man to squeeze the breathing bag for me while I ran indoors and phoned my boss Dr. Bobby Beaver about this circumstance. He listened politely and said,

"Carry on, Zeitlin."

So I carried on: across London through the dense traffic, a couple of hours in the Brompton Hospital, where the hyperbaric technicians looked puzzled but nevertheless drove oxygen under high pressure into his non-functioning body. Then I took him back during rush hour with the patient approximately as dead as on the outward journey.

I had an unholy thought on that journey: would the car drivers who so respectfully moved out of the way of our ambulance done so, had they known the status of its content? Back at the London Chest I took him up to the intensive care unit, set the controls on the mechanical ventilator, and told his nurse that his condition was unchanged, the literal truth. No change from the time 5 hours earlier when I had picked him up. I went home disquieted. In retrospect I should have refused my orders. Instead, I had cooperated in doing violence to poor old Sir X.X.

Chapter 8 LAUGHING GAS IS NOT AMUSING

Let's return to the Whittington Hospital on the high and leafy hills of North London. The Senior Consultant in Anaesthesia was named Otto by his parents, the Belams. I called him 'Sir'. One quiet afternoon Dr. Belam asked me if I would kindly replace him at a dental surgeon's office in a shopfront in nearby Holloway Road.

"All she needs for her extractions is some gas from a McKesson machine. She keeps open on Wednesday evenings for the working men. There are a few guineas attached to this for you. She is very quick. Get there just before six."

The dentist was a middle-aged lady with frosty hair. She met me in her empty waiting room.

"Otto phoned me you'd be coming. Go in there and fiddle with his machine. The first one'll be here in ten minutes. No fillings. Just exodontia on Wednesday evenings."

I knew just enough Latin to guess that the 'ex' in exodontia meant 'out'. Exodontia must be the science of outing teeth, or, as is it called in respectable middle-class circles, 'tooth pulling'.

I had never seen such an anesthesia machine before. I 'fiddled' with it. I peered at the dial at the top. This indicated that by turning the dial one could deliver a mixture of two gases, in precise percentages from zero to one hundred; or, from one hundred to zero. Very ingenious. And it made sense, to be able to vary precisely the percentage of oxygen the patient breathes. I read an engraved label indicating that the McKesson Company in Toledo,

Ohio had made it. I had never encountered an American machine before. I stood back to gain perspective.

Then I saw the ugliness of my situation. The only two gas cylinders attached were one each of nitrous oxide and oxygen. Nitrous oxide is a very weak anesthetic agent; so feeble at rendering people unconscious that it has become known as 'laughing gas', that is, it makes you drunk and giggly. Never before had I given it without adding something more potent, ether and more recently, halothane.

Dr. Frosty the dentist introduced me to the first patient, a muscular builder still in his paint-covered overalls. He was sweating, not from exertion but fear. Anesthesia for dental surgery requires the patient to breathe a gas mixture from a mask that fits over the nose but leaves the mouth accessible. I cursed myself for not even thinking of asking Dr. Belam about taking some Pentothal for intravenous use. I must have been mesmerized by that phrase so rarely used by anesthesiologists about surgeons,

"She's quick."

I applied the nasal mask and dialed a 90 percent nitrous, 10 percent oxygen mixture.

"Please take some deep breaths through your nose," I said. And he did. He closed his eyes but continued to sweat. My free hand counted his pulse rate: about 110 beats per minute. He was not frightened. He was terrified.

"Shall I begin?" she asked.

"Yes," I said because I did not know enough to choose between 'yes' or 'no' and 'yes' seemed more optimistic. I am known as an optimist.

"I can't even open his mouth. Anyway he's too pink. Otto gets them very black and then they relax and I can get the bite-block in – to keep his mouth open," she said kindly.

Too Pink. Very Black. I felt I was trapped in the bell tower of Hampstead Church and the clapper, swinging back and forth was deafening and stunning me.

"Boing, too pink," Then it swung the other way, under the pull of gravity, smashing into me in the middle.

"Boing, very black."

I cut the oxygen to 5 percent. To put it another way, I increased the nitrous oxide to 95 percent. I felt nervous. My hand holding the nose mask felt shaky. The one element drummed into me over and over during my short years in anesthesia was:

"If in doubt give more oxygen."

"What are you going to do? He's still pink and his teeth are clenched," she said, less kindly.

"I dare not give him any less oxygen. I afraid to."

"Well Otto is not, so why are you?

And without waiting for an answer Dr. Frosty said,

"You are no use to me. Go back to the hospital and tell Otto not to send me people without experience. I'll use local, but all these big men hate needles," she said without any kindness at all.

I did as she told me. The next day I never said a word to Dr. Belam, nor he to me; which was odd because she must have complained to him. It seemed as though Otto and I had attended a drunken party each not knowing the other would be there. When we met, sober, the next day neither would acknowledge his obscene but observed behavior to the other.

It was only when I dug around in the medical literature that I came across a description of the anesthesia technique called 'saturation', and it became clear to me that was what Dr. Belam was using on the dentist's patients.

Elmer I. McKesson was born in Walkerton, Indiana in 1881 and died suddenly in 1944. He graduated from Rush Medical College in Chicago, founded in 1837 and named to honor Dr. Benjamin Rush one of the signers of the Declaration of Independence, During McKesson's internship at the Toledo Hospital he became interested in anesthesia and devoted the rest of his professional life to the specialty. A brilliant engineer who ran a successful business, the McKesson Equipment

Company in Toledo, Ohio, he manufactured some of the most sophisticated anesthesia machines ever made. For his time he was remarkably astute in his understanding of what happens to the patient under general anesthesia. All except his one profound misunderstanding of the human body's need for oxygen. Yet his influence was such that incalculable harm was done, particularly to dental patients all over the world.

About 30 years ago all the dentists in the United Kingdom stopped using general anesthesia in their offices because of the many complications including deaths, that resulted. The patients fared just as well and in complete safety when the dentists changed over to local anesthesia. The few patients who required general anesthesia, such as handicapped children, were sent to hospital and received it from a specialist anesthesiologist.

McKesson stated in his various publications that because of nitrous oxide's weakness and in order to use it effectively the patient should be given pure nitrous oxide. Not only did his patients look black (cyanosis) but he advised continuing with the pure nitrous oxide until the patient exhibited 'jactitations' – an old-fashioned word meaning seizures - from oxygen deprivation. Then he gives the game away.

"Anesthesia ... with nitrous oxide is probably due to restricting oxygen in the nerve cell to amounts capable of supporting life functions only."

He imagined, without any proof at all, that by starving the brain of oxygen you produce anesthesia but that the tiny remaining amounts of oxygen are sufficient to keep the brain cells alive. He was guessing.

McKesson was so influential that his technique was widely used in the 1920s and 1930s. I wondered what Dr. Macintosh, the naked professor in Oxford who had interviewed me three years earlier, thought of this. I looked at Macintosh's book published in 1940, Essentials of General Anesthesia with Special reference to Dentistry.

To quote him:

"To be effective in an average patient, its (nitrous oxide's) weak anaes-thetic qualities have to be reinforced deliberately by a reduction of the oxygen intake to such a level that some degree of cyanosis is usually noticeable and is not of serious import."

Even the greatest of us can make errors: John F. Kennedy and Winston Churchill did. I was never again put in a position of being asked to give an anesthetic with insufficient oxygen.

That is not the end of this story. One evening in the late 1970s when we were well settled in the United States our friends Dr. and Mrs. Abroms invited us to dinner. Dr. Abroms is a respected pediatric neurologist. Why is it that I find other people's bookshelves so much more intriguing than my own? I have a bad habit at social gatherings of slipping away and browsing until my wife notices and brings me back. It's not just the gleaming well-dusted, neatly arranged volumes that attract me. If I find something of interest, I look for a chair in a dim corner and start to read.

That particular evening I discovered 'Contributions to the Study of Cerebral Anoxia' by Dr. Cyril Courville. Anoxia, not enough oxygen, is one of the great spooks that haunt all anesthesiologists. I flipped a few pages and just as I heard my wife calling, "Gerald, where are you hiding this time? You're a disgrace to the human race," the words 'nitrous oxide' leapt up at me from the book. I rushed into the jolly drawing room but when no one was looking I scribbled the name 'Cyril Courville' on the napkin from which I munched my mushroom vol au vent.

The following Saturday I dashed off to Harvard's Countway Library of Medicine and found Dr. Courville's 1939 book, Untoward Effects of Nitrous Oxide. Years later, when the Internet gave access to rare-book search sites such as Alibris, I found my own copy.

The book is only 161 pages long but is one of the most terrifying things an anesthesiologist might ever have to read. On page 45 we read the following, which is typical of the many cases he reports:

Case 12: Convulsive seizures and coma following administration of nitrous oxide anesthesia for extraction of teeth. Death after 2 ½ days. Autopsy.

A married painter, 42 years old, having generalized convulsions was admitted to the Cedars of Lebanon Hospital on the afternoon of July 12 1932. The patient was under the influence of the anesthetic for ½ hour. He failed to regain consciousness at the close of the anesthetic, and shortly after developed generalized convulsions.

Here is one paragraph from the detailed autopsy report:

The neurofibrillar structure was found to be altered more or less universally. In the cerebral cortex some of the cells proved to be entirely devoid of argentophilic material. Others showed typical granular degeneration. These changes were especially advanced in the Purkinje cells of the cerebral cortex, where fine and coarse granular fusiform and herudiform degeneration was observed.

You do not need to understand a single word of this pathological jargon in order to realize that this patient's brain had been destroyed. If you really want to get the feel of what this means borrow a copy of this book through the Inter-Library Loan Scheme and look at some of the photos of the slides made from the brains of these unfortunate beings. In the vulgar language of my native country, they are a 'bloody mess'.

It's all too horribly simple. Brain cells die when they have been without oxygen for three to five minutes. Did Dr. McKesson have any excuse for this disastrous idea. I believe not. As long ago as 1868 a Chicago surgeon Edmond Andrews, with an interest in nitrous oxide anesthesia wrote:

'It is my impression that the best proportion of oxygen will be found to be one-fifth by volume, which is the same as in the atmospheric air'.

Dr. Courville was a Professor of Pathology. I have sometimes defined a pathologist as a physician who examines bits of you before it's too late and later, after it's too late. Dr. Courville was also the world's leading expert on the damage caused to the brain by American Indians using their tomahawks to whack open their enemies skulls in war. Just like nitrous oxide, Dr. Courville tells us in one of his monographs that when your Indian friend shows you the handle end of his tomahawk it means he wants to be at peace with you. If he is holding it at the end of the wooden handle you are in trouble. Like nitrous oxide it all depends on how you use it.

Before we leave the subject of nitrous oxide and its use let us take a look at it from another perspective; that of one of the greatest figures in 20th century history, Winston Churchill.

When the Conservative party lost its majority in the House of Commons at the General Election of May 1929 in what used to be Great Britain, Winston Churchill lost his job as Chancellor of the Exchequer. In the next two years his party increasingly shunned him. This was the start of the period in his life now called his 'Wilderness Years'. That ended when war began in September 1939.

His response to these reverses was to write and lecture, both with the additional and important motive of making money. On December 11 1931 he arrived by boat in New York and moved into the newly-built Waldorf Astoria Hotel with his wife Clementine and daughter Diana. That was the start of his third speaking tour of North America.

On the evening of December 13 his old friend, the financier Bernard Baruch, invited him to his Fifth Avenue mansion to meet some mutual friends. Churchill and Baruch had led the effort to produce adequate supplies of munitions for their soldiers in the last two years of what is called The Great War. Both had both lost large sums of money in the stock market crash. Baruch had gambled and regained most of his fortune. Churchill had not and although I have not found any evidence that this was the reason Churchill went to see Baruch that evening it is likely that he went for financial advice. Churchill's finances remained in a precarious state nearly all his life.

After dinner at the Waldorf, undoubtedly lubricated with brandy and champagne Churchill got into a taxi at about 9 p.m. He had forgotten to ask for directions and could not find Baruch's home address in the hotel's telephone book. Churchill later wrote,

"I had been there by daylight on several occasions. I thought it probable I could pick it out from the windows of my taxicab."

For nearly an hour Churchill instructed the driver to drive loops up and down Fifth Avenue to allow him to identify the house. He failed and Churchill lost patience. He told the driver to let him off at a point in the middle of Fifth Avenue believing he could find the building more easily on foot. In two articles published by the London Daily Mail in early January 1932, Churchill described the subsequent events.

"I no sooner got out of the cab than I instinctively turned my eyes to the left. About 200 yards away were the yellow headlights of a swiftly approaching car. I increased my pace toward the pavement about 20 feet away. Suddenly upon my right I was aware of something utterly unexpected and boding mortal peril. I thought. 'I am going to be run down and probably killed'. Then came the blow. I felt it on my forehead and across the thighs."

The right front end of a small truck hit him.
"I lay in the road, a shapeless mass," he wrote.
A small crowd including a policeman gathered and he was lifted into the original taxicab and taken immediately to Lenox Hill Hospital on 77th Street.
Later in his Daily Mail article Churchill describes the events after his arrival at the hospital.

"Soon I am on a bed. Presently come keen, comprehending eyes and deft firm fingers."

The fingers belonged to Dr. Otto Pickhardt, a surgeon on the staff of the Lenox Hill Hospital. He became Churchill's private doctor in the U.S.A. for the next few months.

"We shall have to dress that scalp wound at once," Pickhardt said.
"Will it hurt?"
"Yes."
"I do not wish to be hurt any more," Churchill said.
"The anesthesiologist is already on the way," Pickhardt replied.

The anesthesiologist was Dr. Charles Sanford, one of the very few physicians specializing in anesthesiology in the early 1930s. He spent his whole professional life at the Lenox Hill Hospital.

There are few more vivid descriptions of the patient's experience of general anesthesia than in Churchill's Daily Mail article.

"More lifting and wheeling. The operating room. White glaring lights. The mask of a nitrous oxide inhaler."

Churchill then reflects,

"Whenever I have taken gas or chloroform I always follow this rule. I imagine myself sitting on a chair with my back to a lovely swimming bath into which I am to be tilted and I throw myself backwards; or, again as if one were throwing oneself backwards after a tiring day into a vast armchair. This helps the process of anaesthesia wonderfully. A few deep breaths and one no longer has the power to speak to the world."

He continues,

"With me the nitrous oxide trance usually takes this form; the sanctum is occupied by alien powers. I see the absolute truth and explanation of things, but something is left out which upsets the whole, so by a larger sweep of the mind I have to see a greater truth. It is beyond anything the human mind was meant to master. The process continues

inexorably. Depth beyond depth of unendurable truth opens. I have therefore regarded the nitrous oxide trance as a mere substitution of mental for physical pain. Pain it certainly is: but suddenly these poignant experiences end, and without a perceptible interval consciousness returns. Reassuring words are spoken. I see a beloved face. My wife is smiling."

After a few days in hospital he was discharged back to the Waldorf Astoria. He had suffered widespread bruising and a vertical cut above his eyebrows, the scar from which can be seen in all the thousands of photographs taken later in his life. He had a tube inserted between his ribs, also under a general anesthetic, to drain a hematoma (collection of blood) lying between lung and rib.

But the most frightening occurrence, and in his Daily Mail description it is clear he was quite aware of this, was a complete loss of feeling and ability to move from the waist down while he was still lying in the taxi that took him to the Lenox Hill Hospital. He had suffered a contusion (bruising) of the spinal cord that resolved itself in a few hours. If the blow had been harder he might well have been paralyzed from the waist down, a nearly uniformly fatal injury in 1931. World history might have been different.

While he was recovering he suffered one of his rare but recurrent episodes of depression (he called this his 'Black Dog'). It is also known, and Dr. Courville later wrote about this, that shorter periods of hypoxia (inadequate oxygen) gave rise to lesser complications. I speculate that this was possibly the trigger for Churchill's depression. After all, he was about to embark on huge speaking tour which he loved doing, and for which he was to be paid very liberally.

Churchill forced his sponsor to completely reschedule the tour while he and Mrs. Churchill got onto a boat and spent ten days in the Bahamas recuperating. You might have thought that the sponsor would sue Churchill to compel him to fulfill his contract as originally agreed, but Mrs. Churchill persuaded Dr. Pickhardt to sign statements that Churchill's health required this rest period. Churchill did in fact complete the speaking tour, in the middle of a very severe North American winter, but his sponsor, Louis P. Albers and his fellow investors in the Albers Speakers Bureau went broke six months later. It is not clear whether this was simply the result of the Great Depression or Winston Churchill breaking the terms of their contract.

Chapter 9 TO AMERICA

By March 1965 I had been promoted to Senior Registrar in Anaesthesia at the Middlesex Hospital, Mortimer Street, London W.1.
The Middlesex Hospital was, but no longer is, one of London's
best and most famous teaching hospitals. It has been closed down,
merged into University College Hospital and its building razed.
Recently in London, we drove by in a mini-cab. We saw fine crop
of weeds on the site. The original chapel has been preserved. Sir
Winston Churchill was a patient there for over two months in 1962
after he fractured his hip. I suspect the site of the hospital was
chosen by its founders in the 1740s because of its proximity to The
Cambridge, a rather nice pub across the road.

In 1965 Consultants in Anesthesia wanted as much private
work as they could gather. This meant they had to make themselves available whenever a surgeon's secretary phoned them and
said,

"Professor Turner-Warwick has a couple of cystoscopies at The
London Clinic on Wednesday at about half-past two. Are you available then, Dr. Dinnick?"

The answer was always 'yes' whether or not Dr. Dinnick was
really available. No, meant he was supposed to anesthetize a list
of National Health Service patients on Wednesday afternoon at
The Middlesex. On Wednesday either I, or one of my fellow Senior Registrars would be called to take over Dr. Dinnick's National
Health list at about one-thirty so that he could rush over to the
London Clinic, visit and check the private patient and then anaes-
thetize him or her for Turner-Warwick at 2.30 and then go home
and send a bill for numerous guineas. A guinea is, or was, one
Pound and one Shilling: these days 105 p.

Even though National Health salaries for Consultants were quite generous, living in Central London was expensive. Immediate availability when a surgeon called any time 24 hours a day remained an imperative for success in private practice. We Senior Registrars felt quite sympathetic to our Consultants' financial difficulties and thus we never grumbled about our role, as it were, 'off the bench'. Perhaps we felt some connection to our own aspirations to become Consultants. Sometimes when a Consultant anesthesiologist was booked for two private cases at the same time one of us would be sent as a 'super-sub' to the London Clinic and would end up with a few guinea-crumbs from the Consultants' table, a modest check at the end of the month.

The point is that our superiors considered us fully competent. Otherwise they would not have donated the occasional private patient to us. I had passed all my specialist examinations. I had had every imaginable clinical experience including 18 months at the London Chest Hospital doing cardiothoracic anesthesia, neurosurgical anesthesia at the Maida Vale Hospital for Neurosurgery and so on. I had written and published several papers of clinical and scientific interest in Anaesthesia and The British Journal of Anaesthesia, at that time among the few leading journals in our specialty in the world.

By then we had been married nearly 5 years and had two babies and owned a small house in the far suburbs with a 100 percent mortgage. If it were not for Aideen's professional fees as a freelance violinist running all over the United Kingdom's discovered and undiscovered parts for work, our two babies would have gone hungry. I believe that marasmus, such a threatening word, describes what might have happened to Louise and Jon if there had been a slump in the fiddling business. That is why the conversation I had after lunch one day, with Dr. Peter Dinnick the Chief of Anaesthesia at the Middlesex Hospital, on one of the back stairwells of the hospital remains so utterly clear in my memory; so vivid I can report it word for word:

THE BACK STAIRCASE AT THE MIDDLESEX HOSPITAL

Dr. Dinnick: (in a well-cut suit, going down). "Aah! Zeitlin!"

Dr. Zeitlin: (wearing a 'scrub suit', going up). "Yes. Sir."

Dr. Dinnick; "I think I'll be done at the Clinic by 7. Two hips and a fractured elbow. Why don't you spread the word I'll be buying bitters for the boys at the Cambridge in the Private Bar."

Dr. Zeitlin: "Yes Sir, Thank you Sir. And I'll see the patients coming in for your G.Y.N. list tomorrow."

Dr. Dinnick: "Aah! Zeitlin! Very good."

Dr. Zeitlin: (ascends two steps and is now level with Dr. Dinnick who is about to take the next step down. It is quite clear to Dr. Zeitlin from this that Dr. Dinnick has assumed that the thought of free beer had ended any substantive speech on Dr. Zeitlin's part. Despite my correct assumption about his assumption I looked for and found a mote of courage for my next major pronouncement): "Sir."

Dr. Dinnick (detecting a note of anxiety in that syllable). "What is it Zeitlin? No trouble with a surgeon I hope, old chap?"

Dr. Zeitlin: "Oh No Sir! Not at all Sir. In fact things went very well yesterday with Oswald Eyeball. (Dr. Dinnick's secret name for an amazingly compulsive eye surgeon.) Ha, Ha!"

Dr. Dinnick: "Aah! Very good! Pleased to hear it. But what's troubling you old chap?"

Dr. Zeitlin: "Well, Sir. I was thinking of applying for a Consultant job. Perhaps in a year or two (in a defensive tone of voice). I would value your support Sir. If you think it appropriate. Sir."

Dr. Dinnick: (after a long pause; only one of the modern testing kits now available over-the-counter at Walgreens could decide whether it was a pregnant pause or not)

"Aah! I see now! Let me think for a moment, old chap."

Dr. Zeitlin: "Of course, Sir."

Dr. Dinnick: (after thinking). "Well, Zeitlin you are a bit thin on the ground. (inexperienced, in AmerEnglish). You should think about getting your B.T.A. (BTA was the informal slang for the mystical Been-To-America Diploma).

Dr. Dinnick: (after another thoughtful pause) "Yes, that's the best way. Spend a year in the States, doing research or something useful like that, get published, polish your C.V. so to speak, come back home, spend a little more time with us and then we'll see, won't we."

Dr. Zeitlin: "Oh! Thank you Sir! Jolly good idea Sir!"

Dr. Dinnick: "Well then. See you across the road. About seven. Tell the boys I'm paying. If I'm late put it on my tab."

It was not "a jolly good idea". I know that sounds bitter. I still feel bitter even though poor old Dinnick is now sleeping underground.

What Dinnick did not know, nor would he have cared was that my C.V. was already polished. When I arrived at the Middlesex two years earlier there was no academic program at all for us residents. I persuaded the Consultants to give us two lunchtime lectures a month. If there was one reason why Dinnick wanted me to go to America for a year it was *not* to polish my curriculum vitae. It was simple. He did not want more competition for the gold of private practice if I should be appointed as another Consultant at the Middlesex.

The following week Aideen and I left the babies with her mother and took the Underground to the American Embassy in Grosvenor Square. I have been told recently that the surrounding real estate, some of the fanciest in London, has fallen dramatically in value. No one wants their Spode china tea sets spoiled by an Al Queda car bomb intended for the Embassy.

There we applied for permanent visas to the USA. We told ourselves this was only a precaution. We'd spend a year there, then another perhaps in Australia, see the world, that sort of thing, and then settle down in Jolly Olde England. We had to apply for visas for the babies in addition to our own. On the form we completed for two year old Louise we swore she had never engaged in prostitution or drug-running. This encouraged us so much about the rule of law in the United States that we went and had a cup of tea we could ill afford in an expensive little café near Grosvenor Square.

That September I traveled on one of Sir Samuel Cunard's smaller liners, the SS Sylvania from Liverpool to Boston, Massachusetts. That year in Boston, Massachusetts had been a particularly murderous one. Gangs in South Boston and Revere felt in need of target practice; what could be better than the bodies of their rivals in the drug trade? The news of this sporting activity was so startling and so frequent it reached the British newspapers. Each morning on my way to work I glanced at the Daily Telegraph waiting on our doorstep. If a Boston murder appeared on the front page I took it with me to work and threw it away. If Aideen asked me why the Telegraph had not come when I got home that evening I felt quite justified in lying to her.

"The newsboy has the 'flu."

I did not want her to know anything about Mafia criminal activity despite our positive experience at the American Embassy. This reminds me of a conversation I had years later with my cousin Eli Gottlieb when he came from London to visit us in Boston.

"Gerald, I'm surprised at you bringing your dear wife and children to this dangerous, violent country," he said.

That time I could think of no powerful answer. Clearly he had been watching too many American TV programs; the British love the two-dimensional violence. The next time he came he asked the same question. I asked him,

"Eli, you're quite an historian. How many wars has the U.S.A. been involved in since 1776?

"I'd say about 7 or 8," he said, flattered by my question.

"And how many wars have there been in Western Europe, an area with roughly the same population?"

He thought for a moment, as he nervously approached our neighbor's rose garden which was under attack from some hostile Japanese Beetles. I think he was thinking of Pearl Harbor.

"Oh, Gerald, at least 200," he answered in satisfied tone of voice.

Illogical but nevertheless, 'Touché'.

On the S.S. Sylvania in late September 1965 I shared an Under-class cabin that contained two double bunks. It slept myself and three other gentlemen. One was a Chinese divinity student, very pleasant, but the other two were more interesting, two Irishmen in their 70s who smoked all night and kept the porthole shut.

They had emigrated to America 50 years earlier, illiterate farm-boys from Killarney, and made good. Harold became Postmaster in Medford and Oscar became Chief of Police in Brockton. They never lost touch. They married their colleens and the four of them dreamt their whole American lives that when they collected their pensions they would buy a cottage overlooking the Irish Sea and would live there happily ever after and their grandchildren who had all attended Harvard or Yale and then in turn had become Mayors of their suburban towns or Massachusetts legislators, would visit regularly.

"So … why are you on this boat from Liverpool to Boston?" I asked.

"We are *re-emigrating*. To America," Oscar said, coughing a smoke-ring at the iron ceiling.

"Our wives have already flown home. We're traveling with the luggage, " Harold said.

"We bought a lovely cottage on the beach in Hyannis on Cape Cod. You can walk to the supermarket, go to watch the Celtics in Boston and be home before midnight. The Kennedy compound is down the road and they wave to us when they're in residence."

My question "But why leave Ireland?" was almost swamped as they both interrupted each other.

"We couldn't stand the rain."

"We couldn't afford the income tax."

"We didn't hate the British enough."

"The urinals in the pubs stank."

"We would not have the priests tell us how to live."

"The poverty made me sick"

"Some of the kids had no shoes."

They had become American, an affliction from which there is no return.

I reached the quarter-finals of the deck tennis tournament before we docked in Boston. This is a sport in which you have to catch a rope ring thrown by your opponent over a net on a rolling ship. It results in two handfuls of filthy broken nails. This was of no consequence other than that anesthesiology is a 'hands on' specialty; we do things to patients with our hands. Patients, nurses and surgeons watch us. I did not want have to start with excuses in this brave new world so I scrubbed and scrubbed them in the week before I began work.

We slid into Boston Harbor five days later very early on September 23 1965. A cool, thick mist lay on the city although I could see the tip of the Custom House Tower, pointed out to me by a fellow–passenger at the rail. As we docked I knew for certain this was America. I could not see any streets paved with gold but I did see most of the longshoremen and dockhands smoking cigars. In London only successful businessmen at weddings and clubby Presbyterian stockbrokers smoked cigars. Longshoremen in Liverpool smoked Players cigarettes broken in half: that is if they were not on strike and on the dole.

I walked down the gangplank and stood bewildered as our crate of cribs, clothes and kitchen equipment was dumped at my feet by a gentle, accurate crane driver. How did he know this embarrassing pile of domesticity was mine? The family would arrive a week later by plane.

"Hi Gerry. Nice morning. Roy sent me to pick you up," came a voice out of nowhere "I'm Jeep."

No one, unintroduced, had ever before called me by my first name let alone my nickname. 'Jeep' was rugged with the tight hair only seen on cowboys in Westerns, a composite of all the tough handsome Hollywood film actors with whom I had grown up and aspired to but knew I would never become. He had an accent that I later learned was called Southern Intellectual.

I surmised as we shook hands that this must be Dr. Ellison (Jeep) Pierce, the Vice-Chairman of the Anesthesia Department at the Peter Bent Brigham Hospital, one of the Harvard teaching hospitals. The Peter Bent Brigham Hospital was named in memory of a Vermont native who came to Boston as a young man, started out as a restaurateur and then, like so many of them made a fortune investing in the railroad business. He died in 1877 and in his will stated that the bulk of his fortune was to be used 25 years later to found a hospital for the sick and indigent of Boston. The hospital opened in January 1913 and the first operation there took place on the 28th of that month. The only description of that first operation I have been able to find makes no mention at all of who gave the anesthetic and what agents or techniques were used. Typical.

Until I met him I did not know that Dr. Pierce was called 'Jeep' by one and all. Jeep was to have considerable influence on my career in America and, as we will see, had a profound effect worldwide on the safety of anesthesiology.

'Roy' must have been Dr. Leroy Vandam, the Professor of Anesthesia at the Brigham, the Harvard teaching hospital where I went to work as a junior faculty member. They gave me the title of Instructor in Anesthesia at Harvard Medical School without my asking. I never got an academic promotion, partially because I left academia for the middle years of my American career. There may have been other reasons: I never asked. These days when I give a talk illustrated with slides I put: Gerald L. Zeitlin, MD, FRCA, *Non-Emeritus* Instructor in Anesthesia, Harvard Medical School, Boston, MA on the title page. I can discern how many in the audience are awake from the volume of snickers.

Without a word, Jeep loaded our household goods onto and into his Volvo, one of the tiny early imports to the U.S.A. As he squeezed me into the passenger seat he said,

"I don't suppose Dr. Matson would be very pleased about that."

"Excuse me, but why is that?"

Already I felt less inhibited. None of the 'Sir' business I always used in London.

"He operated on my back. Fixed a protruding disk. Just three weeks ago."

Jeep drove me to the tiny house we had rented for the year we were to spend in America, a house belonging to a local church in a far suburb called Natick. It was so small that I painted the whole interior in one day before the rest of the family arrived by plane a week later.

That evening, after work, Jeep took me to Ken's Steakhouse for supper. I should not have allowed him to order for me.

"What would you like?" he said, passing me an enormous menu.

"Something American. Would you please order for me?" I said.

A steak the size and thickness of a volume of the Encyclopedia Britannica arrived, enough to feed a British family for a week. It was then I began to understand Jeep's sense of humor.

Intermission THE CREMATION OF T.S. ELIOT

Let us go then, you and I,
When the evening is spread out against the sky
Like a patient etherized upon a table:

These are the first three lines of T.S. Eliot's poem 'The Love Song of J. Alfred Prufrock', published in 1915. Ever since I first read the poem I have wondered why he entrances us with the first two lines and then, blam!, hits us in the face with the mundane image in the third. I have searched widely for an explanation why he used that particular image. Later in 'Prufrock' Eliot writes,

It is impossible to say just what I mean.

This just reflects his inherent modesty. I intend to show that Eliot did know just what he meant. In retrospect it seems he found in me an understanding listener, or, for that matter would have, in any Board-Certified anesthesiologist he met.

Eliot died on January 4 1965 and was cremated the same day at the Golders Green Crematorium in London, about a quarter mile from Golders Green Station on the Northern Underground line. That is where I changed from train to bus on my way home from work at the Middlesex Hospital. Instead of mounting my usual number 83 bus, an incomprehensible force compelled me to walk to the Crematorium. That afternoon I had read of his death in the Evening Standard.

Polished hearses hovered there, polluting the front court-yard. They disturbed me, so I walked through an archway into the quiet rose garden behind the crematorium. The rose bushes had been pruned down for the winter but already showed signs of renewed life A gardener whom I asked told me Eliot had just been incinerated.

In life Eliot was known as a reticent man but as his volatile remnants drifted out of the brick tower and far away across the damp sky his soul, that had remained behind, spoke to me.

I heard Eliot say that 'Prufrock' was intended as a paean to anesthesia. Its subject was the escape from the agony of surgery. It seems hard to believe that none of the literati whose writings I consulted could have revealed this. But none of them had undergone the wrenching experiences anesthesiologists, surgeons and their patients have, and that Eliot understood completely. In Prufrock anesthesiologists will find the truth about our practice that Eliot intended with that third line.

For example, further in the poem he says

In the room women come and go
Talking of Michelangelo

That is, our predecessors felt excluded, just looking in. This metaphor reflects anesthesiologists' struggle for status and recognition in the medical firmament.

In the poem's fourth stanza Eliot encapsulates the history of our specialty. It is evident he is talking of the time between October 1846 and now with a profound understanding of our everyday work lives, when he writes:

Time for you and time for me
And time yet for a hundred indecisions

And for a hundred visions and revisions
Before the taking of a toast and tea.

Earlier in the poem he addresses the importance of anesthesiologists acting as perioperative physicians:

Let us go and make our visit.
Oh, do not ask, 'What is it?'

Eliot understood the distress felt when reading the scheduling
white board attached to the Operating Room (O.R.) wall at 6.30
a.m. and finding one has been assigned to the M.R.I. room far
from the Main O.R., and help.

And when I am formulated, sprawling on a pin,
When I am pinned and wriggling on the wall,

His insight into our daily lives is astonishing; for example he
appreciates the significance of doing a 15 hour neurosurgical case
with little hope of more than a single brief caffeine-break:

For I have known them all already, known them all:
Have known the evenings, mornings and afternoons,
I have measured out my life with coffee spoons;

Eliot is aware of the horrid realities of taking in-hospital over-
night call and of having to eat hospital cafeteria food. He is so
distressed by this that he is only able to describe it in poetic terms:

The muttering retreats
Of restless nights in one-night cheap hotels
And sawdust restaurants with oyster-shells:

With his last stanza Eliot transcends these irksomenesses by
revealing the glory and satisfaction our specialty provides. In this

coda he describes the feelings of the patient, waking in the recovery room. The patient 'drowns' in the ecstatic understanding that with our care she has survived the surgery.

> *We have lingered in the chambers of the sea*
> *By sea-girls wreathed in red and brown*
> *Till human voices wake us, and we drown.*

Chapter 10 WHAT IS ANESTHESIA?

In order to answer this question and even though we now live in America I need to look back briefly at my early days working in London hospitals. After several months as an untutored beginner I started to relax. I learned not to react to each fluctuation of the pulse. This was particularly true when the surgeon, deep in the abdomen had to pull on the transverse colon, the large bowel where feces form, in order to get at some valuable object deeper in the belly. When the surgeon lets up, the pulse rate returns to normal. I learned from the few patients whose blood pressure I measured that a fall in the systolic (upper) number of 10 or 20 points was inconsequential and, because by that time I had begun setting up an intravenous infusion in more of the patients as a routine, simply increasing the drip rate was therapeutic. In hindsight I am appalled at the number of anesthetics I gave in those days without an intravenous infusion running and very little, if any, instrumental monitoring.

Giving an anesthetic as a beginner resembled learning to ride a bicycle. Your body and more importantly, what passes for your mind, auto-corrects and you react only to large impediments or variations such as a fit of coughing by the patient or the surgeon saying, "I'm about to clamp the aorta."

Then you watch the blood pressure and urine output like a hawk. 'Like a hawk' is an unsuitable simile: "like a tailor getting the shoulders even" might be better. Hawks float high above the scene of their intended victims, tailors peer closely.

Occasionally, say for a long operation such as a skin reconstruction as in plastic surgery, things were so stable that I would relax and let my mind wander. Most anesthetists if questioned directly would deny this happens but believe me they are not telling the truth. They simply have two awarenesses going at the same time. Only since I retired have I heard the phrase 'multitasking'. I now realize that is what we were doing. Which of the bills would I have to pay at the end of the month and which could I delay? When would the baby stop getting us up three or four times a night? When would I ever find time to study for the FFARCS? Why were starting faculty anesthesiologists in New York getting four times the salary that a consultant got in London? Would I have to do two extra nights on call this week because my fellow Registrar, Remo was down with the 'flu?

I would take a blood pressure, scribble a few squiggles on the written record of the anesthetic and wander into philosophical thoughts.

What is this anesthesia business all about? Where did it come from? Now I have about 200 books on the bookshelves in my home office that in one way or another can be classified under the heading '*The History of Anesthesia*'. Barbara Duncum's magnificent Development of Inhalation Anaesthesia was all I could afford in England.

There have been a few times when we were told, especially by consulting firms, that we were training too many anesthesiologists. In my 40 years we always had and I suspect always will have more work than we can handle. Surgeons and now all the new 'invasive' specialties, particularly cardiologists and radiologists come up with new therapies that need our skills. A good example: the growth of surgery in M.R.I. units and the consequent difficulties for us arising from the powerful magnets therein. They can whisk a steel pen out of your pocket and smash it into a patient in an unexpected instant.

In 1994 the American Society of Anesthesiologists commissioned the services of Abt Associates, a consulting firm, to study future manpower needs in the specialty. After extensive study Abt Associates told us that by the year 2010 we would have trained far too many anesthesiologists for the predicted volume of work.

They were quite wrong – there is nothing remarkable about that – there are still shortages of personnel. The prediction of manpower requirements in many medical specialties is a 'losers' game. A rude person would say that the Abt Associates report was 'in-apt'. But that is not fair. Who would have thought for example, 20 years ago, that a significant part of what cardiac surgeons do, bypassing blocked coronary arteries would be taken over by cardiologists opening these obstructions with balloon-tipped catheters and propping them open with stents.

I am a prime example of that trend. I underwent coronary artery bypass surgery in 1989 and since then have undergone *three* separate and successful angioplasties with stenting. My sludgy coronary arteries are kept open with ingeniously woven wire cylinders put in place via a catheter in my femoral artery.

Let us see if in a few hundred words we can find out why we exist and where we come from. Without anesthesia millions of people would suffer agony every year when they underwent surgery. The terrifying descriptions of surgery without anesthesia at the end of this book testify to this simple fact. I should have said *almost* no surgery would or could be done.

The idea of diminishing human suffering was not always accepted. Historians will tell you that the relief of human pain is an aspect of the great wave of humanitarian thinking that we call the Enlightenment. Another huge subject that, if it should interest you, you can study in several of the books listed in the Bibliography.

Let us think about the straightforward stuff. The chemical structure of ether is quite simple. In 1540 a German scientist, Valerius Cordus discovered that if you took two molecules of alcohol, each molecule a neat arrangement of carbon, hydrogen and oxygen and mixed in a molecule of sulphuric acid, an atom of oxygen was removed and the two molecules of alcohol joined together to give him a new substance, ether. You might argue that if a little alcohol makes you a little sleepy, then, if you combine it with itself it, logically, should make you very sleepy, that is anesthetize you. Scientists reading this, will scornfully say,

"That's naïve chemistry." And they would be correct.

Why did it take about 300 years from the time Valerius did his thing for people to realize that ether could anesthetize you quite safely. It has to do surprisingly, with ethics, concepts of human life. and religion, as they affected the idea that unrelieved pain is not necessarily part of the human condition.

Here is a paradox. Most humans now accept the idea that pain should be treated or relieved, yet we go on with wars, endless wars that probably are the cause of more pain in more people than all the operations and all the untreatable cancers have ever done.

In October 2009 I went the annual meeting of the American Society of Anesthesiologists (ASA) to try to find out if there was anything new about how general anesthesia works. In particular I wanted to know what Dr. George Mashour had to say about how the brain functions during general anesthesia. He is an expert.

I absconded halfway through the lecture in another hall (they are much too big to be called lecture rooms) that preceded Dr. Mashour's. I have a face-saving technique for this. Before the lights dim in a lecture hall I usually 'buddy-up' with whomever sits next me:

"Where are you from?" Where did you train?" we say to each other.

"Oh really, did you know Roy Vandam ? I think he was Senior Resident there in 1964."

"Are your kids in college?"

"Etc."

Then, at the crucial moment, that is 15 minutes before my estimate of the end of *this* lecture I whisper,

"I hope there's a Men's Room close by."

I pick up my papers and creep out ducking under the slide projector's beam of light. I do not return.

Years ago I wrote a series of articles about the American anesthesia scene for the Newsletter of the British Association of Anaesthetists. In one of them I told about my observations of the number of my colleagues who went fast asleep when the lights dimmed for the projected slides during a lecture at the A.S.A. annual meeting. A couple of months later I received an angry letter from the then President of the A.S.A. I still have his letter but do not quite understand what upset him. You, of course know the old joke in which the surgeon addresses the anesthesiologist, saying,

"If the patient's awake, why can't you be?"

Another year I was appointed one of the Delegates from Massachusetts at the annual get-together of the House of Delegates of the A.S.A. – the Parliament of American Anesthesia.

For the last thirty or so years some medical specialties have tried methods by which they, and presumably the public, can rate the competence of their members. That year an enterprising member of the A.S.A. had proposed that his particular method of rating the competence of anesthesiologists be adopted as the official position of the House. He based his rating method on the number of *bad* outcomes that each of us inflicted on patients in the operating room. Most of us felt it was statistically meaningless since, these days, most trained anesthesiologists have no, or, at worst only one or two bad outcomes in a lifetime of giving anesthetics.

I spoke to a number of my politically better-connected, more academically-distinguished colleagues from around the country, suggesting they speak against the resolution. They avoided the matter. So, I, a political neophyte, spoke up with my quaint English accent booming from the microphone set-up. The motion was defeated.

I have a photograph of myself standing at the microphone, taken by the A.S.A's official photographer from the balcony. It gives a fine view of my impending bald spot. Fortunately he had a fast lens and the viewer cannot see how my hands shook.

Before we get to Dr. Mashour, there's something else you should know about the ultimate question of how anesthetic agents work. In 1915 an anesthesiologist from Avon Lake, Ohio named

Dr. Frank H. McMechan, edited the very first ever book on the scientific aspects of anesthesia with each article written by a specialist. Before that time only two practicing anesthesiologists had applied scientific methods to what they were doing. Both of them worked in London: Dr. John Snow in the 1860s and Dr. Goodman Levy during the first decade of the 20th century.

The first article in Dr. McMechan's book, by a PhD called Ralph Lillie is titled 'The Physico-chemical Theory of Anesthesia' and you might expect some kind of reasonable explanation of how general anesthetics put you to sleep. The article is 30 pages long but its message may be summed up by the following extract from the last page.

"Anesthetic action is due primarily to a modification of the plasma-membrane of the cells … etc."

But in all 30 pages I could not find any details of direct evidence as to what that modification consisted of: just a series of hypotheses and speculations. All this means is that the evidence that had been gathered between 1846 and 1915 shows that something is changed at the surface of the nerve-cells in our brains - where consciousness is assumed to reside. These cell membranes as they are called, consist of molecules of proteins and fats all neatly arrayed and interlocking. But so does something happen at the surface of our cells if we spill a boiling kettle on our shins. It does not explain the reversible unconsciousness provided by ether.

Let's jump forward to October 2009 and Dr. Mashour's lecture titled, Unconscious Processes. It was fascinating. He talked about his and others' discoveries that under general anesthesia various parts of the brain did not communicate as well with each other as they do when we are awake.

I left Dr. Mashour feeling disappointed. It is not that his work is not enormously important – it's that I want a comprehensive and 'close-up' explanation of how these chemicals work on the brain cells. I wanted something analogous to an explanation of how local anesthetics work, substances like novocaine or lidocaine that the dentist injects to numb your mouth. It's not difficult to demonstrate they block the passage of electrical activity that carries pain sensation along nerves.

The majority of practicing anesthesiologists are not specialized scientists but in their everyday work they want a simple explanation of what they are doing to patients when they "put them to sleep". I am a member of that group.

Dr. Mashour made one point very clear: anesthesia and sleep are distinctly different states of unconsciousness. He also said, to quote him directly, that there is no single mechanism or "anesthesia center" in the brain that is responsible for the loss of consciousness produced by general anesthesia.

I also wanted to know whether anything had changed since Dr. Lillie in 1915. At great expense I bought a copy of the current issue of the 6th edition of our major textbook, Clinical Anesthesia edited by Dr. Barash.

At the end of Chapter 5 'Mechanisms of Anesthesia and Consciousness' it says,

"The technological revolutions in molecular biology, genetics and cell physiology make it likely that the next decade will provide some answers to the century-old pharmacologic puzzle of the molecular mechanism of anesthesia."

At the moment that is all we know. Here's a fascinating prospect that lies ahead: perhaps when we understand what underlies general anesthesia it will lead us to understand that other great mystery, human consciousness.

I'll end this chapter with a definition from the Oxford Dictionary of the American Language:

EMPIRICAL (adj.) concerned with, or verifiable by observation or experience rather than theory or pure logic.

That is one of the most fascinating aspects of the history of anesthesia. In early 1846 William T.G. Morton, the Boston dentist used *empiricism* when he tried out ether on the dogs roaming around his farm in Wellesley, Massachusetts, just five miles from where I'm writing this. It worked then. And it works now.

Chapter 11 HOW MANY SHALL LIVE AND HOW MANY SHALL DIE

(From the Jewish Prayer book for the Day of Atonement)

The title of this chapter touches on another aspect of anesthesia, life or death. In the prayer book for the Day of Atonement we are asked to confess our sins; this is reinforced by the strong suggestion that if we do not confess sincerely we should consider our own mortality. Even as a child I felt uneasy at that linkage and now if I'm in synagogue at that moment, instead of at home eating lunch, it still makes me uncomfortable.

Back in London, my father went once a month to a lecture at the London Jewish Hospital Medical Society (L.J.H.M.S.). When he came home he would talk about the excitement accompanying the announcement of some new medical discovery. With the callousness and ignorance of youth I politely pretended to listen but took nothing in. Now I wish I had.

One of the founders of the L.J.H.M.S. was Dr. Alfred Goodman Levy, the man who for once and always revealed how chloroform kills and, although it took many years after his 1911 revelations, started the disappearance of chloroform from anesthesia. His story is revealing about the uneven road to safe anesthesia.

In 1890, Cecil Rhodes, the British entrepreneur and founder of the De Beers diamond cartel in South Africa at the end of the 19th century, persuaded the native leader Lobengula to allow him to explore for minerals in Matabeleland. Bulawayo, its capital, could only be reached from the Cape Colony by taking a dangerous journey on an ox-cart. Bulawayo was a typical rough but ready miners' town comparable to those in the American West.

What was a nice Jewish boy Goodman Levy doing in the wilds and woollies of South Africa in the late 1800's? Goodman Levy was born in Melbourne, Australia in 1866. His parents were among the many families who left England for Australia at the time of the Australian Gold Rush.

The now prosperous family returned to England and Alfred studied medicine at University College Hospital in London and qualified in 1892. His first job was as assistant medical officer at the Stoke Newington Dispensary in North London. This dispensary was located on Church Street just round the corner from Cazenove Road. Thirty nine years later, on March 7, 1931 a woman, Ida Zeitlin, gave birth to a male baby at number 89 Cazenove Road. His parents named that baby Gerald Leon Zeitlin. I have his birth certificate, because it's mine.

There is no connection between the two events other than a geographic one. If I had been born 39 years earlier Dr. Levy might well have delivered my mother of me .

Levy had been the first and only qualified physician in Central Africa. Needs must, and among all his other duties he performed a hysterectomy and trephined a skull while he was there. He must have given ether when necessary but so far I have found no direct evidence for this. In 1896 the Matabele natives rose up against the settlers and Goodman was injured in the hand during the ensuing fighting. Soon after, he returned to England and became an anesthesiologist, probably to earn a living while he pursued his love, research.

Back at University College Hospital he worked with Dr. Thomas Lewis, the cardiologist who turned early observations on the electrical activity that accompanies every heartbeat into the modern scientific method of deciding whether the patient's heart is beating regularly or not: in other words, the science of electrocardiography. This important cooperation between two doctors in different fields of medicine, cardiology and anesthesia resulted in the first truly scientific study in our specialty.

In 1959 Dr. J. Alfred Lee, a British anesthesiologist published the fourth edition of his too modestly titled textbook Synopsis of Anaesthesia. During the time I was 'breaking in' I worked for and with Dr. Lee at the Southend General Hospital for one precious month. He was a devoted teacher and the most knowledgeable anesthesiologist I ever met. I used the technique for performing epidural blocks he taught me, unchanged for the four decades encompassing my active practice.

His Synopsis is five hundred and seventy eight pages long. Yet, even the great Dr. Lee was unable to devote more than one paragraph to the single most important question that can be asked about anesthesia. How many people die as a result of an anesthetic? If the answer is greater than zero, we need to ask why *do* people die as a result of the anesthetic? Obvious though it may be, it's worth saying out loud again that anesthesia rarely has any intrinsic beneficial function other than to facilitate the performance of surgery.

It's also obvious that death as a result of anesthesia is fraught. It's worth quoting Dr. Lee on the matter. It seems to me the question was so painful for him to consider that he, the supreme clinician, appeared to avoid it with a legalistic comment.

"In the case of a death on the operating table, legal responsibility will exist only if either the surgeon or the anaesthetist has failed in the proper execution of his functions as a person of professional skill."

In 2011 we anesthesiologists are still embedded in our history and held there by this single thread. Almost everything else has changed in our specialty but all of the tens of thousands of us today, all over the world, whether experienced or a brand new resident at the Massachusetts General Hospital in Boston on July 1 giving his or her first anesthetic, are bound together by the fear of damaging or killing a patient. Sixteen years after the introduction of chloroform, in 1863, the number of *known* deaths in England from chloroform totalled 123. In 1864 The Royal Medical and Chirurgical Society appointed a committee to investigate this disaster.

In the introduction to their report they said,

"Even this large number is probably far short of the aggregate mortality which must have been due to its use in various parts of the world. Many of these deaths, moreover, happened during trivial operations, which without chloroform are not attended with risk to life. Added to these there are cases still in which life is placed in imminent jeopardy during the administration of chloroform, although it is not actually lost."

This last sentence if full of significance for me, and, I suspect everyone giving anesthesia. Although superficially it appears concerned with placing patients in 'imminent jeopardy', the subtext is the *potential* for the anesthesiologist to lose the life placed in his or her care. In various recent surveys anesthesiologists talk about the 'stress' of the job. Of course there are many other causes but underlying them all is this awareness of the potential for harm. Perhaps this is in part why our specialty was the first and leading one to promulgate safety guidelines – something I'll deal with later.

Eventually that Committee came out with its report. They fudged the issue. They recommended the use of mixtures of chloroform and ether, ignoring that each drug acted independently of the other and thus the danger was in no way diminished.

I have studied the status of anesthesia in England during the Edwardian era when it got mixed up in high politics and strangely, in which Winston Churchill became involved. In 1909, forty years after the Royal Society's report, more people died of chloroform than were murdered in England. So far as I have been able to discover, no one was hung by the neck in 1909 for using chloroform.

I am only a sort of historian. People like me have been described as enthusiastic amateurs. We go to the back stacks of ancient libraries to look at the Boston Medical and Surgical Journal or the Lancet, the leading British medical publication. We turn the yellow pages nervously but still they crumble into dust and we worry that a librarian will come along and turn us into dust. When we find an historic treasure we carry the book to the copy machine knowing this is probably the very last time in eternity that anyone will ever look at that particular page - except perhaps those magicians at Google who intend to electronify the world of intellectual activity. Those of us over the age of fifty look at the pages of fracturing words and think that Shakespeare's consolations in the play Cymbeline apply to both ourselves and these unshelved books, comforting us as we approach death together.

"Fear no more the frown of the great/Thou art past the tyrant's stroke;
Care no more to clothe and eat;/To thee the reed is as the oak:
The scepter, learning, physic, must/ All follow this, and come to dust. "

In the middle of the 19th century in the United Kingdom very few doctors specialized in anesthesia. One was Dr. Joseph Clover. If you glance at the front cover of this book you'll see him at work. You will notice he is *monitoring* the patient. Look carefully and decide how he is doing that. The original photograph of Clover hangs in the Nuffield Department of Anaesthetics in Oxford – the place where Professor Macintosh interviewed me!

The next time you are in London please get onto the Underground as I did six years ago, and travel to West Brompton Station on the District Line. Once on the street you will stand next to the main gate of the Brompton Cemetery. Walk down the central path and swing to the left near the Basilica. There you will find Dr. Clover's tomb, white marble engraved in black relief lying recumbent and covered in weeds. I had to clear the weeds before I could read the inscription. He was born in 1825 and died in 1882. His parents, wife and two children are buried there together with him. He became 'chloroformist' to University College Hospital in London.

One year after Morton's demonstration of ether in October 1846, Professor J.Y. Simpson in Edinburgh demonstrated that chloroform was as effective as ether. It was quicker and less irritating for patients to inhale.

My tale is a tale of numbers. What would you think is an acceptable death rate for any particular anesthetic agent or technique? Is one in a thousand acceptable? One in ten thousand? One in two hundred thousand? I would value your opinion. Please tell me. You'll find my Email address at the end of this book.

Of course when I write 'please tell me' you can discern a note of sarcasm, perhaps even despair. Of course, no deaths due to anesthesia would be the ideal. You, the discerning reader will by now have realized that one of the main themes of this book is the question of death or serious damage to the patient due to anesthesia; and whether anything can or has been done about it. The last few chapters of this book cover that part of the story.

In 1874 Clover wrote to the British Medical Journal that he had used chloroform 7000 times but now the first patient had died. His report is long and detailed but it can be condensed into one observation; that, despite the fact that the patient was breathing adequately the force of his pulse weakened and then disappeared and his pupils became widely dilated – the ultimate evidence that the heart was no longer pumping blood to the brain. This is at the heart (please excuse the unintended pun) of the enormous controversy that continued about the use of chloroform until 1911.

One party, mostly the Scots, adherents of Simpson, believed that respiration always failed before the heart stopped and thus gave a warning; the other, that chloroform irritated the heart muscle during light anesthesia with the patient breathing freely and that caused the fatal rhythm called ventricular fibrillation. The next time you walk down an airport corridor to your gate please note the automated defibrillators installed at decent intervals on the walls, in small glass-fronted boxes outlined in red. These of course are for folk who suffer a heart attack on the way to and from their flights and their hearts fibrillate.

I'm sorry to keep introducing my personal pathology into this story – but it's applicable. In the year 2000 my wife took me to see a very modern opera called Akhnaten. The composer, Mr Glass is ingenious because he can write a whole opera using only five notes of the diatonic scale. It's something about a spoiled Egyptian King for whom a Court-maiden lays down a carpet tile for each step he takes, presumably so that his tootsies did not pick up any Methicillin-resistant Staphylococci.

I felt most unwell. I thought it was a case of malignant boredom. Then I felt my pulse. It was beating at a rate of 32 per minute. A couple of days later my cardiologist told me I had heart block and would need a pacemaker to speed my heart up to the normal 70 whacks a minute. The incision on my upper left chest was only 2 inches long, healed up quickly and I felt very much better for the next ten years.

A few of months ago I felt exhausted again though I was not at the opera. I apologize to Mr. Glass. It took 10 years to demonstrate that he was not the cause of my severe bradycardia (slow heart rate). No, the pacemaker battery had died. Dr. Chaudhry, my cardiologist, said he would cut my chest open again remove the dead relic, send it for recycling and place a new one above my left breast. He recommended a cardioverter-defibrillator. If ever I fibrillated the thing would make the diagnosis, think for a moment and then give me a shock and resuscitate me. He delicately opened me up again, put it in, wired me up and as a free bonus added another wire down into my heart. This new machine does so many different things so well that I'll need a new battery in only five years. The way things are going, there's a risk I might live forever. What a mess.

Even more amazing, those magicians at Medtronic the manufacturer, have me set up so that every night at 2 a.m. my pacemaker sends a *wireless signal* to a gadget plugged into the phone jack in the bedroom with all the information about the performance of my heart in the previous twenty four hours. The gadget forwards the information to Debra Braitt at the Lahey Clinic *and* to Medtronic. When I'm in a frisky mood I tell my friends it's also an M.F.M. – a Marital Fidelity Monitor!

One hundred and forty years ago no one knew about defibrillators; actually no one knew what caused sudden cardiac death from chloroform until Dr. Goodman Levy in 1911. Ventricular fibrillation is easy to understand if you realize that the normal heart when it beats, is contracting and squeezing blood out and around the body. Think of a child's balloon filled but not distended with water. Squeeze it suddenly and most of its contents shoot out at one time. Now imagine your hand has lost its power to squeeze; your hand can only quiver helplessly. That is ventricular fibrillation. No water exits. If it's the heart, no oxygen-carrying blood gets delivered to the rest of the body. The defibrillator with its shock, to continue with this image, restores the power to the squeezing hand so it can again work rhythmically.

Let us examine this a little further by going to Harvard Medical School's Countway Library of Medicine. We take the elevator to the basement where the old journals are kept.

We pull out a bound volume of the Lancet from 1862 and look in the index under Chloroform and are directed to page 262 in the section called Medical Annotations. Here are the essential parts of this article:

Death of a Medical Practitioner by Chloroform
We regret to announce another fatal accident during the administration of chloroform for the purpose of producing anaesthesia in a surgical operation. The unhappy !, (author's exclamation point) patient was Dr. Renwick, of Alloa, a member of our own profession, and but twenty-seven years of age. His disease was ingrowing of the great toenail, which it was proposed to remedy by avulsion. Dr. Renwick had previously inhaled chloroform without any bad result; hence, perhaps, a false sense of security. A little of the chloroform was poured upon a towel and he held it to his mouth with his own hands.

The article then describes how a little more chloroform was inhaled to produce a full anesthetic and the operation was completed in two minutes by a Dr. Duncanson. Dr. Renwick did not return to consciousness in the usual time.

Some cold water was thrown on his face to arouse him; but this not having the desired effect, other measures were resorted to, but with a like unfortunate result; and when, after a few minutes his breathing became less frequent and more laboured, and the appearance of his countenance began to change, and his pulse had become nearly imperceptible, serious alarm was felt. Artificial respiration by the modern method was resorted to and in this manner breathing was kept up for half an hour; but, melancholy to relate, his spirit had passed away.

I love the sanctimonious use of the word 'spirit' by the anonymous writer. I have heard a projection that this year (2011) half of all the people now alive will live to more than 100. Have our spirits become more resilient? Of course not.

For our spirits to 'pass away', even though many other of our physiological functions (the way our organs work) may become deranged first, ultimately, the spirits, those poor entrapped waifs, for them to get away from our misbehaving bodies our brains have to stop working; nearly always because they are not receiving enough oxygenated blood, nearly always because our hearts have stopped pumping that sticky liquid uphill.

Then we get the rationalization: *There is some reason to believe that Dr. Renwick was the subject of cardiac disease.*

I ask you, a twenty-seven year old doctor in active practice with cardiac disease?

Then we get what I call the clincher:

The North British Mail mentions that some time ago a gentleman died under the influence of chloroform at Girvan, while undergoing a similar operation.

Let us suppose for the moment that Dr. Joseph Clover's figure of one death from 7000 'properly given' chloroforms was the norm; that is, it was the average experienced by everyone giving chloroform on a regular basis, are we not entitled to ask why for the next 70 or so years after Dr. Simpson first used it no one *acted* upon the observation that this way of dying suddenly did not occur with ether.

"Did you not tell me there were six or seven Commissions of Inquiry into Death under Chloroform during that time?" You say.

All seven Commissions of Inquiry fudged the matter. No one doubted the death rate with chloroform was higher than with ether but its defenders, particularly the Scots, probably because their leader Dr. Simpson introduced chloroform, insisted on continuing with its use. Chloroform is easier to give than ether, works quickly and on the whole has fewer side-effects, such as salivation, coughing, nausea and vomiting than ether. Suppose that when Queen Victoria's daughter Vickie received chloroform for childbirth and her mother commented, "What a blessing she had chloroform.", she had died like so many others. Do you think chloroform use would have continued one more day, rather than the sixty or seventy years it survived?

A lot of surgeons were making a lot of money because of the tremendous ease and apparent safety of chloroform. So what, they must have been thinking: only one case of death in seven thousand. The coroners all said 'Death by Misadventure' and they went home, ate supper and slept peacefully. I have read the case reports of many chloroform deaths; there are hundreds in the online archive of the London Times in the late Victorian era. Not one asks whether the wives or husbands or children asked the meaning of 'Misadventure'.

In 1910 Dr. Levy demonstrated conclusively in cats that in the lighter stages of anesthesia when the patient has high levels of a circulating hormone called adrenaline (epinephrine) in his blood the *combination* of chloroform and adrenaline makes the heart fibrillate. Frightened or nervous patients produce extra adrenaline. What is scarier than having to face an operation? Then Dr. Levy published a paper in 1911 (a year in which there were 2 deaths every three days in the United Kingdom according to the Registrar-General's reports) that conclusively linked the reports of chloroform deaths in humans to precisely what he had observed in cats at University College Hospital.

For the rest of the 20th century the application of science to anesthesia slowly gained ground but with many fits and starts. The little I was taught in my early years was mostly the result of the opinions and experiences of my seniors: very little was the result of carefully controlled experiment.

Chapter 12 WHAT WENT WRONG?

Almost without realizing the implications I had become a faculty member of one of the leading academic anesthesia departments in the United States when we arrived in Boston in 1965. At the end of my year at the Brigham with Dr. Vandam, my friend Dr. Bennie Geffin suggested that if possible I should spend a few months at the Massachusetts General Hospital where the anesthesiologists had begun a vigorous intensive respiratory care program – my first love.

Dr. Donald Todd, the Vice Chairman interviewed and accepted me. Two months later I received a letter from Dr. Dinnick, my chief in London.

"If you don't come back in a few weeks you will have lost your place on the Consultantship ladder," it said in essence.

It took Aideen and myself about fifteen minutes to make the decision to stay. She loved America and Americans. We applied the next day to the Federal Department of Naturalization and Immigration for citizenship.

One overcast morning in early December 1967 I went to work as usual in the operating rooms of the Massachusetts General Hospital, Boston. This famous hospital is known particularly for its historic connection with anesthesia. It's the place where the dentist William T.G. Morton demonstrated to surgeons that by giving a patient ether to inhale he or she would no longer feel the agony of the surgical blade.

I have forgotten the name of the first patient on the orthopedist's list that morning, a young woman of nineteen. I want to call her Sonia. One of my anesthesiologist colleagues had visited her the night before. I spent that evening at home after working most of the previous day and night.

I read in his notes that he considered her to be in the lowest risk category for general anesthesia, that is, in excellent general health. If I had been able to visit her I would have told her about the risks of a general anesthetic if she had asked me. Otherwise I would have reassured her that it had become safer than in the past. I knew that morning I would give a routine anesthetic like thousands of others I had given during the previous nine years.

An XRay had shown spondylolisthesis, a condition of the lower end of the vertebral column in which one vertebra slips forward of the one above giving the patient unremitting pain. These days such a patient would be sent for physiotherapy before surgery is even considered; surgery is now a last resort.

Sonia was the only daughter of a widow who lived in South Boston, an enclave mostly populated by the descendants of Irish émigrés. Earlier that morning her nurse had given Sonia an injection of morphine and scopolamine. Morphine is a narcotic and a sedative; it takes anxiety away. Scopolamine is amnesic, that is, it obliterates memory. This left her drowsy and calm when I first met her.

I started an intravenous infusion of saline in a vein on the back of one hand. I taped a stethoscope to her chest so that I could listen to and monitor her heart sounds during the surgery. We call the start of an anesthetic 'induction'. I used the routine drugs for that time: thiopental and succinylcholine.

She was to be turned onto her stomach for the surgery and I had to maintain control of her airway and breathe for her - something difficult or impossible without an endotracheal tube with the patient's face looking down. I connected the conduits carrying anesthesia gases and vapor from my anesthesia machine to the tube. I had checked the machine's function when I first arrived.

The surgeon and his assistants and nurses stood ready on one side of the patient and when I gave the signal we rolled her face down, like rolling a log of fragile wood, all together without longitudinal twisting. The surgeon taped her to the table so she could not roll off. He then flexed the table so that her lower back made the highest point of a letter 'A' if viewed from the side. I checked her eyes repeatedly during this maneuver to be sure they had not been dragged open. After sterilizing and draping the area the surgeon made an incision over her sacrum and lower back.

It had become routine and the accepted standard for the anesthesiologist to note the pulse rate and blood pressure every 5 minutes. This began when a Boston surgeon visited Dr. Riva-Rocci in Italy at the turn of the century and came back with his blood pressure measuring equipment. I also examined the size of her pupils. I listened carefully for breath sounds on both sides of her now accessible back because endotracheal tubes can become displaced into one or the other lung during the turn.

For half an hour all her vital signs were stable. Then her pulse rate picked up a little more than I would have expected but I assumed that this was due to the stimulus of surgery. I believed she was not, as we say, 'deep enough'. I increased the percentage of the halothane that I had added to the gas mixture she was breathing because nitrous oxide on its own with sufficient oxygen cannot guarantee unconsciousness. Halothane is a volatile liquid. I gave her an extra dose of Demerol, a narcotic, intravenously. These are routine actions and reflect the observation that the amount any given patient needs to suppress subconscious reflex responses to surgery varies from patient to patient. Careful observations made during the 1970s demonstrated that each anesthetic agent had a median 'minimum alveolar concentration' of an inhaled agent to effect this. At the same time those researchers demonstrated wide variations from patient to patient.

These additions brought her pulse rate back below 80 beats per minute. But to my disappointment this lasted only a short while. I could not understand this.

Almost at the same moment I noticed that her fingernails looked dusky, no longer the warm pink I had seen before the operation. She did not use nail polish. We call that color change cyanosis and it can indicate lack of oxygen.

I checked the dials on the anesthesia machine again. She was receiving about 35% percent oxygen in the gas mixture with nitrous oxide. Air has 21 percent oxygen. The duskiness could be explained by venous congestion, that is, the blood flowing back to heart from the veins in her fingers was partially obstructed, because of the extreme position needed for surgical access.

Her blood pressure began to fluctuate more widely than usual. I increased the percentage of halothane but became uneasy. My own heart rate increased, particularly so when *her* heart rate picked up speed again and this time kept climbing. I turned off the nitrous oxide so that she breathed pure oxygen and enough of the halothane to keep her unconscious. A driver on an icy road slows down, pumps the brake gently and repeatedly but when he continues to slide sideways and spin toward oncoming traffic he is no longer in control. That was how I felt.

The surgeon looked away from his deep incision and said the blood there looked dark. As he said that I could no longer hear the heart beating through the stethoscope nor could I feel a pulse at the wrist. I could not hear a measurable blood pressure. I checked all three ways of examining her heart function again, just to be sure.

"I'm afraid she is in cardiac arrest," I said. I was sweating and had a knot in my belly.

"I'll pack and cover the wound and we'll turn her over and resuscitate her."

No questions from the surgeon, just appropriate action.

Once on her back with the table flattened I checked her again. Nothing. Her eye pupils were widely dilated. I could not hear heart sounds nor could I feel a pulse either at the wrist or deep in her neck where the carotid arteries lie.

The surgeon began external cardiac compressions and I turned off everything except the oxygen. I drew up adrenaline into a syringe and he injected it between two ribs directly into the chamber of the heart after making certain the needle lay inside a heart chamber – proven by aspirating blood flowing freely back into the barrel of the syringe.

There was nothing to be said and no one said anything, the slowest minutes of my whole life. I asked the circulating nurse to urgently page whichever of my colleagues was free to help. Before anyone arrived we saw a sudden flush in her complexion, and listening I heard a heart beat.

"When things go wrong in the operating room, you and *only you* are responsible," Dr. Alsop had told me.

We stood in silence except for me speaking out the frequent blood pressure and pulse readings. Even though her circulation had been restored she showed no signs of waking up, something that should have occurred by now in a routine anesthetic with the patient breathing only oxygen. Her pupils remained dilated but were now constricting when I shone a light into them – an encouraging sign.

"I think we should abandon the operation and come back another day," I said, trying to keep my voice steady. "I cannot tell you why this has happened."

That was the most distressing thing I ever had to say during my forty or so years as a clinical anesthesiologist. Where had all those years of study, training, experience, attendance at lectures and listening to my colleagues gone? At that moment I felt – "For nothing".

"I cannot tell you why this has happened."

The surgeon asked, "I would like to turn her on her side and close the wound properly under sterile conditions?"

"Let's watch her a few minutes more and if she remains stable you can go ahead," I said.

At that moment a neurologist arrived. The surgeon had paged him. The neurologist also looked at her pupils and tested her reflexes.

"I think I should do a lumber puncture to measure the pressure and get some spinal fluid to rule out an intracerebral bleed,"

he said. He was thinking of the rare possibility that she had ruptured an aneurysm in her brain.

I did not think that was necessary because it was so unlikely.
But it was hard to argue against additional information in a crisis.
I knew and the surgeon knew that whatever had occurred was due
either to the anesthetic or the surgery. We looked at each other.
Each of us said,

"Go ahead."

The neurologist did his lumber puncture and drew off some
spinal fluid for examination in the laboratory. Then the surgeon
closed the wound and his nurse applied the dressings. We took the
patient to the recovery room with the breathing tube still in place
and connected it to oxygen. By now Sonia breathed by herself.

"I'm going to tell the mother what happened," the surgeon
said.

"I would like to come with you," I said.

I did not know what I would say or how I would react but my
instincts told me two things,

"Be brave. Get it over with."

By that time my colleagues and several surgeons had arrived.

"The lawyers tell us to say as little as possible. It would be better
if you did not go. You might say something unfortunate. You might
admit liability," one said.

I did not go.

I now know that was a mistake. When something goes wrong in
medical care the patient's family wants empathy and honesty. Most
people understand that most doctors are doing their best within
the limits, and there are many limits, of medical science. It was
the first of several occasions when I came to distrust the impact of
lawyers on medical care.

Late that afternoon I visited the patient in the intensive care
unit. Clearly her brain function had improved. She was chewing on
the endotracheal tube. I removed the tube and sat by her bed for
a while. I was nervous her mother would arrive to visit and again I
could not think what I would say. Sonia was breathing normally but

had not woken up in the way a patient recovering from an uneventful anesthetic would have done by that time.

I was due to go to New York the next day to attend a postgraduate educational course. I told my colleagues I would cancel so that I could watch the patient.

"You must go," they said. "If you don't go it might look as though you are guilty of something and admit liability."

So I went. I doubt I actually took anything in. My mind was far away. I could not sleep and it was not from the taxis hooting all night. Every time I closed my eyes I saw a young woman with fixed dilated pupils. I reminded myself she was improving before I left. I tried to convince myself of a good outcome.

I returned to Boston at the weekend. When I went in to work on Monday morning I went to her floor and a nurse told me Sonia had died. An autopsy had revealed an overwhelming septic meningitis, probably the result of pushing the lumber puncture needle though a contaminated wound. That came after the cardiac arrest and was not my fault. It did nothing to alleviate my distress.

My colleagues comforted me.

"It happens to everyone. Eventually," they said.

I felt guilt and despair. The crisis had started on my watch. I had an overwhelming sense that I should visit the mother - to what end I still did not know. How could I explain such a thing and at the same time try to comfort her?

I did not tell my wife about the tragedy at that time. We had two small children and she was restarting her career as a professional musician. In any case, my colleagues told me, that's what happens when you become an anesthesiologist. Without their support I cannot imagine what I would have done.

I did tell my wife when I discovered a year later that I had become a defendant in a malpractice suit. The mother had, or rather, her attorney had sued the hospital, the surgeon and me for $500,000. Later they dropped the others and I became the only defendant. On the face of it the arrest was due to or in some way related to something I had done. How could a hospital that provided me with all the equipment and drugs I needed be held liable? How could a surgeon performing a routine operation he had done many times before with complete safety be held liable?

The hospital provided me with $100,000 worth of liability insurance. Where on earth would the remaining $400,000 come from? Would I remain in debt for the rest of my life?

At that point I told my own attorney Mr. Charlie Burgess what had happened. It was then I discovered that lawyers do not show their feelings, and that's just as well. They are like the British generals in the First World War who had absolutely no idea of what an attack by an infantry brigade was like; terrifying screaming blood. They stayed comfortably in their chateaux 20 miles behind the line. They could hear the guns booming in the distance and planned the strategies of attack and defense. Lawyers do the same. They have to be manipulators of words, ideas and attitudes, standing back from my fear and guilt.

Charlie told me I would have to attend a deposition at which the plaintiff's attorney would question me, and an expert, an anesthesiologist flown in from California would arrive to testify that I had been either incompetent or neglectful. A Court Reporter would transcribe everything that was said and that document would become part of the evidence if the matter went to trial. When I heard that, it reinforced my questions for myself: had I been incompetent or inadequate or neglectful? At that moment my only comfort was to look back at nine years of taking care of patients in the operating room without a single serious adverse outcome for which I could be held responsible.

It reinforced my realization that part of being an anesthesiologist is confidence: confidence in your own skill and judgment. Knowledge and technical skill by themselves were inadequate. I also began to realize that resilience in the face of tragedy is part of the life we have chosen. When in my later life residents anxiously questioned me about the risk of a malpractice suit, I could think of no better answer than,

"Practice with a conscience."

The two depositions seemed like a bitter and irrelevant joke. The plaintiff's expert did not show up, either time. The plaintiff's lawyer hacked away at me. Charlie and the lawyer for my insurance company tried to protect me. The plaintiff's lawyer hacked not with any specifics of the case but by trying to prove that my residency and postgraduate diploma from the United Kingdom did not meet the standards of the equivalent in the USA. The most revealing moment came when the Court Reporter said, at about 11 a.m.,

"Gentlemen, may we take a break?"

They all readily agreed. I watched as the plaintiff's attorney slowly moved toward my defense attorney. A moment before they had been cats hissing at each other with their tails erect. They shook hands. One put his arm around the other's shoulder and offered a cigarette from an engraved gold case. They sat close, exhaling bonhomie like two beer-sodden veterans delighted to meet again. They proceeded to question each other about the achievements of their two college-age sons both studying for the Bar. I sat there like a mortally wounded mouse whose corpse they had been fighting over.

A year later the lawyers reached a settlement.

Many years later I was asked to become an assessor for the American Society of Anesthesiologists Closed Claims Project. This project is one in which medical liability insurance companies allow experienced anesthesiologists to read the documentation of malpractice claims that are closed: that is, won, lost or settled. The result of this effort is by far the largest database of adverse outcomes in anesthesia. The findings have led to many improvements in the safety of anesthesia. As I read those files I saw that the financial settlements for plaintiffs bore little relationship to the degree of neglect by a physician – rather, it was the result of haggling between lawyers. The phrase that struck me most in their correspondence was,

"This is worth xxxx Dollars."

Then I would read a riposte. I thought I was reading a transcript of the haggling that occurs on Saturday evenings as the poorer housewives go to pick up a left-over box of bananas before the fruit market closes in Boston's Italian Quarter.

Sonia's bereaved mother received five thousand dollars less legal fees from a settlement between the lawyers. I never understood whether I was considered guilty or not as seen by The Law. When I asked Charlie, all he said was,

"Gerald. We reached a favorable settlement."

I have told this sad and disturbing tale because it touches on many of the issues that still surround our specialty. In 1967 there were not too many of us. We each know many of the others. My story is not unique.

Writing this was difficult and painful and I still get a knot in my stomach when I think of that December day. The case was discussed at the Morbidity and Mortality conference held once a month and which all the members of the anesthesia department attend. We did not settle on any particular cause for the cardiac arrest.

In hindsight I know for sure that there *were* three possible causes:

I did something wrong although I do not believe I was neglectful.

Or the patient suffered from a metabolic defect that had only been described in the Australian and British literature shortly before the event. This is a rare but often lethal genetic predisposition to an abnormal response to some anesthetic agents. The metabolism of the patient's muscles speeds up as though they had been asked suddenly to run a mile in four minutes when they, of course are not. This leads to a cascade of events called hypermetabolism. The condition is called Malignant Hyperthermia. Now we have an antidote but in 1969 we did not. Dr. Henry Rosen-berg , the Director of the Malignant Hyperthermia Association of the U.S.A. recently assured me that the condition was unknown among anesthesiologists in the United States in 1967.

Or else Sonia had suffered a venous air embolism, something that is known as a risk when the operation field is the highest point of the patient's body. This allows air to be sucked into open veins and leads to froth on the right side of the heart, a lethal event.

All this happened forty-two years ago. I still feel guilty because a young woman died.

Chapter 13 PRIVATE PRACTICE

I have often been asked: How can an anesthesiologist establish a private practice? After all we do not have our own patients the way a surgeon or an internist has. We are analogous to pathologists and radiologists in that we are doctors' doctors. In other words, we are consultants. Without going into the complicated history of the relationship between hospitals, surgeons, the law and anesthesiologists the usual pattern these days is for a group of anesthesiologists to form a partnership. The partnership signs a contract with the Board of Management of a particular hospital or a group of hospitals to cover surgical, obstetric, intensive care and pain therapy services but retains the right to bill patients individually. In return the partnership is obliged to provide coverage 24 hours a day and three hundred and sixty five days a year.

Chuck Slater made me his partner one year after I joined him in private practice at the Union Hospital in Lynn, on the North Shore of Boston. He hired me three years after our arrival in the U.S.A. I told Chuck I would spend a couple of years as his partner and then return to an academic position – mainly because I loved teaching. We stayed together for 15 years! When I discussed a written employment contract with Chuck he said,

"If we cannot trust each other with a handshake no amount of legalistic paperwork will keep us together." And that was how things stood for the years we stayed together.

It was an exciting time because it soon became clear to me that Chuck would impose high standards of perioperative care of patients whether our surgical colleagues liked them or not. Several examples come to mind: surgeons were performing tonsillectomies without allowing us to insert breathing tubes to protect the child's airway; mothers in labor were still being given heavy sedation usually a drug called scopolamine, the effect of which was to make them act crazily: vascular surgeons were operating on patients with concomitant heart disease without any of the sophisticated invasive monitoring that was becoming standard by then; very sick patients were sent to the intensive care unit (ICU) connected to breathing machines without anyone with ICU expertise to monitor them. Our surgical colleagues did not put up much resistance to our suggested changes because they saw their patients do well.

We each took a lot of call at night and weekends. Later, I will describe some of the consequences of this. But it was also a unique experience, not least because at that time many anesthesiologists in small hospitals were not involved in the postoperative care of surgical patients. We became respected members of the medical staff. For me it was the realization that all medical students have at some time; the idea of becoming a healer and an expert. It was good for my medical ego.

Let us call our third partner in those early days George McCutcheon. He had graduated from the University College San Francisco residency program with a fine reputation and seemed both bright and capable. He was married to a pretty girl and had two gorgeous toddlers. A year after my arrival Chuck told me that George had received a lucrative job offer at a hospital in New Hampshire. He took some vacation time we owed him and we gave him a farewell party. I remember thinking that anesthesia group in New Hampshire must have offered him a very lucrative contract because he left so suddenly. That was when we hired Michael.

Years later I discovered that George had been making preoperative visits on young female patients without having a chaperone in the room when he examined them. There had been complaints. Chuck hid all this from me. He was terrified I would leave. He would have had to be available in the hospital all by himself 24 hours a day, seven days a week, as specified in our contract with the hospital.

At that time Lynn was a city fading away economically because its primary industry, shoe manufacture, was going abroad. Fortunately we had the General Electric Aero Engine plant near the harbor in Lynn. Lynn once again has become an émigré community instead of the settled Irish and Italian communities from earlier immigration. The towns on the North Shore of Boston such as Revere, Saugus and Lynn harbored criminals and some of the drug trade. The male physical therapists whom we hired to help us in the ICU told me they always carried a handgun in their glove compartments. Some of the surgeons who operated at the downtown Lynn Hospital as well at our more suburban Union Hospital did the same.

One evening, making preoperative rounds I visited a healthy-looking gentleman booked for a hernia repair on the morrow. We did our medical business. He was friendly and asked me about my English accent. I had time and we chatted some more. He asked me about my family and about my relationship with my wife. I was slightly confused by this until he handed me a calling card. All it had on it was a phone number, no name. As I said 'good night' he said, in the nicest possible way,

"Doc, if you ever have any special needs just call that number."

I thanked him. Fortunately it was late and no one saw me blush as I left.

The fun began a few nights later. I was on call. It was quiet. I was checking out with Maryanne at the switchboard when her phone buzzed.

"Doc, don't leave. They got a gunshot," she said

I ran down to the Emergency Room (ER, for those who love television). The ER doc told me,

"He's got bits of aluminum in him all over. It's rather embarrassing but I have called the neurosurgeon on call, the thoracic surgeon, that abdominal lady, two orthopods, a hand man and the plastics guy. And the radiologists; they never get up at night if they can help it. I've ordered ten units of blood and I'm just about to start the second intravenous line (IV). The lab people are coming in if you need more."

Later he became a 'television doctor'.

Henry, our patient was tall, muscular and his beautifully tailored clothing was covered in blood. Telephone booths are made of steel covered in anodized aluminum to prevent rusting and erosion. It would have saved us a lot of trouble if the gentleman sitting in a Cadillac under a tree in full leaf on the other side of Route 1 North had been more accurate with his rifle and hit Henry in the heart. He must have been nervous because he hit the metal stanchion of the payphone where Henry was dialing. This disintegrated into a spray of metal that was quite unselective which of Henry's organs it penetrated. It penetrated them all.

What do you call too many surgeons who keep getting in each other's way? A jostle of surgeons? A chat of surgeons?

As each of them arrived in the room after scrubbing up they asked me,

"Gerry, where do you think he's losing the most blood?

All I knew was that I had a patient with healthy heart, lungs and kidneys and that I had plenty of blood available for transfusion and his vital signs were quite stable. Because these surgeons operated on different days they only met at social occasions. This turned into a social occasion. I heard as much discussion as to which private school in Swampscott was best as there was about whether the left pulmonary artery had been lacerated.

At 6 a.m. I left the patient with normal vital signs on a respirator in the ICU. I phoned Chuck. He was already up, doing his treadmill.

"I'm going home. I'm sure you'll manage without me. Take a look at Henry P. in the ICU before the O.R."

After I showered and dressed I checked out in the lobby with MaryAnne at the switchboard. Two gentlemen wearing dark blue Brooks Brothers suits and crisp white shirts approached me and shook my hand.

"Thank you very much Dr. Zeitlin. We understand Henry is doing well in the ICU. They said we could go up as soon as he's settled."

Few people remember or even know the name of the anesthesiologist. These two gentlemen, in the middle of the night had the access to get my name. You do not need me to explain what business they were in.

One late evening in the early 1970s I was writing preoperative orders at the nurses' station on West One. Those are often the quietest hours on a ward. All the nursing attentions have been given and most of the patients are watching television before settling down for the night. A nurse came out of a room at the end of the corridor and ran up to me.

"Please doctor, go to room 112. Please go now," her voice high and urgent.

A pale wasted woman lay in the bed near the window. The light was off. It was only when I turned it on that I saw the horizontal cut across her throat and the last few feeble spurts of blood out of the wound. Then I saw a man sitting in the visitors' chair, sobbing. He carefully handed me an old-fashioned open blade barber's razor with the handle first.

"I had to do it Doc. I had to. They could not fix her pain. She had too much pain. Please call the police for me. Please look at her and make sure she has gone."

She had indeed 'gone' when I examined her: too late to even start an intravenous infusion and call a vascular surgeon. He had cut right through a carotid artery.

The police soon came and when I explained they took the husband gently away. I later heard he was confined to the Danvers Mental Hospital for a while but released to his children soon after.

As recently as the 1970s the agony of advanced malignant disease was poorly treated. The reasoning behind this probably was due to unnecessary worry about the risks of addiction. There is no upper limit to the dose of narcotic that must be given to such a patient when you are reasonably certain the patient will soon die.

Just about that time Dr. Cecily Saunders started the hospice movement in London. The care of the dying patient in pain includes adequate pain relief without worrying about the dosage needed.

One last anecdote. One afternoon I was called to the E.R. to see my surgical colleague Dr. John Bucchiere. You will meet him again later. He was passing a kidney stone. I'm sure many readers will have been asked by a doctor or nurse,

"Please rate your pain for me on a one to ten scale."

I did not have to ask this of Dr. John. He was at least a ten. The E.R. doc asked me to give him Demerol, a powerful synthetic narcotic, intravenously. He was uncomfortable doing this but knew that anesthesiologists did it every day. Dr. John is well-built and needed lots and lots. All of a sudden his pain vanished.

Dr. John's mantra to me in the Operating Room on the few occasions I had to delay him, was always,

"Whatever turns you on Gerry."

Now he smiled at me,

"That turned you on Gerry, didn't it?'

Chapter 14 SOME SURGEONS

Surgeons come in all sizes, shapes and genders. I never wanted to be a surgeon. I was always much more interested in the way the body works than in its anatomy, whether healthy or diseased. Without surgeons, without their knowledge, skill, judgment (in my opinion far and away their most important attribute) and their, let's say it out loud, their courage, where would we all be? Where would I be? I would be down there; and on my gravestone it would say,

"Please Come and Visit Me Occasionally for a Chat and a Joke."
Gerald L. Zeitlin, 1931 - ?

An anesthesiologist's experience of taking care of any particular surgeon's patient is only somewhat linked to the surgeon's skill and experience and much more to his or her personality in the operating room. We all have our most favorite and least favorite surgeons. We only talk about this covertly.

Here are a few examples from private practice:

Dr. Kanada came to us with a reputation from his residency as a brilliant and up to date urologist. My two partners, Chuck and Michael and I had about 40 years experience between us taking care of every imaginable situation that can face an anesthesiologist. Michael had spent a year on the beach in Viet Nam resuscitating and anesthetizing the most gravely torn apart young soldiers and civilians. Chuck had been an Associate Professor at the Massachusetts General Hospital before entering private practice where he was considered an exemplary leader and I had been 'through the mill' in many different hospital settings and circumstances before settling in Britain's Great and Former Transatlantic colony. But Dr. Kanada knew everything better than we did. He knew what form of anesthesia was best from his one week's experience as a medical student; he knew which patients did or did not need further study of their cardiac function before going ahead. He was impossible.

At our monthly meetings to discuss what we did not have time to discuss in the middle of the daily schedule the Kanada Problem arose frequently. For a while we had no good solution. Chuck claims he thought of the answer but I know for sure it was my idea. Michael's mind was mostly on how to lower his golf score and his temperament was such that neither well-behaved nor temperamental surgeons bothered him.

My solution was to smother Dr. Kanada with love. Before he started his first case one of us would meet him in the changing room.

"Harold, there's some fresh coffee in the lounge. Estelle tried this new kind from the A and P. It's delicious," one of us told him.

Even the most irritable surgeon cannot resist good coffee. The poor chaps have to get up each morning even earlier than we do – about 5.00 a.m. They have to 'make rounds' that is, visit all the patients they have at all the hospitals where they admit and operate. They might have to drive 50 miles and stop at three hospitals before starting the day's operating.

By discreet enquiry from the nurses, who knew all the gossip, we discovered that Mrs. Kanada was pregnant with twins, in addition to caring for Samantha, age 4 and Thelonius age 2.

"How is Mrs. Kanada feeling? Does she have any help with the little ones?"

Like taking a hair drier to peppermint-stick ice cream he dribbled sweetness and became our greatest ally.

Then there was Dr. John Bucchiere, also a urologist. He specialized in Transurethral Resection of the Prostate known by most of the patients living in Lynn, as the 'prostrate'. As you surely understand these patients were elderly gentlemen who, although suffering from inability to urinate on command, also suffered from arteriosclerosis usually of the heart and sometimes of the brain, osteosclerosis, that is, rust covered spinal columns and otosclerosis – they were hard of hearing. But all they cared about was being able to enjoy a couple of beers without consequent drainage difficulties. These patients required a spinal anesthetic to numb their lower halves and particularly careful monitoring, so that Dr. B. could do his reaming safely and without hurting them. But spinals often lead to a temporary and sometimes drastic fall in blood pressure, which is a bad thing if you have arteriosclerosis. On the operating table we attached an EKG monitor before giving the spinal and sometimes we would see an ugly slump in the ST segment. That simply means a part of the heart was not getting enough oxygen. I, for example would say,

"Dr. John. I think we need to get a cardiac consult."

"Whatever turns you on Gerry," his answer was always the same.

And he would sit with the scrub nurse, endlessly patient, discussing the Red Sox's latest slump while the cardiologist gave his opinion whether or not it was safe to go ahead.

Dr. Jules, a bony orthopedic surgeon was always in a hurry; too hurried to scrub properly and too hurried to look at the Xrays that had been taken in his office and that the circulating nurse had extracted from their brown cardboard envelope. She affixed them to the viewing screen in the orthopedic operating room.

"Let's get cracking," was his mantra; I always thought but never dared say, how singularly inappropriate for an orthopod. On this particular day the operation booked was an ankle fusion to relieve the constant pain the patient suffered from an old injury that would not heal. The patient was otherwise healthy and preferred a general anesthetic to a spinal. The nurse scrubbed and draped the leg with sterile towels. Dr. Jules applied a tourniquet and made the incision on the inside surface of the ankle. All was quiet. I was completing the chart on which every anesthesiologist records the patient's vital signs. Then I heard, from the other end,

"There's nothing wrong in here." Pause, while Dr. Jules consulted the Xrays.

"Dammit. Wrong side," He looked at me for the first time that morning. "Zeitlin. It's the anesthesiologist's responsibility to tell the surgeon which side. There's bound to be legal trouble. Hope you're well insured."

"Good try, my man," I thought but did not say.

He prepped, draped and cut the other ankle..

The patient went to the recovery room when all the sutures were in place, made an uneventful recovery and went home five days later with a plaster cast on one ankle and a bandage on the other.

I never heard another word either from the patient or his lawyer. Indeed I never ever exchanged another word with Dr. Jules.

Conversely: about 10 years ago in the Spring the parents of an eight-year-old girl noticed she had a golf ball sized protrusion on her right lower abdomen. It came and went but when it appeared it was somewhat painful.

A surgeon told them,

"Your child has a hernia and I should operate on it otherwise her bowel might get stuck in it. Let's arrange to do it in a couple of months when her summer vacation begins."

The parents agreed. Two months later they took her to the hospital in the university town where they live. The nurses were most kind to the child, admitted her and undressed her.

"We have to mark the operative site." said the Head Nurse and drew a large 'X' on the left lower abdomen. The hernia did not show itself that morning.

"But the hernia is on the right." said the parents.

"No. It's on the left," said the Head Nurse. "It says so on the form I received from the surgeon's office."

The parents were adamant. When the surgeon and the anesthesiologist arrived a stalemate ensued. The anesthesiologist left the admitting area telling the Head Nurse to call him when they were absolutely certain.

The surgeon said his office notes were still in his office but his office was closed that Monday morning. The operation was delayed for two hours while the surgeon drove to and from his office. His original notes said 'Right-sided hernia.'.

Clearly human error had intervened. The operation and the anesthetic went very smoothly and the child came home at 2 p.m., feeling fine. That child is our granddaughter, Rachel.

A little later we caught her climbing onto the kitchen counter and quietly appropriating chocolate chip cookies for herself!

Neurosurgeons sometimes have to perform what is called a posterior fossa exploration; they have to open the back of the skull, the part on the pillow if you sleep on your back. From the anesthesiologist's point of view this involves at least two particular dangers. Sitting an anesthetized patient up can lead to drastic falls in blood pressure and if the surgeon, peering deep into the cerebellum should miss the fact that air is being sucked into an open vein that air will very quickly reach the right side of the heart. The heart was not designed to pump froth.

Please do the following. Go out to the nearest liquor store and buy a bottle of dark Guinness, shake it up and then pour it into a tall glass. Get a straw (I admit very un-Irish) and place the far end at the bottom of the glass - most satisfying. Then withdraw its tip into the froth, also known as the head, and suck. That is unsatisfying. That's what's in the heart if air gets into it..

One day, a few years earlier, when I was still a junior faculty member at the Massachusetts General Hospital, Dr. Sower, the famous neurosurgeon booked such an operation. For my resident and I this meant introducing a long catheter from the neck into the right side of the heart so that if air did enter, which we hoped to detect with a Doppler device taped to the patient's chest, we could aspirate (suck out) the bubbles of air. We had to put in two intravenous lines and a catheter into an artery to watch the blood pressure second by second after anesthetizing the patient. This leads to a tangle of wires and plastic lines under the sterile drapes

141

the surgeon requires. While we were struggling with all this the patient suddenly reared up and almost broke from the devices holding her in the sitting position on the table. The surgeon made an angry comment.

Dr. Sower had quietly walked in after scrubbing and without so much as a 'Good Morning' made his incision. At that point we had the patient lightly anesthetized for fear of dropping the blood pressure.

That was three years after I had arrived in the United States and I had discovered that one of the glories of this country is that you must speak up. No timidity based on hierarchies.

"Where I come from it is customary for the surgeon to ask the anesthesiologist if he may begin. Seems things are different here in the Colonies," I said aloud, putting on my best BBC English.

I was told this reverberated round the hospital. Passive-aggressive, I agree; but it reflects how many of us felt about our status at that time.

If you persist in the habit that I have acquired in my later days of eating a Cadbury Milk and Nut bar every day, that stuff gets laid down, not surprisingly, as brown fat. If you have the money to spend you will be tempted to go to Dr. Handsome or Dr. Beautiful for a suction lipectomy. Yes, it's exactly what it sounds like. They make a few holes in the skin of your belly and roam around your fat stores with a cylindrical steel vacuum cleaner that looks like one of those attachments that come with your new Hoover for getting the dust out of corners. It's an 'OK, Not-to-Worry' operation except that physiologically it acts like a large burn under the skin. Burns lead to enormous losses of body fluids and in fact are sometimes an unrecognized cause of death. One afternoon at New England Surgicare in Boston, many years later, one of our cosmetic surgeons Dr. Safrica an intelligent pleasant fellow, did a vigorous lipectomy. Before leaving to pick up his kids from school he checked with me.

"Her B.P is a little on the low side, but we'll keep her here until she makes some urine," I told him.

The production of urine is the hallmark of an adequate volume of bodily fluids.

Three hours, 5 litres of electrolyte fluid and 4 litres of plasma intravenously later she provided us with a few drops of urine and we admitted her to the main hospital for observation. The Board of Surgicare met the next day and placed a strict limit of 1 liter of fat per aspiration.

Intermission CAST A DEEP SLEEP

It's time for another rest from all this *sturm und drang*. This intermission requires a little activity on your part, not too different from getting another beer from the 'fridge while watching the Cup Final or the World Series.

Please fetch your Old Testament off the shelf (the Chumash if you're Jewish) and turn to Chapter 2: Verse 21, of Genesis.

And the LORD God caused a deep sleep to fall upon Adam, and he slept: and he took one of his ribs, and closed up the flesh thereof, instead;

Other than the observation that the Lord God acted as both the anesthesiologist and the surgeon (after all She/He *is* omnipotent) this one sentence could have been a dictated if old-fashioned operative note in your local hospital in 2011. In fact, in 2011 if the anesthesiologist and surgeon do not dictate their notes they will not get paid.

Let's look at the verse with a little more care.

And the Lord God caused a deep sleep to fall upon Adam, and he slept:

Adam has entered the Lahey Clinic in Burlington, Massachusetts. The surgeon (Lord God #2) has booked him for a rib resection under general anesthesia. A week earlier Adam visited the preoperative clinic and the anesthesiologist assigned to see him found that he was in excellent health and thus in the lowest risk category for anesthesia, not least because he lives on a vegetarian diet, mostly apples.

On the appointed morning I, the appointed anesthesiologist (a.k.a. Lord God #1) start an intravenous infusion after making him comfortable with a pillow and assuring him of the safety of anesthesia, give Adam a dose of Propofol sufficient to *cause a deep sleep to fall upon him*. Then I passed an endotracheal breathing tube through which nitrous oxide, oxygen and isoflurane flowed for Adam to breathe, *and he slept.*

And He took one of his ribs, and closed up the flesh thereof, instead:

In my opinion that surgeon (Lord God #2) is an excellent chest woman, not only because she is quick, the most desirable attribute of any surgeon, whether heavenly or like most of them earthbound and she rapidly closed the incision. That is, *she closed up the flesh thereof, instead.*

Instead of what? Instead of just a few whacking great nylon sutures that leave marks on the patient's skin that resemble the perforations on a piece of Matzoh, she did an elegant subcuticular (concealed under the skin) closure. In a couple of months Eve would hardly be able to see Adam's incision before he put his pajama top on.

To study this matter in more depth I recently spent an afternoon at the Old Testament Bookstore on Harvard Street in Brookline, Massachusetts. One of my non-believer friends had told me the Five Books of Moses (Old Testament) were not written by Moses. I wanted to find out for myself, because if they *were* written by Moses then it seemed to me that our specialty's origins are even older than is commonly believed. I approached the young man behind the counter and asked,

"Do you have a section with books about who wrote the Five Books of Moses?'

"You'll find them over there." he said pointing to a stack at the side of his spacious establishment. He leaned over the counter and said quietly,

"Are you Jewish?"

"Sort of." I answered.

I am short and old with a fringe of gray hair and despairingly overweight but otherwise not easily pigeonholed other than I still speak with a Hampstead Garden Suburb-in-London accent – unchanged after 45 years in the USA, a loyal citizen and Clinton Democrat. Now he felt more confident.

"Have you never heard of *Moishe Rabbeinu* (Moses, our Teacher). He wrote them. It's in the name. The Five Books *of Moses.* How can you not know that?"

"If that is so, why are you pointing over there? To the bookshelf at the end of the room," I said, quick as a bunny.

His sigh was neither melancholy nor despairing, more a sigh of resignation.

"There *are* different opinions. Even among us. And, I have to make a living."

I only bought one book and that was because it was the only one I browsed through that I could understand: Richard Elliott Friedman's "Who Wrote the Bible', now in paperback. When I went to pay, the young man asked me about my particular interest. I answered,

"Genesis. Chapter 2, Verse 21," I answered neatly.

As though the holy text was a part of his being he smiled as he recited in Hebrew, (translation from the Soncino Bible).

"VaYapel (And He Caused to Fall Upon), *Adonay Elohim* (The Lord God), *Tardemah* (A Deep Sleep), *Al-HaAdam* (Unto Adam), *Veyishan* (And He Slept): *VaYikach* (And He Took) *Achat Mizalotav* (A Single Rib), *VaYisgar Basar* (And Closed Up the Flesh Thereof), *Tachtenah* (Instead)."

"Aaah, now I see. You are a doctor and you want to increase your practice here in our community. So you are studying the relevant parts of Bereshit (Genesis). The Bible teaches us everything we need to know," he continued with a smile.

147

"No. I'm an anesthesiologist and a surgeon told me the other day he would treat me with more respect because he had heard in church that God was my predecessor."

He did not take the bait because another customer showed up at the desk.

Prof. Friedman is only one of many scholars, all cautious and seemingly meticulous that appear to have proven that the Old Testament (Five Books of Moses) was written by four separate scribes whose work was later combined into one. Almost nothing is known about these four other than their dates. Chapter 2 of Genesis was written by 'J', a scribe who lived in the Kingdom of Judah 950 years BCE (Before the Common Era) or, if you prefer 950 B.C.

"So what?" You say.

My point is that approximately 2750 years before a chemical anesthetic, ether, was given to a living, suffering human, undergoing surgery, *someone or, some people had the idea, or if you prefer, the concept.*

The most important three words in Chapter 2, Verse 21 are:

"VaYapel." ... (And He Caused to) fall upon, in the active voice sense."

"Tardemah." ... "A Deep Sleep."

And, *"VaYishan."* ... And he slept.

Can you not agree that a precise translation of the *meanings* of these three words might help us understand whether 'J' and you and I are talking about the same things.

So I wrote to our daughter-in-law Lisa's friend, Michelle Lynn-Sachs who is a faculty member of the Jewish Theological Seminary in New York. She referred me to two of her professorial colleagues. I also wrote to Professor Friedman. That all three even bothered to reply to a variably-observant pretend historian shows what generous people they must be.

Professor Kalmanovsky said that 'going on the Bible, *'tardemah'* does seem to indicate some kind of 'special' sleep. She said she often uses the word 'trance'. She admitted that the removal of Adam's rib seemed lot like surgery to her.

Professor Allon Pratt, in his modest reply said, 'my instinctive feeling is that *'tardemah'* has to do with the moment of falling asleep. Aha! – we call that general anesthesia. He continues with the infinitive of *'tardemah'* which is *'leyahadrem'* meaning, TO FALL ASLEEP (his upper case), even with a touch of passive spice to it – notice my intentional non-scientific lingo.'

Then comes my great moment: Professor Pratt wrote 'whereas *"vayishan"* has to do with continuous sleep'. That is what we call the 'maintenance' phase of an anesthetic. I really must take him out to dinner the next time we're in New York. I wonder if he's Kosher.

Professor Friedman said he could see why Genesis 2: 21 rings a particular bell for an anesthesiologist; but, he cautioned me in not reading too much into what are, after all, just three words in Hebrew by the author of an elegant narrative in circa ninth century BCE. He gave examples in which the word *'tardemah'* refers to a sleep that affects an entire military force (in Samuel) or elsewhere refers to the stage of sleep in which one dreams (in Job).

Despite these varied translations and cautions I believe that the *idea* or, if you prefer, the *concept* of general anesthesia for surgery is about 2750 years old.

I wondered if I could find any artistic depictions of this event. There are lots, both old and new. But they all fudge the central question: despite the specificity of the description in the good old Genesis 2: 21 they all show some kind of airy-fairy nonsense with God floating around the edge of the picture covered in robes. Adam is lying intact and mostly naked apparently wondering what movie is on that evening and Eve floats charmingly in the ether (sorry about that) up in the trees looking like a post-pubertal nymph. No cuts and no blood. But worst of all Adam is wide awake. Now if God had given him a numbing anesthetic, that is a spinal or an epidural, it might just be acceptable. But 'J' is quite definite: *"Tardemah"* equals a deep sleep. The other thing I noticed is that

God, no matter whether obstetrician, midwife or anesthesiologist, is always depicted as male.

The one exception is the drawing by Michael Wohlgemuth in the Nuremberg Chronicle of 1493. One of Wohlgemuth's pupils was Albert Durer. They both made woodcuts of great sophistication to illustrate the increasing numbers of books being printed at that time.

In Wohlgemuth, Adam lies on his left side on a grassy bank. Obstetricians would strongly approve of this if Adam was a she and was having a baby, because when the pregnant person lies on her back the baby compresses the great abdominal vein, the vena cava and reduces blood flow back to the heart, and the laboring woman's blood pressure can fall drastically. Adam props his head up on his left elbow. It's difficult to see whether his eyes are open or shut. At any rate he looks at peace. Eve is gently sliding out of a circular incision *below* the rib cage, more in the area of the right lobe of the liver. She is being politely helped out with God's left hand guiding her. She looks demure and relaxed and her hair is nicely done with a sort of flowing coif. God is blessing her with his right hand making the sign of the cross.

No bleeding, no agony, but at least there is an incision.

If you let your mind roam while gazing on this scene you'll start asking questions such as: Did Lord God No. 1 know about epidural (numbing) anesthesia? Does Adam wonder whether the postoperative incisional pain was worth the product? Why did the surgeon promise he would do a rib resection but instead used a hepatectomy incision to get Eve out? Should Adam go see a lawyer and sue? Does the Lord have decent malpractice insurance coverage?

You can only draw one conclusion: the four early scribes understood modern anesthesia whereas the Dark Ages' chaps did not. We had to wait for the Enlightenment.

Chapter 15 OPERATING ROOMS

Operating room suites are usually dreary and forbidding with low ceilings and buzzing neon lighting. Surgery is often a life-changing event for the patient. You would think that some of the money spent on gigantic, thrilling entry halls to hospitals similar to the sky-scratching atria of Hyatt hotels would be spent on humanizing operating rooms (O.Rs). Two examples of these extravagances can be seen at the palatial entrances to the Brigham and Women's Hospital in Boston and the Mayo Clinic in Rochester, Minnesota. The concealment of operating suites is a hangover from the time before 1846 when the screaming and the blood were kept hidden. Come on, chaps – I mean you - you administrators, with your enormous budgets, get with it. It's 2011, not 1845.

What goes on in operating suites is probably the most lucrative part of a hospital, but administrators seem frightened of visiting us down in the mines. During my five years at the Lahey Clinic I only remember Dr. Robert Wise, the C.E.O. of the hospital coming down to us twice. On both occasions the patient either was or was likely to become a major donor. I do not mean this as criticism of Dr. Wise. We are good friends now. It's another of the ingrained ways of doing things in hospitals. Much of medical practice is still bound by tradition. It's as though the 'there's something nasty in the woodshed' idea of operating rooms still pervades the minds of the medical intelligentsia, the thinkers like endocrinologists and neurologists who do not actually *do things to patients*.

Talking of Dr. Wise, let me tell you about his Salary Committee. During my third year at the Lahey I suffered my second heart attack and shortly after underwent coronary artery bypass surgery. I was back at work full-time in 10 weeks – about as short a recovery period as is possible after such surgery. At the end of that year my salary increase was, wait for it – zero. One percent would have made me a happy man. We had two of our three children in college. Before my next Lahey anniversary I applied to be interviewed by the Salary Committee. The Salary Committee consisted of Dr. Wise, Dr. Fager, a neurosurgeon and Dr. Libertino. the Chief of Urology. Dr. Libertino was unavailable. Dr. Fager was paged immediately after we shook hands and vanished.

"Gerry, I understand you have an interest in and write about medical history. Did I ever tell you I won a prize in High School for an essay on William Morton, your ether man." Dr. Wise said.

He used the rest of the allotted 15 minutes crawling on his hands and knees and scrabbling in the lower drawers of a row of file cabinets. His secretary came in.

"Dr. Wise. They are waiting for you at the Board of Management."

So, again, that was that. I apologize to Dr. Wise. It must be hard balancing the books of a hospital. Financing of acute medical, that is, in-hospital medical care in the United States is yet another of those fascinating topics that I cannot deal with here.

Operating rooms (O.R's) in America, salle d'operation in France, Operationssaal in Germany but Operating Theatre in England. Are the surgeons in the country of my birth more demonstrative, more expressive than in the USA? Do they bring the curtain down amid thundering applause? The only difference I could discern is that, on the whole they were faster in the land of Shakespeare. Why were they faster? Because if they finished their list before the surgeon in the next room they would have the pick of the raisin-filled rock cakes made by Sister's (O.R. Head Nurse) ex-husband who lived with her and took care of the children and for that time in history was in that shameful position of being a 'home father' who loved to cook and fill in the Football Pools. Tax laws in England at that time favored the single. I doubt the Internal Revenue had the nerve to inspect their bedroom.

When I was young we only did our anesthesia stuff on a table in an operating room or the delivery room and very rarely in Casualty (the E.R.) or XRay. Now we do it all over: in the lithotripsy room, in the M.R.I. unit where our cheap steel watches fly off our wrists into the giant magnet possibly banging into the patient on the way, in intensive care units, in invasive cardiology units where cardiologists make us nervous by stopping the heart almost casually while they insert some life-prolonging electrical gadgetry, in free-standing day surgery units where, allegedly, all the patients are young and healthy and surgery is 'minor' meaning they can go home for afternoon tea and lastly and most scarily, in cosmetic surgeons offices. Scary, because plastic surgeons sometimes do not have resuscitating equipment and appropriate drugs in their surgeries.

My wife and I go to Sarasota, Florida each year for the three winter months. Every year in the Florida papers I read of tragedies in plastic surgeons' offices. Not many; but if *your* mother undergoing that facelift had a cardiac arrest and the needed drugs were unavailable it's likely you will sit up and take notice.

No one talks about what it's like to work in an operating room; what it's like to work in a noisy, freezing pale-green tiled room without windows sometimes for twelve or more hours a day. The rooms in England were cold and dank. I think dank is the best word if it means chilly, moist motionless air. In the USA every room I ever worked in was freezing. Modern operating rooms have a laminar airflow system that changes the air and filters it 400 to 500 times per hour. That breeze by itself has a cooling effect. You have to add the effect of the air-conditioning. The anesthesiologist cannot move far from the head of the table and thus generates little of his or her own heat. The surgeons and the scrub nurse are heavily gowned and gain heat from the overhead lamp and stand near and use electronic equipment that adds to their heat gain. The anesthesiologist like everyone else starts with a layer of 'scrubs', and down below a pair of cotton trousers of standardized length.

I am short and chubby and again T.S. Eliot represented me when he wrote, later, in Prufrock,

I grow old … I grow old
I shall wear the bottoms of my trousers rolled

That is excellent advice for someone like me forced to wear scrub trousers designed for six-footers. Up top we wear a short-sleeved cotton T-shirt with a deep V-neck. I have a suprasternal notch that is particularly sensitive to cold. To find that notch please place the middle finger of your left hand on your breast-bone move it upwards in the midline and it will sink into a neat lit-tle hollow below your larynx. I solved that by wearing two tops, the under one back to front and the outer one the right way round. I looked like a priest.

In later years still suffering from malignant *hypothermia*, I wrapped myself in blankets but that posed an ethical problem. There were barely enough blankets in the blanket warmer for the rush of incoming patients as 'day surgery' grew in volume. Dr. Sessler, a perceptive chap in Cleveland, has demonstrated bad effects if patients are allowed to cool too much during surgery: lit-tle things like an increase in the incidence of perioperative heart attacks, bleeding and infection. My suffering became a secondary consideration. I asked my wife to buy me more vests (undershirts in the USA).

I have previously referred to my case of athlete's foot – a misno-mer if there ever was one. Anyone less athletic than me cannot be imagined. One of the therapies recommended by dermatologists is to 'keep the affected part cool'. To cool my feet even more than they were already, I wore my 'theatre shoes' with laces untied and cut crude ventilation holes near their front ends..

Soon after entering the world of work I discovered that the state of shortness and chubbiness had its advantages. The nurses and the orderlies and sometimes even the surgeons regarded me as sort of Teddy Bear, someone to be petted. The circulating nurse would say,

"Dr. Z.. You'll trip and hurt yourself if you don't tie your shoe-laces."

I was too ashamed to admit the real reason; what real red-blooded American, that I became by naturalization as soon as I was allowed to after arriving in Boston, would admit he was disa-bled by a fungus or two?

"It is intentional, Marguerite. I do want to trip up. I want break a tiny bone in my foot and then I won't have to work for a couple of months and everyone will bring me tea and éclairs q4h (every four hours)," I told her.

The anesthesiologist is given a stool to sit on covered in hard black rubber, hardly ever a chair with a back support. That's probably why I suffer from chronic backache in my senescence.

Let's get back to operating rooms by looking at the worst and the best and then go on to the most curious. Some of the worst belonged to the Brigham and Women's Hospital in Boston, Mas-sachusetts, one of the Harvard teaching hospitals. Toward the end of my working lifetime I returned to academia at the Brigham after years in private practice. One great advantage to the life of an anesthesiologist is that our skills are portable. We carry them in our heads and in our hands.

I loved working with the residents but hated the 32 operating room suite. My first year in the USA was also spent at the Brigham but at that time it was the Peter Bent Brigham Hospital. In the old building there were only eight operating rooms, four in a row on each side of a central corridor.

A new and splendid hospital was planned at that time to stand on what was then the muddiest, iciest parking lot in Boston. That part of Boston at the foot of Mission Hill once lay in the huge area of marshland that came under the title of Boston Harbor and was later reclaimed for construction using landfill. In the late 1960s and 1970s the Peter Bent Brigham Hospital and the Boston Lying-In Hospital merged. I suppose you 'lay-in' to have your baby.

155

Our youngest, Richard Til, was born in the old 'Lying-In'. One of the men who revived the use of epidural blocks for childbirth in this country Dr. Jess Weiss, gave my wife her epidural at 4 a.m. one summer morning. A few days later he suffered his first heart attack. In my paranoid way I suspected a connection. For years after, whenever I met Jess at some committee meeting or other I felt guilty about his health.

The merged entity was called the Affiliated Hospitals - later renamed the Brigham and Women's Hospital. I heard that the reason the new operating room suite was built two stories below grade was that we were at the height of the Cold War and was done for safety. Have you ever tried to find your way out of the Hampton Court Maze in England? It is extraordinarily difficult but at least you can see the sky at all times. Now take that maze down two floors with nothing but artificial light and air conditioning and corridors branching left and right without logic. Working there was good training for future work in the coal-mining industry. There was little or no storage space for heavy equipment and so it sat in the corridors, obstructing the movement of patients on stretchers. A few days before the inspectors from the Hospital Accreditation people arrived all this equipment disappeared, to be temporarily stored – who knows where? It was then an unpleasant and stressful place in which to work.

A few days ago Dr. Jim Philip took a few of us on a tour of those same rooms. They have been upgraded: they are now large, bright airy and cheerful. I plan to fake my London County Council Birth Certificate and take twenty-five years off my age. Then I'll apply for a faculty position at the Brigham and go back to work in that subterranean elegance.

For the last three years before I retired I was sent to a Day Surgery Centre down the road from the Brigham. I think this was done by the Chairman of the Department because once the residents discovered I had been in private practice they were not at all interested in the working of the alveolo-capillary membrane of the lung, one of the few subjects on which I considered myself an expert. Instead they asked me two questions with monotonous regularity.

"Dr. Zeitlin, will I be sued?"

And,

"Dr. Zeitlin, I'm a $180,000 in debt. How much do you think I'll make in private practice in Orlando?" when they knew me better, and judged I would not split on them.

They all wanted to go to Orlando. They were all so knowledgeable and intelligent and had volunteered in Bangladesh tracking down malaria-laden mosquitoes or trying to get the men to use condoms, but now they all wanted was to live and work in Orlando.

Some of the Brigham surgeons brought their patients to the Surgicentre if they were suitable for 'one day surgery'. This was located on the second floor of a modern medical office building and had windows everywhere except in the operating rooms themselves. We were happy, relaxed, efficient and safe. It was also an interesting place. Some mornings from the windows in the patients' waiting room we saw Mr. Michael Dukakis, Presidential aspirant, and by then a professor at Northeastern University walking to work. We watched with respect as he picked up trash lying around on the sidewalk and dropped it into the nearest bin. He's a man of action and civic responsibility.

Some of the older English operating theatres I worked in had windows to the exterior. You knew what the weather was like and that there was a world out there. But this disappeared when they were closed off or bricked in on the false assumption that exterior air carried bad bacteria, a belief with no scientific foundation. Medical ideas go in circles over the decades.

Here is a curiosity. After telling you about the artificiality of the operating room environment I'm about to contradict myself. All surgeons are rightly afraid of their patients acquiring bacterial infections during the period when the wound is open. The enormous growth in the number and variety of operations during the Victorian era depended on three things. First of course, the arrival of anesthesia. Then the introduction of antisepsis, that is, sloshing the surgeon's hands and the whole of the area of the surgery with antiseptic solutions that kill bacteria and lastly, the change to

157

aseptic methods in which everything that touches the patient, drapes and instruments have been previously heat-treated and thus sterilized. Of course we all wear masks and clean clothing.

Orthopedic surgeons are more worried than most about infection. Infected bones and joints are difficult to treat. Unfortunately infections still occur occasionally. In the 1980s the orthopods introduced ultra-violet lighting with their bactericidal power into the operating room they used at the Union Hospital where I worked in private practice. At first we tried to protect ourselves using sunscreen on our hands and faces, that is our exposed parts. We got badly burnt. Then we added hoods, heavy dark goggles and two or three pairs of surgical gloves and we swathed the patients' heads. That was an improvement but for me had one serious disadvantage – I felt I had 'lost touch' with the patient. It became much more difficult to feel the pulse and observe the skin color and the size of the eye pupils. I was told to stop complaining and rely on our new measuring instruments. I was old-fashioned enough that I found this unsatisfactory.

So I had our technicians build me a 'house' in which I could sit and be protected against the UV. I was the architect. They took four or five mobile poles that were intended for hanging intravenous equipment and made the ceiling and walls by using layers upon layers of cotton surgical drapes.

I have always been concerned about my stomach: put another way I get irritable and irrational when I'm hungry. Let's say I'm stuck at the end of a long day with another very long orthopedic case in the UV room. All my colleagues have gone – there's no one to give me a break. My 'house' enabled one of our techs to nip down to the kitchen and smuggle a tuna salad sandwich and a Coke into my little house. I have never revealed this secret before to a waiting world.

I think the most peculiar operating theatre I ever encountered was the one built for neurosurgery at the Whittington Hospital in London while I was a resident there in the early 60s. The senior neurosurgeon suffering from the usual skull opacity, refused to wear a headlamp and the title of his oft-repeated song was,

"I Can't See a Thing."

The hospital authorities bought and installed an expensive lighting system from France. The whole ceiling was a concave upward curve of lights so that no matter where Mr. Cantseeathing's head was positioned, light would get into the patient's cerebral depths at all times. By chance I gave the anesthetic for the first case done there and Mr. C. seemed happy. As usual, a few instruments were dropped onto the floor surrounding the table but this surgeon wanted complete silence and the circulating nurse did not, as is usual, pick them up. He performed a long and picky operation and I noticed that these instruments were migrating, slowly and fitfully, by themselves, toward the sides of the room.

As I have previously explained there is a lot of time in an operation like this for the anesthesiologist to speculate upon the eternal verities and now I wondered if magnets had been built into the walls of this theatre, analogous to built-in vacuum systems in modern houses. Then I had another thought. Very discreetly I lay down on the floor after winking at the circulator, I could see that the floor was convex upwards in the middle! Later we discovered the builders had merely dropped equal vertical distances from the ceiling when they built the floor. The reconstruction cost the National Health Service a lot of money.

Operating rooms have interesting floors and hereby hangs a tale – to which I have exclusive rights. So far as I know nobody else in the whole wide world knows this tale because I have the only remaining copies of the supporting documents. What's so great about having documents about floors? Please be patient. It's an explosive story. I came in at the very end of it.

After 15 years in private practice with Chuck and Michael I moved to the Lahey Clinic, a multi-specialty Clinic, modeled on the Mayo Clinic. The hospital and the clinic share a single building in Burlington, Massachusetts with obvious advantages to the patient.

Your physician can walk with you down the corridor to get the opinion of a colleague. Everyone is on salary although that is determined to some extent by productivity, seniority and special skills.

The Lahey Clinic was founded by Dr. Frank Lahey in 1923 in downtown Boston. Although I never met him, he died in 1953, I hold a special place for him in my historical heart. He was one of the very few surgeons in the first half of the 20th century who saw the importance for his patients of having excellent anesthesia. He is the only surgeon to whom the American Society of Anesthesiologists presented a Certificate of Honor. This still hangs on the office wall of the Anesthesia Department at the Lahey.

When Frank Lahey founded his eponymous clinic in 1923 he first hired one of the few specialist gastroenterologists in the country at that time, Dr. Sara Jordan. His next hire was an anesthesiologist, also one of the very few specialists at that time, Dr. Lincoln Sise. If you enter the main lobby at the Lahey Clinic you will see three large portraits: Dr. Lahey, Dr. Jordan and a recent CEO, Dr. Wise. I wonder why no portrait of Dr. Sise. I'm going to write to the new C.E.O. and ask.

In the anesthesia department's conference/lunch room at the Lahey there stood at the far end a regiment of file cabinets. I asked my colleague Dr. Jim Jovenich who had worked there for many years,

"Would anyone mind if I browsed through those cabinets?"

"We have intended throwing out those old papers for years. Somehow we never got around to it." Jim replied. That is how I got my exclusive historical scoop, as the newspapermen say.

In the 1920s and early 1930s anesthesiologists only had three inhalational general anesthetic agents of real use, ether, chloroform and nitrous oxide. They were all gases or vapors the patient had to inhale. A few anesthesiologists had experimented with chemicals introduced into the rectum or into a vein. Their effects were unpredictable and did not really catch on until a decade later. Ether was safe but flammable and unpleasant for the patient, chloroform caused irregular activity of the heart and killed patients and nitrous oxide was such a weak agent that on its own for it to be useful, the patient had to be deprived of oxygen. In sum very little had changed in the previous 70 years. Chemists and physicians had for a long time searched for an anesthetic agent that was powerful enough to put the patient to sleep quickly and pleasantly and could be used with a very high percentage of oxygen in the gas mixture. In 1880, a Dr. Freund prepared a gas he called trimethylene. Its chemical diagram can be drawn as a circle and so it was renamed cyclopropane.

In 1929 a pharmacologist with the lovely name Dr. Yandell Henderson, working at the Toronto General Hospital experimented with cyclopropane to see if it might be a useful anesthetic gas. The description of his third experiment on an animal says it all; not just about cyclopropane but how different medical research was 70 years ago.

"Experiment 3: Feb 1, 1929. A cat of 1.5 Kg. At 1.40 p.m. the animal was placed in an anaesthetizing tank and at 1.50 p.m. a gas mixture of 15.4 per cent of cyclopropane in air and oxygen was admitted. The cat slowly sank down with no stage of excitement, and was apparently anaesthetized in four or five minutes. It did not respond to poking.

When removed from the tank the cat winked and moved its tongue in one minute, sat up and walked about in three minutes. In five minutes it purred when petted. It was quite normal a week later."

I find it hard to believe that he actually had the nerve to submit a paper to the Canadian Medical Association Journal with the words, "it did not respond to poking". What was the editor thinking when he accepted it for publication? Poking!?

In 1934 Dr. Ralph Waters, the head of the first real academic department of anesthesia in the world, academic in the sense that he developed a highly organized program of teaching and research, reported on cyclopropane's use in two thousand patients undergoing surgery in the course of one year at the University of Wisconsin. He found that it was powerful enough to allow the use of lots of oxygen and when used carefully, that is, with close monitoring of the heart's action, had few dangers. In passing he mentions that it was explosive.

What makes cyclopropane explode? Sparks, visible or not perceptible from static electricity. You know what static electricity is – the sharp tingle when you remove your nylon undergarments and the air is dry. What happens when cyclopropane explodes when a patient is breathing it? Often the patient dies and sometimes the bystanders, nurses, anesthesiologists and surgeons are injured.

The first cyclopropane explosion was *reported* in 1938 but it certainly happened earlier. A carefully done estimate for 1939 told us that in that year alone there were 93 cyclopropane explosions.

One evening when I was on-call for emergencies at the Lahey, I was too tired to go home and planned to spend the night at the hospital. It was still too early to go to bed so I started to go through the file cabinets in our conference room. I found all kinds of interesting correspondence from the past as far back as the mid 1930s and one fat file with the most astounding detail of a death from a cyclopropane explosion at the Lahey Clinic in 1938. To be precise, it occurred on the morning of October 31 1938, the morning after Orson Welles scared the life out of millions of Americans with his realistic radio adaptation of H.G.Wells's 'War of the Worlds'.

This one tragedy had a more profound impact on the practice of anesthesia than much of the detailed research that was beginning to take place in the late 1930s: not because of any scientific discovery but because of the personality and vision of one man, a surgeon, Dr. Frank Lahey.

In 1938 the doctors at the Lahey Clinic examined patients at, what else, a Clinic, in a fine brick building at the inner end of Commonwealth Avenue, one of the main roads leading from the wealthy Western suburbs of Boston toward downtown. The patients attending Dr. Lahey's emporium sometimes had to be admitted to hospital if, say, they had pneumonia or had suffered a heart attack. Dr. Lahey was a surgeon and you can only do surgery in a hospital. He and his growing numbers of colleagues obtained 'privileges', the right to admit and treat a patient at two non-Harvard hospitals, the New England Deaconess and the Baptist.

Why do I mention 'non-Harvard'? Because in 1923 when Lahey first came up with idea of a clinic where all the doctors would be on salary instead of charging their own fees, it was met with much opposition from the 'academic' doctors. Although they were in theory devoted to teaching and were so, they were also devoted to making lots of money if they were successful and popular.

One year after Waters' publication about cyclopropane in 1935 Drs. Sise, Woodbridge and Eversole the three anesthesiologists now working with Dr. Lahey, published a paper about the use of the agent in the operating room based on their experience in 184 patients. They called it a 'valuable' new agent. They only remarked on its explosibility in a way that someone new to its use would merely be aware of that as a possibility. To me that sounds like the captain of a submarine about to embark on a deep sea expedition being told that he might at some unpredictable point run out of fuel and then suppressing or minimizing that possibility.

On the morning of October 31 1938 a 44 year-old woman, Mary Lahiff with a lump in her breast was brought to the operating room at the Baptist Hospital for excision of the lump. She belonged to a poor Irish émigré family and worked as a clerk in the office of a coal delivery merchant. The 'triple-decker' house where she lived with her parents in Cambridge still stands. I have photographs of the house. It is no different from thousands of similar houses built in the inner Boston suburbs like South Boston where successive waves of émigrés moved as soon as they got work.

The anesthetic was actually performed by a nurse anesthetist supervised by a staff physician anesthesiologist, Dr. Urban Eversole. It's interesting that although Dr. Lahey went round the country trumpeting the fact that he only asked physicians to give anesthesia to his patients, he also employed nurse anesthetists. There is also good evidence that the anesthesiologists at the Lahey Clinic, although quite well paid, never shared in the year-end bonuses Dr. Lahey handed out. Money talks. Hypocrisy abounds.

Years later after he retired Dr. Eversole described what happened on a videotaped interview for our historical museum and library, The Wood Library/Museum of Anesthesiology in Park Ridge, Illinois.

"It was a very disturbing situation as you may well imagine. I was giving anesthesia in the adjoining room (at the Baptist Hospital). One of the nurse anesthetists, Miss Bernice Edgar, was giving this anesthesia for a breast operation. It was just about over when we heard the bang in the next room. It was not Dr. Lahey operating on that patient. Immediately I turned my patient over to the resident, went into the adjoining room and examined the patient. She seemed alright (at that time). An immediate bronchoscopy was performed but nothing untoward was seen (but) she died about 18 hours later. She had progressive emphysema (air in the body where it should not be) clear to the knees. At autopsy a rupture of the posterior pharyngeal wall (the throat) was found that had been bypassed at the bronchoscopy."

Dr. Lahey stopped the use of cyclopropane immediately. He took charge of the situation. Prior to that, when a patient died on the operating table, no matter what the cause, it was kept as quiet as possible.

"Your father was too ill to take the anesthetic," they would tell the family of the deceased. I am willing to bet that if those of you who read this book ask their grandparents or their great-aunts and uncles,

"Did you ever hear of anyone who died on the operating table? What were you told about the cause of death?", many of your older relatives will tell you,

"That's what Uncle Freddie died of. They told us he couldn't take the ether."

My friend and colleague in Australia Dr. Rodney Westhorpe, gave the main historical lecture, the Lewis Wright, at the annual meeting of the American Society of Anesthesiologists a couple of years ago. The title of his paper was, "He took it well, didn't he?" This is what a surgeon said to the anesthesiologist at the end of a long and difficult case. Not one word or acknowledgement that the anesthesiologist had brought the patient through some devastating physiological insults.

Anesthesia was a convenient scapegoat for death on or soon after, 'the table.' My wife is a professional violinist and because of that I have become interested in the lives of great classical music performers. In the mid-1930s Emanuel Feuermann, a classical 'cellist emigrated to the United States from Germany as a result of Hitler's persecution of the Jews. At that time expert musicians considered that he either was or would soon become the greatest of all performing 'cellists. Soon after his arrival he was concertizing with the most successful American orchestras.

In April 1942 he underwent a hemorrhoidectomy at a small private hospital in California and died soon after. At his funeral, Toscanini, the famous conductor is said to have cried out,

"This was murder."

Various biographies, not excluding the 1950 edition of the Oxford Companion to Music wrote that Feuermann 'died of the anesthetic' or, 'he was allergic to the morphine he received.' Five summers ago my wife and I attended a chamber music concert in Wellfleet on Cape Cod. One of the players in the quartet was Bernard Greenhouse, then aged 90! After the concert I approached Mr. Greenhouse and congratulated him on his performance.

"Mr. Greenhouse, did you ever meet Emanuel Feuermann?" I asked him.

This captured his attention.

"Did I know Feuermann? What a question? I took lessons from him when I was a student in the early 40s," he answered.

"Mr. Greenhouse, I am a retired physician so I hope you will not mind a difficult question. It is said and it is written that Feuermann died of the anesthetic."

"I have heard the same but it is not true. He died of an overwhelming infection, peritonitis as the result of a botched hemorrhoid operation," Mr. Greenhouse told me.

The morning after Mary Lahiff died Dr. Lahey did something remarkable: he issued a press release. He made the death public and used that as a platform to decide whether the use of cyclopropane should continue. By 1938 he was very successful and hugely influential. His stature in the profession led to the his being consulted on President Roosevelt's failing health in early 1945.

In one of those file cabinet drawers I found the original typewritten copy of the press release.

Mary Lahiff is buried in the Mount Auburn Catholic Cemetery in Cambridge, Massachsuetts. The headstone is a simple granite slab and is engraved with "Mary Lahiff, October 31, 1938". I still visit her occasionally. Recently I wrote to the Massachusetts Catholic Cemetery Organization. Did they have any more information about Mary than one reads on her headstone? They did not. Her family presumably was too poor and therefore unimportant. I looked through all the Boston newspapers of that era on microfilm at the Boston Public Library. I could not find an obituary for Mary, not even a death notice. Yet she is central to one of the great developments of modern anesthesia, that of the non-explosive inhalational agents.

"Your death was not in vain. Although you were humble and completely unknown you were the start of a revolution in surgery and anesthesiology," I think when I visit her.

A few weeks after the tragedy Dr. Lahey convened a meeting of leading anesthesiologists and physicists to try to decide whether cyclopropane should be abandoned. After a discussion that went on well after midnight Dr. Lahey concluded that cyclopropane use would continue with the understanding that antistatic precautions would be even more strictly enforced. This led to several major research efforts to come up with solutions to *prevent* cyclopropane explosions. The central problem was the unpredictable settlement of static electric charges on the anesthesiologist, the anesthesia equipment, the patient and the operating table.

Professor Horton of the Massachusetts Institute of Technology, incidentally one of the developers of 'sonar', the way in which ships during wartime detected the presence of hostile submarines, made an 'intercoupler' – a device connecting all the places where static might collect so that they would all have the same degree of charge and sparks would not jump. Horton, for the first time since the introduction of cyclopropane had actually measured the electrical charges in different parts of the operating scene by reconstructing it with the same equipment and personnel as on the day of the tragedy, rather like a crime-scene investigation. Even though there had been a relative humidity in the air of over 60%, he found '*that an anesthetist wearing cotton garments acquired a potential of several hundred volts merely by sliding forward on the cushioned stool and then rising.*'

The National Fire Protection Association became heavily involved in the writing of safety regulations. The Intercoupler was the least of the many ingenious devices and maneuvers developed to prevent sparking but the most important and the one I was introduced to in my early days was the wearing of conductive shoes. The idea was that we wore shoes or disposable shoe covers that connected us electrically to ground thus allowing charges accumulating on our bodies to leak away. Accompanying this we had to step on machines each day that registered whether or not we were conductive enough.

That is my roundabout way of getting you back to floors – they also had to be conductive. This was usually achieved by using terrazzo tiles with copper conductive strips in between, through which the static charges were supposed to leak to ground instead of accumulating on the equipment. Once, when I was working at the Brigham in the 1990s I came across an old operating table with a metal link chain hanging from its underside and dragging on the floor – another way of conducting static charges away. Not one of the residents I quizzed about this knew what it was. Not should you expect them to know. They were reared in an era of non-explosive agents.

Then the Second World War came, and except for the arrival of the first intravenous induction anesthetic agent, sodium pentothal, for general use, nothing much else changed. The dismal newspaper articles continued to appear. Please note the dates.

New York Times, April 16 1940
EXPLOSION OF ANESTHETIC GAS KILLS WOMAN PATIENT AT SLOANE HOSPITAL
An explosion of cyclopropane gas, a commonly used anesthetic, in the rubber pressure bag of an anesthetic unit in Sloane Hospital for Women shortly before 9 o'clock yesterday morning caused the death a few hours later of Mrs. Duncan Dunbar Sutphen Jr. of Dobbs Ferry, socially prominent wife of the son of the president of the silk firm A.D. Julliard &Co.
Mrs. Sutphen, 31 year –old mother of two children, had entered the hospital Sunday night for a minor gynecological operation.

Julliard was a successful silk merchant who gave the large sum of money required to found the Julliard School of Music in Manhattan – one of the premier conservatories in America.

St. Louis Post-Dispatch: November 2, 1960
PATIENT DIES IN BLAST OF ANESTETIC (sic) MACHINE
Reuben J. Lee, a Lewiston, Idaho business man, died at St. Joseph's Hospital about an hour after a machine used to administer an anesthetic exploded when he was undergoing abdominal surgery. His doctor said death resulted from lung damage caused by the explosion.

New York Herald Tribune: April 3 1963
ANESTHETIC BLAST KILLED PUBLISHER, CITY AID (sic) SAYS
Daniel J. Mahoney, 74, publisher of the Miami (Fla.)News died from the results of an anesthetic explosion while he was being operated on at Doctors Hospital, East End Avenue at 87th. In his statement Dr. Helpern (Chief Medical Examiner) said, in part that "there was an explosion of

the anesthetic which injured the windpipe. This injury was the direct and immediate cause of death. The anesthetic was cyclopropane."

In the July 1964 issue of a leading American scientific journal, Dr. Carl Walter, a Professor of Surgery in Harvard Medical School published an article titled, 'Anesthetic Explosions: A Continuing Threat' He wrote:

"An elderly surgeon, now demised, had opposed the "nonsense" of National Fire Protection Association Code 56 on the basis of lifelong experience, He was convinced of the safety of the operating rooms in the hospital where he was chief of staff. One evening he insisted on viewing an appendectomy on his teenage son. He climbed onto the viewing stand clad in leather-soled shoes, woolen (sic) trousers, a long cotton coat, cap and mask. After the procedure was completed and the dressing was being applied, he stopped to pat his lad's cheek. There was an explosion that killed the boy and propelled the father into the corridor."

These extracts come from American newspapers. There is no reason to believe that a survey of British or French or Indian or even Argentinian newspapers would read differently.

The only thing a little different about Mrs. Sutphen's death was the name of the anesthesiologist, Dr. Virginia Apgar. Dr. Apgar as any reader who has had a baby or two might well know, was the inventor of the Apgar Score, the enumeration method for assessing a newborn baby's condition. Dr. Apgar is the only anesthesiologist ever to have appeared on a United States postage stamp. Cyclopropane was no respecter of rank, hospital sophistication or money. I will not bore you with a discussion of its chemical structure other than to say that a high school chemistry student will tell you that just by looking at its formula on a blackboard he or she can see its inherent instability.

Why were anesthesiologists in the 1930s so enthusiastic in adopting its use? It was powerful and could be given with lots of oxygen and hardly affected the action of the heart and the lungs at all. Cyclopropane had such allure that they 'stuck their heads in the sand' about its explosibility. It is remarkable that when Dr. Ralph Waters, the academic leader of anesthesia in the U.S.A. during the early part of the 20th century retired to an orange grove in Florida he would have nothing more to do with the specialty. I wonder whether it was his guilt about his influence in the general adoption of cyclopropane. My 'historical' colleagues disagree!

I used cyclopropane for my first two years as a resident in London but only to put frightened children to sleep quickly and easily. We almost always used a 'gas' or 'inhalation' induction of anesthesia in children to avoid sticking them with an intravenous needle. That was done by a colleague after the child was anesthetized. All that my various superiors, Senior Residents and Consultants said about cyclopropane was, "Be careful."

But they never actually articulated what I should be careful about. Was I supposed to develop some intangible foresight when an explosion was about to happen? I never dared ask. I developed what I called, secretly, 'anticipatory shell-shock'. I avoided it by simply turning the cyclopropane off and continuing with ether; or better, the new, non-explosive vapor that had just appeared called halothane. Years later when I rose in the ranks I discovered that most of my senior colleagues used cyclopropane with apprehension. Compressed liquid cyclopropane came in an orange colored cylinder that turned into a vapor when released at room temperature. To this day orange is my least favorite colour. My favorite is Royal Blue even though I gave up my British citizenship 40 years ago and became a red-blooded American. As I tell all my American acquaintances,

"I am a loyal American citizen, I just talk funny."

Although I never suffered an intraoperative explosion I did have some experience of explosions of a different sort. I had grown up in London during the war. Some days on the way to school after a night of German bombing I would see a pile of rubble sloping into a street filled with ambulances and cranes and women brewing cups of tea for the men pulling at the ruins. A week later the rubble-removers arrived and the week after that I would see a gap between two houses like my top back teeth after the dentist pulled a molar, a healthy tooth/house on each side. Then it was fenced off and would start to grow fantastic weeds and wild flowers. As a boy I sometimes wondered if they grew so well because of the blood from the people that died there. My father used to fertilize his dahlias with bags of dried blood. I had always assumed it was the dried blood of beef cows or mutton sheep.

I was a 14 year-old schoolboy in the early Spring of 1945, toward the end of the war in Europe, The Allied armies had pushed the Germans out of France but had not yet overcome their rocket launching sites. We lived in a house at 230 Finchley Road in the variably posh North London suburb of Hampstead. My brother David and I shared a ground-floor bedroom and our recollections are identical. In the middle of the night of March 17 we were woken by a painful pressure in our ears and on our eyeballs. Then, accompanying a roaring noise there came a feeling of being sucked at as we watched the ceiling plaster crack, disintegrate and slowly settle on us in a thick dust cloud.

"That was a German V2 rocket," David said and I agreed.

Our parents rushed in, inspected us and found we were whole. They told us not to worry, that we were safe. Worry was the last thing on our minds. Excitement pervaded the rest of our night. After an early breakfast we were allowed out to check the damage. The last ambulance was leaving from where the Hampstead Public Library once stood, five houses along the road. Holding on to each other we peered into a deep hole that had replaced the library. That hole in the London clay was lined with bricks and books and splintered shelves. At the bottom we saw a cricket ball. One of us scrambled down and retrieved it. Later we sometimes wondered whether or not its owner was dead. I do not remember feeling guilty.

Solly Zuckerman was a South African doctor and scientist doing research on apes at the University of Oxford during the years between the two wars. In 1939 when the war became imminent, a newly organized Scientific Department of the Ministry of Home Security recruited him to study the question of whether people sheltering from bombing raids would be injured by shock waves traveling through the surrounding soil. From this he moved on to investigate why soldiers and civilians died within twenty-four hours of having stood near an explosion despite showing *no* sign of external injury. Using small animals he demonstrated that between 18 and 50 feet from the site of an explosion all the animals died, but only because of the drastic effect of the pressure wave on their delicate lung tissues. In one of his lectures he described the death of a young man 12 hours after a bomb exploded in his bedroom yet he had suffered minimal external injury. Autopsy disclosed widespread lung hemorrhages.

This allows us to discuss *beneficial* explosions. Here comes a paradox. In 1969, twenty four years after the end of the war in Europe, German physicists working for Dornier Systems, a company that manufactured bombers during the war, wondered whether shock waves could be used for medical purposes. They focused them on kidney stones and discovered that they imposed mechanical stresses that exceeded the strength of the stones' brittle substance. They also showed that shock waves could be transmitted undiminished in force though water and they could be focused. Until that time stones stuck in the kidney had to be removed through a long and, postoperatively, a painful incision. The physicists combined these findings into a machine called a lithotripter and in Munich in 1980 their colleagues reported the successful fragmentation of large kidney stones in 20 patients.

In 1987 the Lahey Clinic in Boston where I was then working, my urologist colleague Dr. Robert Roth persuaded the Clinic to buy a lithotripter. It was not known which anesthetic technique would allow the best results in pulverizing the stones because patients must breathe or be ventilated artificially with all of them. The movement of the diaphragm with breathing controls the vertical movement of the kidney, potentially moving the stone out of the focus of the shockwave. I tried to answer this question in consort with Dr. Roth.

We demonstrated that there was no difference in the success of fragmenting the stones no matter whether we used very small breaths or medium size breaths under general anesthesia or if we numbed the patient with an epidural block and let them breathe on their own. Our conclusion was that the focus of the shock wave was nowhere near as sharp as had been previously supposed. If ever there was a real case of swords into ploughshares, lithotripsy was it.

Back in the mid-1950s when I was a medical student at the Oxford Medical School I boarded with Mr. and Mrs. Eyles on the second floor of their 5-story brick townhouse near the hospital. They were kind to me, too kind. Many evenings when Mr. Eyles heard me turn the key in the front door he would yell up from their basement apartment,

"Doc, join me for a snifter. You need something. You've had a terrible day, I know."

Down I went and was handed a mixture of gin, brandy and elderberry wine. An hour later I went to my room to study, so befuddled I could not define the difference between appendicitis and early labor pains. I saw exam trouble looming.

From then on I spent my evenings in the library. I may have avoided the Eyles's booze but I could not avoid using the sole bathroom on the top floor. The water was heated in a device clamped to the wall over the tub, called an Ascot heater. A ring of gas jets heated the water. To save gas we students were instructed to turn off the pilot light after each use. You had to take your own matches with your towel and clean underwear.

One summer evening I did this but there was only one match in my box and the pilot would not light. Down I went three flights and up again with my new box of matches. I struck a match. It flared vigorously and the next thing I knew I was lying at the other end of the bathroom with a thudding pain in the back of my head, smelling of singed hair. I could hear screaming from down below. Mr. and Mrs. E. were enjoying their snifters in the back garden when the whole bathroom window together with its frame dropped at their feet. I had forgotten to turn off the gas to the pilot when I went down for more matches.

Science and life sometimes move in circles. In 1955 the fuel in water heaters was 'coal-gas' – a mixture of distillates from newly mined coal. The explosive component is methane – what we call natural gas today. At the beginning of the 19th century the young British scientist Humphry Davy (later Sir Humphry) invented a miner's safety lamp that revealed but did not ignite dangerous concentrations of methane in coal mines, to this day the cause of tragic mine explosions. Years before this invention Davy *suggested* the use of nitrous oxide as an anesthetic agent for surgery. He never did anything about it!

Chapter 16 DR. HARRY BEECHER

Anesthesiology is a specialty where the most serious outcome, death, is *not* necessarily the consequence of the patient's illness; merely, if that is the right word, the result of incompetence, lack of attention, lack of knowledge or choosing an anesthetic agent or technique that was the wrong one for a particular surgical situation.

I suspect that this is the underlying reason why I and many of my colleagues are so fascinated with our history. *The history of anesthesiology is the history of the struggle for safety.*

Even though my story is now firmly settled in the United States, let's return for a moment to the Whittington Hospital in London. Mr. Embry became my friend. And very, very slowly he told me … how should I put it? Things, actually secrets. He made me his confidante. It was as though knowing these 'things' and not sharing them, was a burden to him. I suspected that a plane crashing at the airport and the death of passengers, being out in the open, in the newspapers, would not disturb him very much.

"Doc Zed." He would start while I was drawing up my drugs into syringes for the next case and he was cleaning my Boyle machine.

"Doc Zed."

"Yes, Mr. Embry? What is it?" I would say in an encouraging sort of way, "Did I draw the curare into the wrong syringe?"

"Oh, no. No. It's not you that's drawing it into the wrong syringe. Oh no. That's just my point. You are drawing it into the right syringe."

Then he would say,

"Excuse me doc Zed. I'm out of glass cleaner. I'm going to the workroom for some more."

And he would not return until I wheeled the patient into the theatre and I was left in a state of unununderstanding. Is there such a word? If not, I don't care: it's the only way I can describe what Mr. Embry was doing to me.

The next day, as though only a few seconds had passed,

"Yes, you always draw the curare into the right size syringe. And you put the atropine into that little two cc. chap. But that one, five ago, I think it was, he was casual. And she paid the price."

It took me a few minutes of mental acrobatics, like doing The Times crossword puzzle when you are a complete beginner, to work it out. 'Five ago' was my predecessor five times removed. 'Atropine, curare, wrong size syringes, casual'. That five-times-ago predecessor must have given the patient curare at the *end* of the operation and sent her back to her bed on the ward with paralyzed muscles. It's likely no one noticed she was not breathing adequately, that she *could not* breathe adequately and she died what we call a respiratory death.

I wanted to ask one of the consultants, particularly Dr. Otto Belam who had been Chief of Anaesthesia at The Whittington for many years, whether he had ever had a death on the table for which he was responsible; but I could not. It was like asking a sword-swallower,

"Where, actually, does the sword go?"

So I asked Dr. Belam,

"Is there a good book about the history of anesthesia."

"The best by far is Duncum. I'm sure H.K.Lewis will have a second hand copy."

H.K. Lewis was the biggest and best medical bookseller in the land. I bought Barbara Duncum's 'The Development of Inhalation Anaesthesia'. I still own that copy.

As much as anyone who enjoys sitting in an armchair by the fire reading frightening books, I enjoyed reading frightening books. The first few chapters of Duncum's book reveal how we anesthetists came into being; the concept of surgery free of agony starting with the ideas and animal experiments of thoughtful ingenious men in the United Kingdom and being made into an everyday medical tool by young, economically ambitious men in the United States. Perhaps this was even a reflection of the characteristics that both unite and separate the two countries. That ether was a consistently successful chemical in achieving this desirable end is proven by the historical fact that within one year of William Morton's demonstration of ether's power, at 10.16 a.m. on the morning of October 16 1846 to the assembled surgical greats at the Massachusetts General Hospital, its use had spread to the whole of the known world. In 1846 it took two to three weeks for a ship to sail from Boston to Liverpool and two to three months from London to Sydney.

We have plenty of written accounts and imagined pictorial representations of that great moment in the history of surgery. I have something better, says he boastfully, and untruthfully.

These days all anesthesiologists keep minute by minute written notations of blood pressure, pulse rate, breathing, electrocardiogram, the inspired oxygen level, the state of the patient's oxygenation, the amount of carbon dioxide being expired, the urine output, the percentages of inspired anesthetic vapors and doses of intravenous agents given, the amounts of salty solutions given intravenously and bags of blood and other blood components transfused, doses of antibiotics given intravenously at the polite request of the surgeon, the level of muscle paralysis to assist the surgeon, the patient's temperature both on the surface and on the inside, whether air is going into both lungs and whether when the last suture is in and the dressings are on the patient can take a deep breath, cough and "squeeze my fingers until you hurt me."

"You're surgery is over Mr. Truman and you did well. Dr. Veidenheimer was very pleased how things went. He is out talking to your wife and brother-in-law and he will be in to see you as soon as you get to the recovery room. I know it hurts like Hell but as soon as we get to Recovery I'll give you the Demerol left over in this syringe and you'll be much more comfortable," you tell the patient as you wheel him into his slot in the recovery room.

It's a wonder we have time to actually observe the patient. In 1846 all they noted was that the patient inhaled from a glass jar with an ether soaked sponge in it. He moaned a little while Dr. Warren made an incision in his neck and tied off a few enlarged veins.

"I knew something was happening, a little scratching on my neck *but no pain*," the young man said afterwards.

"Gentlemen," Dr. Warren, the surgeon, is alleged to have said, "This is no humbug."

The thing I have that is better, resulted from my sending a message to my old friend Dr. George Battit the most senior clinical anesthesiologist at the M.G.H. and luring him into my plot. Dr. Battit is as respectable an anesthesiologist as you will find anywhere but he entered into my fraud with enthusiasm. He sent me a contemporary preprinted anesthesia record and faked up the name and date of birth and date of admission stamp that is made up for every patient who enters hospital these days. His fake was that of the Famous First Anesthetized Patient, a young man called Edward Gilbert Abbott and the date stamp reads October 16 1846. I completed the fake by writing in a few notations of the likely pulse rate and respiration and skin color - all that was noted in those days by way of monitoring. This was my 'something better'.

I framed it and exhibited at the World Congress of Anesthesiology in Sydney, Australia about 20 years ago and no one remarked that there was anything unusual about it. It seemed obvious to me that the idea, prevalent in the heads of our present-day young trainee anesthesiologists that 'things have always been like this' is widespread.

To test this last hypothesis even further I submitted another invention of mine – another fake anesthesia record that I alleged to have found behind a dusty statue in the Ether Dome at the M.G.H. where William Morton did his thing, to the Bulletin of Anesthesia History; and *they published it!* My history-obsessed colleagues are among the cleverest and most knowledgeable doctors I know: either they did not notice the spoof or, they merely thought,

"Let's be kind to that madman Zeitlin and publish his junk. Maybe then he'll be quiet and just fade away."

I spent two years on the anesthesiology faculty at the Massachusetts General. Like most Professors and Chairmen of anesthesiology departments Dr. Harry Beecher did not have too much time to actually give anesthesia; there was too much committee work and European travel to recruit cheap labor to permit that. Mostly he gave anesthesia to the well-heeled patients secreted in the plushy rooms of the private wing, the Phillips House.

Dr. Beecher was only the second full Professor of Anesthesia in the world. The first was Dr. Robert Macintosh who interviewed me in Oxford.

Early one evening I was called to the Phillips House to do a pre-operative visit for a patient for whom Dr. Beecher was booked to give anesthesia the next day and was unable to do his own preoperative visit. She was a sweet older lady but she looked at me anxiously when I said I had come to talk to her about the anesthesia.

"You ... you are not Dr. Beecher, are you?" Her voice had the whisper of fear.

"No, I'm not Dr. Beecher. I am a member of the anesthesia department."

"Oh, thank goodness for that. You seem very nice," she said, more relaxed now.

I had already guessed what was worrying her but I did not have the guts to tell her that it *would be* Dr. Beecher on the morrow.

We chatted some more, mostly how remarkably good the food was for a hospital.

"I had Dr. Beecher for the other hip. I didn't wake up for three days and I smelled of ether for weeks," she said before I wished her 'good night'.

I mumbled some nonsense about everyone's metabolism being different but I knew the truth from the few times I was asked to relieve, that is, take over the anesthetic from Dr. Beecher. His patients were in *deep, deep* ether anesthesia, almost apneic, the fancy term for the moment when your breathing stops, with the plunger pushed all the way down in three bottles of ether in series. If nothing else proves that ether is a safe anesthetic in its approximately 130 year history it's the survival of the patients anesthetized by Harry Beecher; and it was not just because they were rich and well-nourished, merely the inherent safety of ether. Harry Beecher had another side. He was, like so many great men, a paradox. He was one of the greatest 'conceptualists' in the modern history of medicine. All I mean is that he made important observations and had great ideas.

The study of deaths associated with anesthesia has gained the attention of leading anesthesiologists from the very beginning to the present. Beecher was no exception. Between 1948 and 1952 he and his colleague Dr. Donald Todd gathered records of nearly 600,000 anesthesias given at 10 hospitals in the U.S.A. Their figures were correct but their conclusion was wrong. They concluded that the paralyzing drug curare, was the main cause of death during or after an anesthetic leading us to believe that there was something inherently poisonous about the drug, perhaps analogous to chloroform, which was indeed so.

As I have discussed earlier, an important part of a general anesthetic is to provide the surgeon with a patient whose muscles are relaxed. It would be more accurate to say paralyzed. The flaw in the Beecher-Todd study was their failure to recognize that because during the period of their study anesthetists did not fully understand that curare paralyzes the muscles of breathing as much as it did the abdominal muscles, they were sending patients to the recovery room breathing inadequately. There were even then, excellent antidotes, so-called reversal agents, available – but they were not understood initially and thus not used.

Beecher's subsequent contributions were so important that they still influence medicine into the 21st century. I will summarize them briefly.

Until Beecher thought and wrote about it in 1952 the scientific study of new drugs for use in humans was hampered by the idea that if a drug works in sufficient cases it can be released for general use. No one had previously asked the question,

"How well does a drug work for a particular illness compared to doing nothing?"

In modern language, of course, this means comparing the benefits of a drug to those of using placebo controls: or, as Beecher put it, 'the study of subjective responses'. These observations began when he was a doctor in the U.S. Army on the Anzio beachhead in Italy in January 1944. He did this work when, on average one German shell exploded every minute in the pitifully small grip the Allies had established there but were unable to expand for several months. It was on the battlefield that he noted that soldiers injured in combat seemed to need much less morphine than similarly injured young men away from combat. He developed the hypothesis that an important aspect of pain was its *meaning* to the patient. Perhaps it was that an injured soldier regarded himself as fortunate and knew he would go home alive.

In 1966 the New England Journal of Medicine published a paper by Beecher on the ethics of performing scientific experiments on humans without their full comprehension of the risks. This caused a furor and its beneficial echoes still reverberate and influence medical research today.

The power of his paper came from the examples of unethical behavior he gave. I'll just quote one.

Live cancer cells were injected into 22 human subjects as part of a study of immunity to cancer. According to a recent review, the subjects (who were) hospitalized patients were merely told they would be receiving 'some cells'. The word cancer was entirely omitted.

In his summary and conclusions Beecher is quite clear.

The ethical approach to experimentation in man has several components; two are more important than the others, the first being informed consent. ... It is absolutely essential to strive for it for moral, sociological and legal reasons. The statement that consent has been obtained has little meaning unless the subject or his guardian is capable of understanding what is to be undertaken and unless hazards are made clear. If these are not known, this too, should be stated. In such a situation the subject at least knows he is to be a participant in an experiment. Secondly, there is the more reliable safeguard provided by the presence of an intelligent, informed, conscientious, compassionate and responsible investigator.

Some 40 years later this is completely accepted as normal practice in medical research. But in the last 40 years there has been a tremendous growth in what may be described as 'invasive' procedures such as passing catheters into the heart or sticking needles into livers to get samples of tissue. But it is the everyday procedures in surgery and anesthesia that have brought the need for informed consent in clinical practice to the fore. What this should mean is to explain risks to patients and balancing the potential gain from surgery and anesthesia against those risks.

Let us see what the leaders of my specialty have to say about this. One of the most prominent textbooks for our specialty is the Sixth Edition of Clinical Anesthesia edited by Dr. Paul Barash and similar intellectual aristocrats. Chapter 4 is titled 'Anesthetic Risk, Quality Improvement and Liability. Let me quote:

The requirement that the consent be informed *is somewhat more opaque.*

And the authors continue:

Most states have adopted a 'reasonable patient' standard, which requires that the physician disclose risks that a reasonable patient under similar circumstances would want to know to make an informed decision.

Only a lawyer could dream up nonsensical circular reasoning like this sentence. Did you ever see the French movie 'La Ronde'? Lover A has an affair with Lover B; Lover B has an affair with Lover C, and so on up to Lover H who has an affair with Lover A. It's a piece of imaginative and entertaining nonsense not unlike 'Most states ...' which is a piece of dreary tautology and only goes to show once again how the practice of medicine has been dirtied by legal interference.

When I was in practice I did not sit down with each patient and enumerate the risks of knocking out a tooth, cardiac arrest, permanent neuropathy, paralysis and death. And except for terrified new residents in anesthesia I doubt if more than a small minority of my colleagues do so. If a patient asked me a direct question I spent as much time as I was able telling him or her of the risks but I emphasized the huge improvements in safety over my professional lifetime - which is the central theme of this book.

As a practical matter it almost always is the nurse who admits the patient either the night before surgery or as we now do almost always on the morning of, who gets her to sign the consent. It is an almost meaningless ritual because no nurse can be expected to understand let alone explain the potential for harm from anesthesia.

I was sued, and rightly so, for the one unexpected outcome a patient suffered in my hands. I have already described this tragedy. The fact that both the patient and her mother signed an 'informed' consent made no difference to the suit. The consent was not even mentioned during the depositions.

Later, Harry Beecher headed a Committee of Harvard Medical School physicians to examine the definition of brain death. Why was this important and timely? Because in the decade preceding 1968 resuscitative procedures had improved hugely but sometimes by the time the heart was restarted the brain had been damaged.

Again, let me illustrate this from my own experience. Anesthesiologists are nearly always included in the team that deals with 'codes', the obscure term used for the rush of people trying to bring the incipient dead back to life. Our particular skills are needed to maintain breathing and monitor the vital signs while the others do their cardiac stuff. One will not work without the other.

One afternoon, back in Good Olde England at the Whittington Hospital I was called to a code on a very elderly gentleman. Attempts to revive him went on and on with no real improvement and I was focused on trying to ventilate him adequately when I felt a finger poking my back. There stood Dr. Belam, my boss. Without a word he used the poking finger to indicate a scene taking place outside the nearest window. Immediately behind the Whittington lies the Highgate Cemetery. I looked and saw an interment. I stopped squeezing the breathing bag and the others turned their gaze out of the window. They took the hint. We let the poor old man go in peace.

The Harvard docs had become more and more aware that the result quite often is an individual whose heart continues to beat but whose brain is irreversibly damaged. They also felt that the criteria for the definition of death were so obsolete that controversy arose in obtaining organs for transplantation. Without relating the ethical and religious aspects of this matter they came up with the simple idea that examining the patient's neurological status every twenty-four hours would allow informed judgment to be made about the desirability of continued support of vital function in the absence of brain activity.

Dr. Henry Beecher's life was a paradox but his influence on humanitarian medicine remains with us.

When I first applied for the job at M.G.H. Dr. Donald Todd, Dr. Beecher's most senior associate, hired me. Dr. Beecher was traveling in Europe at that time.

Except for taking over his patients in the Phillips House operating room (he must have thought I was reliable enough to do be given this responsibility, or just did not care) I had no contact at all with Dr. Beecher during those two years. When the news became public that I was leaving, Dr. Beecher became my instant friend. He invited me to his office one afternoon and offered me whisky from a bottle he kept in his desk. He invited me to lunch the next day to join him at the special table in the dining room reserved for the Professors and Chiefs of the various services and introduced me as one of his talented young men from Europe. But I already had an understanding with Chuck. Dr. Beecher, I thought, it's too little, too late, too hypocritical.

One incident toward the end of my time at MGH showed I had acquired a mite of self-confidence, the American way. Dr. Donald Todd approached me one day.

"Ahem, Gerald. About your countryman, Dr. O'Dorr. It appears from a complaint by Dr. Cope who was doing a thyroidectomy that he and his assistants standing near the head of the table became aware that Dr. O'Dorr is not in the habit of using underarm deodorant. Is that a British custom, may I ask?" said Dr. Todd.

"Well Donald, deodorant used to be considered namby-pamby but you know, I have been away for three years," I answered cautiously.

You should note I did not say 'away from home'. I had just become an American citizen with the intention of taking the full Massachusetts Medical Licensing exam and then the specialist exam for the American Boards in Anesthesiology. I had sworn to a judge standing on the podium of Fanueil Hall in Boston that I would be faithful to the American flag and similar useful symbols.

"It's rather awkward for me … you know … to ask him. Being a countryman … ahem, … I wonder if you wouldn't mind talking … to him," Dr. Todd always had a hesitation in his speech. This was more like a car running out of gas.

"It's not my job. Donald," I said as I walked away..

I left MGH soon after that and never found out whether 'namby-pamby' carried the day or not.

Chapter 17 **THE PATIENT**

So far we have only looked at anesthesia from the outside, that is, from the point of view of what we now call providers. Ugh! What a distasteful word. What about patients' experiences of anesthesia? There are not too many descriptions available but those that we can find are quite revealing.

Why not start with mine? When I was five years old I developed acute otitis media, that is, an infection of the middle ear. When I was five years old we had no antibiotics. The sulphonamide drugs, the very earliest of the antibacterials had just made their appearance.

I had a terrible earache. My father called in a well-known ear, nose and throat surgeon. He recommended a myringotomy. A myringotomy means piercing the eardrum with a sharp-pointed knife to let the pus in the middle ear escape. They crept up on me. The pain was the worst thing ever in my little life. I remember screaming. I remember being comforted and then getting better. That was surgery without anesthesia.

My next surgery was different. I was 58, in the full flower of my working, marital and fathering life. I had just survived my second heart attack. Dr. Alexander, my cardiologist sent me to a famous cardiologist at the Beth Israel Hospital in Boston – to Dr. Baim who had recently and successfully started doing in the USA what Dr. Gruenzig had begun in Switzerland; namely threading a long and sinuous catheter through a hole in the femoral artery back up into the aorta. The aorta is the biggest highway carrying oxygenated blood from the heart to the brain and the kidneys and also into the small but vital coronary arteries that feed the heart itself. The coronary arteries are like the waiter at the Ritz who helps himself to a couple of fries on the way from the kitchen with a platter for the guests at the window table. The guests do not notice but the food supply remains efficient. My coronaries had become silted with a kind of gucky rust called atheroma. This, in my case was the result of long-standing high blood pressure and bad genes.

Dr. Baim did not show up when they took me down to the cardiac catheterization lab. An unnamed assistant of Dr. Baim's did the job; actually did not do the job, could not thread the catheter with the inflatable balloon at its tip through the blockages in my coronary arteries. I'll never know and have not had the courage to enquire whether if Dr. Baim had kept his promise to Dr. Alexander to attend to me himself he would more likely have opened up my coronaries. I remained unimproved.

"Gerald, do you ever get seasick?' Dr. Alexander asked when he saw me in his clinic the following week and showed the video of blood struggling through narrowings in my coronaries.

Was he going to send me on an ocean voyage hoping the air would clear my coronaries? Perhaps he thought the Cold War would erupt into a Hot War and a Communist submarine would torpedo my boat. That would solve my, and his problem. He did not know that my late and beloved father-in-law, Dr. Jimmy, who also suffered from severe coronary disease used to take trips on cargo boats that carried passengers from London. That was Jimmy's way albeit briefly, of putting the stresses of his family practice out of mind. I still have the letter Jimmy wrote to me describing what it was like to have a heart attack on a small freighter in mid-Atlantic not knowing whether he would die at sea, alone among strangers. The captain had a few doses of morphine and a syringe. It took nearly a week to reach the nearest port, Curacoa, where, after weeks in hospital he recovered just enough to fly home.

On March 16 1989 my life started to improve. That day I was admitted to the New England Deaconess Hospital. That same day Dick Cheney was strongly supported by Congress for the position of Secretary of Defense for the cautious George Bush, George the First. I think that was coincidental.

That evening Dr. Jim Gessner a senior member of the Anesthesiology department came to see me. I had asked him to take care of me while Dr. David Shahian, a cardiac surgeon operated on me. Dr. Gessner spent a long time comforting and reassuring me. He asked if I would like a sleeping pill that night.

"Yes, please," I said, "I'm pretty anxious. Not so much for me. More for the wife and children. The children will miss my bad jokes if I go away. I won't know anything about that journey. I'll be under your anesthetic."

Jim Gessner is a serious, conscientious man. I would guess he appreciated my feeble humor as much as the T.S.A. men at the security gates in American airports appreciate jokes explosive toothpaste tubes.

Next morning, early, a nurse came into my room and gave me an injection of a strong sedative into my postero-inferior aspect. An orderly put me on a stretcher and wheeled me down to the operating room floor. He then transferred me, using a rolling device similar to a miniature baggage claim at Logan Airport onto an operating table.

Jim Gessner arrived and started intravenous infusions, one in each arm; no longer the steel Gordh needle but a strong flexible plastic sheath. Initially he dripped a salt solution called Lactated Ringer's solution from a plastic bag connected to each sheath. Then he strapped one of my hands to a board so the that the undersurface (non-hairy) part of my wrist was exposed and after feeling with his finger tips for the pulse in my radial artery he did more or less the same as he had done with my two veins. This sheath however, he connected to a transducer, which is a gadget that transforms a pressure wave in a liquid, the blood pressure in my artery, into an electronic signal that would allow him to watch the pressure generated by my heart every beat for the next several hours.

Jim painted my neck with an antiseptic solution and using his three dimensional imagination passed another catheter into my right internal jugular vein. This is a 'blind' procedure that sometimes leads to catheterization of the innominate artery or the apex of a lung, both quite undesirable occurrences. The one bleeds with vigor; the other allows air where the Good Lord did not intend. He passed a flexible wire through this and over that flexible wire he passed a Swan-Ganz catheter which is a device with a balloon at its tip that goes through the great veins returning blood from the head to the right side of the heart; then on through the heart and into the pulmonary artery so that he could measure the pressure in the pulmonary artery. This is another but less direct way of following how well the heart is pumping.

I was wheeled into the operating room. Jim injected the usual drugs into one of the intravenous solutions and after about a minute during which time he breathed for me with 100% oxygen he passed the breathing tube. He connected this tube to a machine that he set to breathe automatically for me. He passed a wire called a thermistor into my esophagus, my gullet. This was connected to a device that displayed the temperature of the core of my body. Think of it this way. You pick up an apple in the supermarket and it feels cool because it is being kept so. But, is that its temperature? Most would argue that you would need to stick a thermometer down into the core to get a scientifically satisfying answer. Jim put an oximeter clip on my finger. That showed him continuously what percentage of the hemoglobin pigment in my red blood cells had an oxygen molecule attached to it. Anything over about 94% is acceptable. You are going to hear more about this device.

Then he connected the tubes that carry anesthetic gases and vapors into my lungs to a device that displayed the amount of carbon dioxide I was exhaling at each breath. This was displayed in terms called partial pressure; it is measured as though it was the weight of a column of mercury, usually written as $pCO2$ in mm. Hg. Silly isn't it, but it's a nod to our history. Anything between 30 and 50 is acceptable.

Than a nurse stripped me naked and wearing sterile gloves washed my penis with an antiseptic solution, squeezed some jelly into its internal conduit and inserted a catheter into my bladder and connected the outside end to a calibrated plastic bag to monitor my output of urine. At the end of the catheter inside my bladder she inflated a small balloon so it did not slip out.

Then she painted my front with cold antiseptic solution from neck to toes. She covered me with lots of sterile drapes leaving my chest and both legs exposed.

The assistant readied a gadget like an enlarged version of the device used by the dentist to keep your mouth open during a long and weary root canal. This was used to pull the two halves of my breastbone and thus the attached rib cage, apart, using a special saw. Sometimes the surgeon has to use a flexible nail file called a Gigli saw, actually an abrasive wire, under the breastbone and saw it lengthwise. He did this by pulling the ends back and forth like two lumbermen sawing a felled tree trunk with one of those double-handed saws; except, to make the image accurate they would have had to saw the trunk from the underside to the top: awkward. This gadget was invented by Leonardo Gigli an Italian obstetrician for helping babies out by enlarging ladies' pelvises and later used by neurosurgeons to open the skull, something all brain surgeons have to do from time to time.

Then the exciting stuff began. Dr. Shahian inserted tubes into the big veins and arteries near my heart and these were connected to a heart-lung machine run by an experienced, highly trained perfusionist. Perfusionists in my opinion, do not get the credit and fame they are due. Without them the surgeon could not operate on a quiet still heart and the patient's brain and kidneys, those two most vital organs, would not get enough oxygenated blood during the tedious yet worrying period while the surgeon does his stuff. The machine also provides continuous anesthesia and cools the patient to protect the brain because at low temperatures the brain needs so much less oxygen.

OK, fine, except Dr. Shahian encountered a problem.

The heart is surrounded by a smooth bag called the pericardium. Think of it as a Ziploc bag lubricated with WD 40, inside

191

which the heart beats. Sometimes when a person has had a heart attack the outer surface of the heart becomes inflamed and clearly, so might the pericardium. Mostly when you get over the heart attack and the dead part of the heart heals into a scar, the pericardium also quiets down. Sometimes though the pericardium is so inflamed that it has to heal and *itself becomes scarred.* That means the surgeon is faced with a very thickened rigid Ziploc bag before he can even get at the heart. That was what Dr. Shahian found inside me.

Nevertheless, Dr. Shahian worked intensely, removing the pericardium, freeing up one of my internal mammary arteries, a healthy artery lying under my breastbone, and using pieces of my leg vein, connected my aorta, as it leaves the left side of the heart to four of my silted up coronary arteries. They sewed these conduits in place *beyond* the obstructions with minute sutures. My life depended on the accuracy and smoothness of these new conduits. The proof of Dr. Shahian's expertise lies in my survival for another 21 years. Before that he had stopped my heart from beating with a solution of what I like to call Heartstopper which sounds like a name for a new lipstick.

For the common or garden storyteller like me it's difficult to explain death. Rabbis, Archbishops and Popes have encyclicals available to them. Kings' fools like Yorick in Hamlet, pathologists and white-coated indifferent mortuary attendants have proformas to use. But what about real people, the rest of us? We use words like 'loss' or 'absence' or 'the late (Charlie Brown)'.

So pity the poor inarticulate anesthesiologist, perfusionist or heart surgeon when the patient is on cardiopulmonary bypass. Is he dead or is he not?

The heart is still, in my case for a very long time: one cannot measure the blood pressure in the ordinary way because that depends on the presence of a pulse wave. Jim Gessner had even turned off his (my?) respirator because the bypass machine was acting as a locum tenens for my lungs. Please refrain from asking questions whether my brain or my kidneys were getting enough oxygen to keep their sensitive cells alive.

As it turned out my pancreas, one of my sweetbreads, was the only part that suffered. I developed 'pump pancreatitis' on the third day after the operation. This showed itself as an 'ileus', that is the normal peristalsis (forward squeezing movement) of my intestines stopped. My guts filled with increasing amounts of painful gas. Every Professor of Gastroenterology (Harvardian or not) came to see me and examined me using the erect finger index technique. They all left, muttering,

"This could only happen to a doctor-patient."

In the not-so–good old days Jim Gessner's anesthetic would have been blamed. The ileus got better on its own and my pancreas has survived another twenty-two years. So far as I know.

All the while everyone is fixated on my heart. Quite right, but who was watching *me*? Of course you know the answer: Dr. Gessner.

Then Dr. Shahian got all the air bubbles out of my heart, Grand Central, and also out of the big underground tunnels into and out of that nexus. It would not do for a bubble of air to travel up to my brain and lodge in a place where it would cut off supplies of oxygenated blood to that part that stores the stories I tell over and over again to whomever I can trap into listening. Then the perfusionist moved off slowly into the wings as Dr. Shahian gave my heart a little shock and it started to beat. He and his assistants put me together. They use wires like twisties for freezer bags - here we go again with my obsession with food. They must have been stainless steel because you can still see them on my chest XRay. I have never seen any rust oozing out of my cleavage.

Cunningly, Jim does nothing special, leaves the breathing tube in, takes me to the Intensive Care Unit where I am connected to a different breathing machine and am monitored as though I was still in the operating room. What is a modern Intensive Care Unit? It's a place where the patient is watched as carefully and precisely as though he or she were still undergoing surgery. That is why you need skilled intensive care nurses.

And all that is one reason why modern medicine is so expensive. All this rubbish about medical costs consuming 17% of the

America's Gross Domestic Product (GDP). So what? What percentage of the GDP is consumed trying to kill warlike tribesmen in Afghanistan, chaps who want to live and kill each other the way they always have and not have a MacDonalds or a J.C.Penney at every corner? And, who kicked the British and the Russians out and undoubtedly will do the same to us. I feel sick every time I think of the young American boys being unloaded in boxes at that Air Force base. For what?

By now it is teatime for Dr. Shahian, Jim Gessner and all the other unnamed heroes of my war with death. I bet all they got was rewarmed coffee and dreadful peanut butter crackers instead of a decent cup of tea and cucumber sandwiches on buttered brown bread with the crusts cut off. Dr. Shahian does not leave until he is absolutely certain I am stable and not bleeding.

That night was boring for everyone but me. I remained unaware. My heart was beating, the machine was breathing for me, my kidneys were making urine and all the numbers on all the monitors made my night nurse feel comfortable. Every so often when I looked like waking up and ordering a taxi to take me home the nurse gave me a dose of sedative via the intravenous.

The very first paper I ever published in the English anesthesia literature was about the use of mechanical ventilation in patients who had just undergone open-heart surgery. The theory was that having a machine do the breathing for the patient reduced the amount of work the heart had to do to supply the muscles of breathing with oxygen and energy during those critical early hours. Little did I think nearly thirty years earlier that I would become one of those patients I wrote about!

Next morning, Dr. Shahian and his residents came by and told Jim Gessner that from their point of view it was OK to remove my breathing tube. He did that after passing a catheter down the breathing tube to aspirate secretions that have accumulated. By then I breathed on my own and that evening the nurses sat me out of bed. What do they think they are doing, those nurses? Do they think Zeitlin is Tarzan? Next they'll have him swinging from tree to tree.

By Sunday afternoon I was removed to a regular hospital bed on a regular hospital floor.

My first awareness since Thursday evening when Jim said 'good night', was Sunday afternoon with my wife telling me to stop complaining about the physiotherapist who was banging on my pain-wracked chest to help me cough up my secretions. Winston Churchill's manners were better than mine. When he woke up from surgery with anesthesia at the Lenox Hill Hospital in 1931 after his accident on Fifth Avenue, you will remember he said:

"I see a beloved face. My wife is smiling."

As always, Churchill said it best. He had spoken for me, fifty-eight years earlier.

It was almost three days since Jim Gessner had given me the sleeping pill to swallow on Thursday evening. Those three days were, and still are a complete blank. Now I know what it's like to be dead, except that Jim Gessner brought me back to life.

This experience raises another and so far unanswered question. Is there any difference between general anesthesia, that is, chemically induced unconsciousness and the obliteration of memory. Perhaps they are the same thing. That is why I told you my Thursday evening to Sunday afternoon story. Whatever it was that James Gessner, MD, a graduate of Harvard Medical School in 1972, gave me, I completely avoided the pain and suffering that would otherwise have attended my open-heart operation.

Suppose now that Jim did not have the tools or drugs that he had in 1989. I know the comparison is not entirely logical but let us see if we can find a description by a patient of her surgery *before* the introduction of useful general anesthesia in 1846. Please read the last chapter of this book.

That brings me to a profoundly important but little discussed aspect of modern anesthesia. I, like so many of my colleagues accept the fact that certain drugs, particularly the benzodiazepines such as Valium, Dalmane and especially the shorter-acting one that is used intravenously, Versed (midazolam) are what we call amnesics, they obliterate memory. So what? You say again. Many times friends and relatives when they discover what I used to do, tell me,

"Dr. Joint said I would be awake, just a little sedated for my nervousness but that I would be able to watch what he's doing on the TV screen. The anesthesiologist said he would just give me a tiny dose of Versed. Now I'm upset with both of them. I do not remember a thing."

About three years after I joined Chuck in private practice I hurt my back badly pulling a canoe out of Lake Ossippee. I was sent to a neurosurgeon who put me in hospital for nine (can you imagine that in 2011, nine days) and with physiotherapy I got better. Dr. Arena also put me on thrice a day Valium. I am told that Aideen brought the kids to visit me every other day and my old friend Jonathan from London came to visit. I remember absolutely nothing of those nine days.

It was when I read Oliver Sacks's brilliant book 'The Man Who Mistook His Wife for a Hat" that I realized the implications of this. His Chapter 2 is titled The Lost Mariner and tells the tale of a patient who for neurological reasons had lost the memory of all his life prior to the moment that Sacks met him. Then as the interview proceeds, he immediately loses the memory of what has already been said and done that day. It is a quotation at the beginning of that chapter from the memoirs of the film maker Luis Bunuel that struck me as I was thinking, as I sometimes do about that aspect of anesthesia and sedation, that is the temporary loss of memory. This is what Bunuel says,

You have to begin to lose your memory, if only in bits and pieces, to realize that memory is what makes our lives. Life without memory is no life at all ... Our memory is our coherence, our reason, our feeling, even our action. Without it we are nothing,

If you agree with Bunuel and I do, you will realize how remark-able are the actions of anesthetics and sedatives. They excise pieces of our lifelong memory formation with all the associated implica-tions described by Bunuel but they do it *in a reversible way*. Don't you think that is remarkable? Drugs that can obliterate pieces of your life without damaging the rest?

Chapter 18 ADDICTION

One ordinary morning, in the middle of an ordinary week about 1980 I arrived at work at the Union Hospital operating room. The three children had eaten an ordinary breakfast and gone to their ordinary school and my wife had already started an ordinary violin lesson in our ordinary home studio before I left for work. In the ordinary way I finished dressing in the car on the way to work; do the zip up, fasten the belt, button the shirt and tie the knot in the tie.

Chuck and Michael always reached the hospital before I did. I never got over the shock when I first went to work at the Brigham Hospital in Boston in 1965 of discovering that surgery begins at 7.30 a.m. in the United States compared to 9 a.m. in the United Kingdom.

That ordinary morning Chuck was preparing a patient who was to undergo resection of a colon cancer and Michael was upstairs giving a caudal epidural to relieve the pain suffered by a laboring lady. I had been appointed the 'floor-runner' for the day; I was to be the general factotum. I had to help the nurse anesthestists, three intelligent, reliable ladies, start their cases. I had to be available to see patients coming in that morning. We were already seeing the beginnings of day-case surgery when patients no longer came into the hospital the night before. I had to check the patient in the intensive care unit. I had to visit patients who were not receiving adequate pain relief, the pain, the result of their surgery the day before. I had to pacify an irritable neurosurgeon, let us call him Dr. Cortex, who complained to me that his craniotomy scheduled to start in Room 4 at 10 a.m. was delayed until noon because the 8 a.m. surgeon in Room 4, let us call him Dr. Intimate, had changed the operation from a pelvic floor repair for prolapse of the uterus to a pelvic floor repair plus an abdominal hysterectomy. When I approached Dr. Intimate gently about this unexpected change he said,

"I promised the patient I would do both just before she went to sleep," to which I had no answer. Dr. Cortex followed me round the hospital, grizzling,

"It's just not right. My patient has raised intracranial pressure, his just bleeds a little."

Chuck and Michael also contradict this but what follows is another of my great contributions to the science of anesthesia.

"Dr. Cortex, if you feel so strongly about this, why don't you go into Room 4 and discuss the matter with Dr. Intimate, directly, to his face?" I said.

This resulted in an immediate cure. Dr. Cortex, without a word slid off to the doctor's sitting room and read the Wall Street Journal until he got the call later that morning that his patient was ready.

I was standing in the O.R. corridor wondering if I could safely slip out for a quick coffee when Jennifer, the operating room Head Nurse (Theatre Sister) linked her arm with mine. I knew from past experience this was a prelude to trouble. This time it was the prelude to one of the strangest questions I had ever been asked by someone who was not an anesthesiologist.

"Dr. Zeitlin. How much Demerol (Pethidine) would you use for an appendectomy (appendicectomy) that took 45 minutes skin to skin?" she said.

'Skin to skin' is the vulgar term we use for the period starting with the surgeon's incision and ending when he puts in the last suture and cleans up the mess in preparation for the dressing.

"That depends on the size, the age and the physical status of the patient. Also some unquantifiable factors such as the response to the halothane which varies from patient to patient," I replied. There was something serious in the way she asked me the question so I answered it as objectively as I was able. Halothane was the non-explosive and powerful inhalation agent that entered general use in the early 1960s.

There was a troubled tone to her next question.

"Have you ever used 800 milligrams for such a case?"

"Never," I answered without hesitation.

"That's what Dr. Williamson used for just such a case last night," she said as she walked away.

When the surgeons on Boston's North Shore realized all three of us were Board-Certified and capable they brought us more and more work. We asked our nurse anesthetists to do the elective work during the day and kept one of us free to supervise them and make ourselves immediately available. That meant we were 'on-call' every third night (or every second night if one of us was on vacation or sick) and every third weekend. When I had my first heart attack in 1981 Chuck and Michael took call every second night for three months. They got some extra help but not much. We should all be so lucky to have such partners.

Our contract with the hospital which gave us exclusive rights to the anesthesia service there, was dependent on our providing 24 hour a day coverage 365 days a year. We also guaranteed to provide the same degree of coverage to the obstetricians who asked us to provide pain relief to nearly all their patients and we had to be available at very short notice for emergency Caesarian deliveries. In our later years the Massachusetts Legislature mandated that the full surgical team had to be at the ready within 30 minutes of the moment that the obstetrician decided the laboring mother required an emergency Caesarian Section to save the baby's life.

The three of us were in our forties and the burden began to worry us. We all suffered from Chronic Fatigue Syndrome. But, unlike the modern illness whose existence and cause remain dubious, ours came from, well, fatigue. We began to hire moonlighters who would come in at about 6 p.m. - mostly well recommended residents from the Massachusetts General Hospital. We have subsequently discovered that more than half of them in later years went on to become full Professors and Chairmen of Anesthesia departments. We have one President of the American Society of Anesthesiologists in our collection! We provided secondary coverage for each other, and our moonlighters from home.

This was not enough to make our workload tolerable. We needed a full-time, regular 'moonlighter'. I forget how we found Dr. Williamson but he had done his training in the Navy and was about to take his Board examination; he would soon become a fully qualified specialist in anesthesiology. He needed to support a family while he was studying. Chuck interviewed him and told us he was mature and experienced clinically. We heard good reports from the surgeons whose patients he had anesthetized at night and our fatigue problem improved. We paid him well.

That was why Jennifer's question on that ordinary morning seemed like an unexpected punch on the nose. I waited until lunch to tell Chuck and Michael. There could be little doubt Dr. Williamson was addicted to narcotics and had somehow hidden this when he worked at the Chelsea Naval Hospital. Jennifer had asked me the important and perceptive question.

Chuck screwed up his courage. Underneath his solemn exterior there lurks the kindest of hearts. But he had to face Dr. Williamson with the direct question.

"Are you or are you not …?"

Dr. Williamson strenuously and indignantly denied he was an addict and told Chuck he was interfering with his, Williamson's, clinical judgment. But the nurses, who were the ones to get the narcotics for us to use from a double-locked cabinet, were now alerted and the pattern continued.

"Frankly I don't know whether you are or are not using, but you have worked your last night here," Chuck eventually told Dr. Williamson.

Chuck gave him a bonus check and shook his hands wishing him well. Dr. Williamson's denials were so vehement that Chuck was unable to recommend where he could and should have gone for treatment. In retrospect, that was a mistake.

Let us slip back a few years to a small suburban hospital in England where, in one of the operating theatres only children had surgery. The ceilings were painted with scenes from Alice in Wonderland and the nurses had fashioned huggable bear-shaped toys out of whose ursine nostrils came a steady stream of nitrous oxide and oxygen and a low concentration of ether. We called this a 'steal' induction for children, nearly all terrified of needles.

A pleasant lady anesthesiologist worked in this room. One morning, my case was cancelled and I asked her permission to watch her anesthetize a child. I saw a miracle of kindness and efficiency. I stayed and chatted for a while. She took a clean dry surgical sponge and poured a little ether onto it. She folded the sponge into a small square, put it in her mouth, in her cheek and sucked gently.

"Very relaxing," she said and smiled sweetly at me.

I left. I said nothing and did nothing. I was very junior. Later, I heard on the grapevine that she had fallen asleep while giving a child, and herself, the new more powerful agent halothane. The child died.

In 1960 a British anesthesiologist Dr. W. Stanley Sykes published the first of a three volume history of anesthesia titled 'Essays on the First Hundred Years of Anaesthesia.' He died before the third volume could be published but another, able British anesthesiologist Dr. Richard Ellis completed the third volume from the notes collected by Dr. Sykes. It is a tragic irony that Dr. Ellis himself died from an as yet unrevealed complication of anesthesia after a minor procedure about 25 years later.

In the Preface to Volume 1, Dr. Sykes, with erudition, discusses various safety devices invented as early as 1868 designed to warn anesthesiologists when the pressure in their oxygen tanks was low.

He wrote,

"A safety device of this sort would probably have prevented part of a recent tragedy. The reference is to an ex-consultant anaesthetist who

acquired the habit of inhaling the anaesthetic himself. During the semi-stupor produced by this an oxygen cylinder ran out and the patient, a child, died on the table.

The anaesthetist lost his job, got a goal (jail) sentence and was struck off the register."

Anesthesiologists more or less are the only doctors who regularly administer the drugs they prescribe. Nearly all others write a prescription that is administered by a nurse for patients in hospital. Or, the patient takes a prescription to a pharmacist who dispenses it and writes precise instructions on the bottle.

It is this simple difference that leads to our particular problem. Although hard numbers for rates of drug abuse are difficult to obtain there are published studies suggesting that opiate misuse among anesthesiologists is higher than in other specialties. A survey done in the USA 8 years ago found the incidence of known drug abuse to be 1% among anesthesia faculty and 1.6% among our residents. The American Society of Anesthesiologists leadership has been aware of this and has tried very hard to prevent these tragedies. It has an active Task Force on Chemical Dependence.

Two aspects of this sad situation remain unresolved. First, should an anesthesiologist who has once become drug dependent *ever* be allowed back into the operating room no matter how effective his or her rehabilitation seems to have been? What is the evidence that a drug-dependent anesthesiologist may harm a patient?

The answer to the first is still under active debate, as recently as last year in our leading journal, Anesthesiology.

I have a totally unproven theory, shared by some but not all my colleagues, about drug-dependence in our community. I believe that young doctors with that tendency choose anesthesiology as a specialty. I realize this is harsh and adds to the burden of my academic colleagues who every year make choices about whom to admit to their residency programs.

Chapter 19 AWAKE

If the makers of the 2009 movie 'Awake' had asked my advice it would have been a blockbuster. I would have done it for free except for my First Class round trip airfare to Hollywood, a pleasure I aspire to but will never otherwise achieve.

They did not invite me and it grossed only 14.3 million dollars in the weeks after its release. The average cost of making a feature film in 2007, when 'Awake' appeared, stillborn, was about 70 million dollars.

I would have told the director to have a scene in which the anesthesiologist carelessly picks up a syringe that he has not labeled and that contains say, a muscle relaxant instead of the narcotic he believes he is giving. I would have told the director to show the delivery van from the British Oxygen Gas Corporation filling the oxygen tanks behind the hospital with nitrous oxide. The delivery man played by Steve Martin would have scratched his head wondering why the fittings from his hose to the tank did not quite fit. I would have told the director to make his anesthesiologist a drug addict; one who has figured out how to penetrate an ampoule of fentanyl with a hot needle and aspirate the good stuff for himself and replace it with saline for the unfortunate patient. I would have made the anesthesiologist a Board-certified, conscientious resident who has been on-call and without sleep for 48 hours. I wonder why I never went into the film business?

This movie has almost nothing to do with awareness during anesthesia. It's about Cardiac Grand Larceny and the villains are caught. A more appropriate if somewhat lengthy title would have been the rock lyric below that describes the almost indescribable plot:

'You stole my heart
Yeah you packed it up
And you took it away from me
You stole my heart
Yeah it followed you up on the train
When you left me
You stole my heart'

This movie is an irrelevant piece of trash and a morbid insult to those few patients who are indeed aware of something during surgery. What is the truth about awareness?

I did not know of any patient I anesthetized during 40 years in the operating room who was aware of any part of his or her surgery. Nor did I hear tell of any such by my many colleagues through the years. That proves nothing. Patients rarely complain or even speak up because they are so grateful for the care. There is a stage of the anesthetic process called analgesia during which the patient may be aware of what is happening but feels no pain. This was true of the famous first public anesthetic at the Ether Dome and many more times during the early days. This is called analgesia.

In a later chapter I will describe the remarkable piece of research about the underbelly of anesthesiology called the American Society of Anesthesiologists Closed Claims Project. It is an ingenious way of studying untoward incidents and outcomes associated with anesthesia from the records of malpractice suits held in the files of insurance companies.

In 1999 the leaders of this project studied 79 malpractice claims in which a patient alleged they were aware of the surgery while under anesthesia. Of these claims 18 were situations in which the patient said they were awake during surgery but paralyzed; the rest alleged they could recall events during general anesthesia. Other studies have reported incidences of awareness at a frequency of 1 in 300 for a mix of all surgeries other than obstetric and cardiac. In the latter two the incidence is about 1 in 200 and in trauma cases about 1 in 75. Quite often the anesthesiologist has to be cautious about the concentrations of the agents he or she is using because of fear of the birth of a depressed baby and in trauma cases, because of the fear of making a bad situation, by depressing the low blood pressure from major blood loss, worse.

Many of these cases *were* the result of errors, most notably, picking up the wrong syringe and the patient receives a dose of an agent that does not 'deepen' anesthesia, The incidence of claims was higher for women; there is no good explanation for this other than a suggestion that women are more likely to sue than men. We do not know why.

Some of these cases of apparent awareness result from a failure by the patient to understand what is the intention of certain types of anesthesia. The best example I can think of is arthroscopy of the knee joint. The surgeon looks into the knee with a fine telescope and if necessary removes a torn cartilage. This involves two or three very small incisions. The surgeon fills the knee joint with a local anesthetic and often asks us to sedate the patient either because the patient is nervous or because lying flat on your back on a hard table can become most uncomfortable. A few patients either, because they are unable to comprehend this or, because the anesthesiologist or the surgeon has failed to properly explain, remain aware of the surroundings and procedures in the operating room.

The people who study these Closed Claims are quite explicit about the flaws in their method of studying adverse events arising from anesthesia. The project is of such great interest that I will devote a whole chapter to it, later.

We cannot leave this important subject without fully discussing two related matters: can patients who are under general anesthesia learn and then recall what they have heard even though they were totally unaware of the surgery? Is there any way by which we can monitor brain function in such a way that we'll know at all times whether the patient is aware or not.

Dr. Richard (Dick) Blacher, a psychiatrist, lives up our street and we are friends. Dick is the one of the few psychiatrists who studied the mental disturbances that sometimes follow open-heart surgery. He belongs to a small group of doctors who raised the possibility that a patient can learn and memorize when under a general anesthetic. Dick was also the first and only psychiatrist ever to write an Editorial in our leading journal, Anesthesiology.

The subject of learning and memory while under otherwise 'perfect' general anesthesia is of more than academic interest. One day, I suspect it will be part of our understanding of what general anesthesia is, its relationship to ordinary sleep and perhaps open the door to new and even better methods and agents than we have at present. Again, this is too large a subject to discuss in detail here.

The question of monitoring brain function under general anesthesia to determine whether the patient is or is not oblivious to the surgery is central to what we do. I can only outline this matter. One good way to approach this is through a three-part historical review of the question.

What dose of an anesthetic agent should I, the anesthesiologist give the patient to ensure she will be unaware of the surgery, yet not so much as to depress her vital functions or cause other disturbances such as irregular heartbeat? You have had a glimpse of this in the chapters on chloroform and ether.

Part One: You will remember my earlier description of empiricism in anesthesia. To put it crudely, give the amount that works but does not harm. This brings us to the work of Dr. Arthur Guedel a brilliant but self-trained anesthesiologist who in addition to setting up a family practice in 1909 in Indianapolis gave anesthetics to supplement his income.

The United States entered the First World War in April 1917 and in November of 1917 became heavily engaged on the Western Front in France with a growing stream of casualties requiring surgery. Six major medical schools sent volunteer surgical teams to France. Hundreds of surgeons and nurses went but only *one* anesthesiologist with any experience, Dr. Guedel. He arrived at an American base hospital in the town of Chaumont, Southeast of Paris. He realized the only way to anesthetize the flood of injured

soldiers safely was to train nurses and corpsmen using the key principles of safe ether anesthesia. Obviously he could not be present
during surgery at all the American base hospitals at the same time.
He responded to this in two ways.

He devised a chart based on his own clinical observations of
patients under ether. The eye signs and the respiratory signs of
deepening anesthesia are clear and consistent in all patients. He
divided the depth of anesthesia into a set of reproducible and
diagrammaticable stages and planes. The most important sign
his 'students' learned was the point at which the anesthesia was
too 'deep'; that is, the point at which the patient was about to
stop breathing. That point can be a deliberate part of a modern
anesthesia technique.

When I started my career in London, often all by myself with
no guidance, I was in many respects in a similar position to those
corpsmen – even though I was a licensed physician. Dr. Guedel's
chart is clearly reproduced in Dr. Goldman's little red book – my
great comfort in times of uncertainty and worry.

Dr. Guedel's other contribution was to obtain a motor-bike
from the army and race from one hospital to the next to assure
himself about the safety of the ether anesthetics. One day, I hope
to go to Chaumont to see for myself whether any historical relics
of Guedel's activities remain to be discovered. Recently I found an
old picture postcard of that base hospital on EBay!

Part Two: In 1976 two anesthesiologists, Drs. Peter Winter and
Ted Eger developed a way of comparing the 'strength' or 'power'
of the increasing number of inhalational anesthetic vapors that
were being developed for our use. If you know how 'strong' a
vapor is you also get a much more precise idea of how much is too
much; that is, what concentrations are safe to give most patients.
What they did was almost laughably simple – I wish I had thought
of it. I would not be rich but I would be famous.

They anesthetized patients with say, halothane using a wide range
of concentrations. They measured the concentration of halothane
in the lungs of these patients. They called the concentration at which

50 percent of the patients moved when the surgeon made the incision and 50 percent did not, the agent's MAC, or minimal alveolar concentration. Every agent has its own consistent MAC.

Part Three: More recently, probably because of concerns about awareness, attempts have been made to use the wave forms from an electroencephalograph (EEG). These patterns change more or less consistently as anesthesia is deepened. A device in which a computer integrates the EEG waveforms into something called a Bispectral Index (BIS) has been developed. I have been retired for a decade and never used it but my colleagues still in practice have doubts about its clinical value. It might be a useful weapon on the defense side in the medico-legal arena. Some studies seem to show the use of the BIS device might actually *increase* the incidence of awareness by misleading the anesthesiologist into giving too little. As this book was being prepared for the press Dr. Avidan and his colleagues published a remarkable paper in the New England Journal of Medicine. Again I lack space but here are their two key findings.

In a group of approximately 6000 patients at high risk for awareness during surgery more patients recalled awareness in the group whose 'depth of anesthesia' was monitored by a BIS device than in the group in which the concentration of the main anesthetic (causing oblivion) agent was carefully monitored. The other finding is comforting: depending on the monitoring method used the incidence of awareness ranged from 1 in 400 to 1 in 1400. May I please remind you these were fragile patients who would tolerate higher concentrations of agents very poorly.

Intermission PAINTINGS ON A WALL

Let us go now, you and I, back to the Countway Library of Medicine, Harvard Medical School's library. Before we get into the elevator that takes us down to the basement where we'll find, shelved and bound, virtually all the medical journals ever published in the last two hundred years I stop and show you the two the huge paintings on the wall of the lobby. The first is the most famous: *The First Operation under Ether by Robert Hinckley.*

"What? Why?" you say in a loud astonished voice.

"Hush, please do not raise your voice," I plead in a whisper, "Some of the finest medical brains in the country are studying here."

"Well. Yes … but," you say, now quietly. "Why paint a picture of someone giving an anesthetic? There must surely be more important medical events to commemorate with such a fine painting." I decide that truth overrides *la politesse.*

"Well, no," I say. "Historians consider that the event displayed in the picture, the dentist William T.G. Morton giving ether to a young man about to undergo surgery for a vascular tumor under his jaw by the most famous surgeon in Boston Dr. John C. Warren, is probably America's greatest single contribution to the advancement of medicine."

"How so?" you ask.

"Before this event, the so-called Ether Demonstration, surgeons were vastly limited as to what operations they could do. They had to be very, very quick and the patients screamed and had to be held down."

"I would like to know more about all this," you say.

"There are innumerable books and movies about the event. In my opinion the best-written and best-informed book is 'Ether Day' by Julie Fenster. You can buy a used copy in good condition for as little as $1.99 on Amazon. She is a bit weak on the science but powerful about the complex drama behind the and following the Great Event. I don't want to spoil it for you but Morton was no hero. He was a farm boy who became a small-time criminal, took up dentistry and had the courage to give ether in public – but, all for money," I answer.

We move on to the next picture. It is 'The First Successful Kidney Transplantation' by Joel Babb.

"Seems a more important painting to me. An operation; now that is a really important event to paint," you say.

I keep silent. You look at my grim visage. You are perceptive. You blush a little and say in a soothing voice,

"Well … I suppose they are equally important."

"Without the first the second could not have taken place. How would you like to be awake when you are donating a kidney to your beloved sister-in-law dying of kidney disease?" I answer.

There is a feature of this painting that only an anesthesiologist would notice. The faces of all the surgeons and nurses can be seen but not that of the anesthesiologist. Mr. Babb the artist, only painted the back of his head. I know you think this is Zeitlin once again getting all excited about the status and appearance of anesthesia and anesthesiologists but this man is Professor Leroy Vandam, my first chief in the United States. He is the man who invited me to join his department in 1965. Dr. Vandam was and is still regarded as a central figure in the intellectual development of the specialty in the second half of the last century.

I know that you think this book is too full of coincidences but last October I discovered that Mr. Babb was holding an exhibition of his work in one of the elegant galleries on Newbury Street in downtown Boston, the Vose Gallery. Aideen and I went to see it. Joel Babb is a superb example of what I will call the ultrarealistic/

perspectivist school of painters. I wrote to Mr. Babb, trying to conceal my irritation, about the back of Dr. Vandam's head.

This is part of what he kindly replied:

"*Dr. (Francis) Moore* (the Chief of Surgery at the Brigham) *interviewed me in his office. Once he had decided to give me a chance as his artist, he brought in Dr. Murray* (the surgeon who had performed all the research and actually performed the transplant) *and Dr. Vandam, as co-commissioners of the painting.*

Further on he writes,

"*I think Dr. Vandam, as a fellow artist tried to buffer the strong managerial disposition of Dr. Moore.*" Dr. Vandam painted lovely watercolors. I have one he gave me after I (nervously) gave him an anesthetic for hand surgery.

Until I read that sentence by Mr. Babb I had entirely forgotten an incident that occurred during my first year with Dr. Vandam. One of the aspects in my curriculum vitae that had apparently appealed to Dr. Vandam when he offered me the job, was my experience in London with various mechanical ventilators; that is, machines that do the breathing for patients to relieve the anesthesiologist or intensivist of the need to hand squeeze a bag, and do it more efficiently. Machines do not tire nor does their attention wander.

At the Brigham I was supposed attend the once-a-month 'intensive care' rounds as the representative of the anesthesia department. I only got there once that year because the operating rooms were so busy.

In front of a large group of physicians, surgeons and visitors Dr. Moore set out to demean me by asking questions about a brand new and extremely complicated machine that had just arrived from Sweden called the Craafoord Ventilator. I had never seen one before. Having read about it I understood the principles on which it worked but Moore hammered away at me about details, trying to humiliate me. Years later Dr. Vandam told me of similar battles he had with Dr. Moore, notably his decades long effort to break the anesthesia department out from under Dr. Moore's thumb.

There is really no reason for relating this nasty story other than to help you understand that these struggles for the independence of anesthesia from surgery took place everywhere during the second half of the 20th century.

Chapter 20 MALPRACTICE

1975 was a worrisome year for anesthesia in the United States. That same year I was elected to represent District 3 of the Massachusetts Society of Anesthesiologists (M.S.A.) and became a member of its Executive Committee. At that time about 450 anesthesiologists worked in the whole of Massachusetts.

One of the reasons why doctors largely did not enter anesthesiology training before World War 2 was the command surgeons had over their ability to charge. I leave you to guess how they used this power. I do know that in private surgical practice in London the standard ratio was 5 to 1 in favor of the surgeon. If an anesthesiologist in private practice in the U.K. tried to charge more he would be dropped by the surgeon. In the USA, the political battles to change this situation could provide the material for a whole and separate book.

Not the least of these battles was a class-action suit brought by the Department of Justice against the members of the American Society of Anesthesiologists alleging restraint of trade because we were using a relative fee schedule. A relative fee schedule compares the severity of every operation known to surgeons. Each operation was given a certain number of points but *the dollar value of a point was determined by each individual anesthesiologist without any collusion.* Because of this the Department of Justice was unable to prove that this action was anti-competitive and their suit failed. You will remember my wife's anesthesiologist Dr. Jess Weiss. He led our society in defending this action.

That year, 1975, a sudden increase in amount of the premiums we had to pay for malpractice insurance coverage disturbed us. How did this come about? How did the insurance companies get away with what appeared to be greed? What evidence did they have to support their efforts to increase our premiums by as much as 80% in a single year? How did we respond?

This story reveals why it is so important for doctors to become involved in the political process. I know from personal experience that the last thing a young doctor wants is to have to attend a fundraising cocktail party for his or her local candidate for Congress. I once attended a fund-raiser for Barney Frank and later met him several times during our society's congressional visits to Washington DC. He was pretty hostile the first time but much more receptive to our needs on subsequent visits. We discovered the change was the result of having undergone successful coronary bypass surgery!

What is a malpractice crisis? We struggled with two of those beasts in the late decades of the last century. It's a crisis of affordability and availability.

"So what?" you mutter, "it's just about doctors and their incomes; nothing to do with us, the patients."

You would be quite wrong. All physicians need to carry malpractice insurance in case of a bad outcome of treatment whether the doctor is at fault or not, and the patient or his family sues successfully. If it is warranted the patient and her family are compensated for the injury. Without insurance this would not be possible. There is nothing new about suing doctors. I have a book describing just that in the mid-Victorian era in both the U.K. and the U.S.A.

In early 1975 the Massachusetts Society of Anesthesiologists established an Ad Hoc Committee on Liability and Malpractice. Here are a few extracts of the first report written by its Chairman, Dr. Richard Kemp.

Prior to 1970 Massachusetts was fourth from the bottom in its liability insurance rates. Medical liability suits have increased spectacularly since then – 2000 estimated new cases in litigation, one law firm estimated to have 740 cases pending (Author's note: cases against all specialties, not just anesthesia). *In 1962 the insurance coverage premium for an anesthesiologist* *was a meager $40 (per annum). In 1970 the average was $922 and in 1974 an insurance company called Argonaut that wrote many such policies was charging $4139. Another company called St. Paul Fire and Marine arbitrarily stopped writing policies for anesthesiologists and plastic surgeons.*

Insurance companies classify all physicians into one of five categories of risk; they placed a high-risk specialty with the likelihood of a big award into Category 5. That's where they placed us the anesthesiologists, together with the obstetricians and neurosurgeons. At the bottom of the risk scale a family doctor who did no surgery it was Category 1. Premiums were proportional to risk. The insurance companies estimated this by studying their losses associated with each specialty.

Dr. Kemp then describes a meeting he attended in the office of the Insurance Commissioner for Massachusetts to which all seven of the relevant insurance companies sent representatives. They all either planned to withdraw from the malpractice market in the coming year, or, at least double their premiums. Dr. Kemp concluded his report by writing,

A number of society members have candidly said they will leave anesthesia rather than face the possibility of personal financial ruin.

At that point the Executive Committee of the Massachusetts Society of Anesthesiologists (M.S.A.) did something remarkable. We retained the services of legal counsel to represent us in front of legislators and government officials.

To understand the need for this try to imagine the following scenario. Suppose Chuck, my partner, or for that matter any one of our 450 members had been chosen to represent the M.S.A. at a hearing at the State House in Boston on a given Tuesday at 1 p.m. He had been on call on Monday. He finished the last case in the operating room at 8 .30 p.m. – an add-on, a ruptured bowel in a frail elderly lady. He took her to the Intensive Care Unit and organized her mechanical ventilation program and wrote the orders for all her life-support medications. Then he had to visit 13 patients booked for surgery on Tuesday. It's now 11.30 p.m and all was quiet. He drops by the delivery room for a last look and the midwife tells him a multip has just come in, in active labor. At midnight Chuck and Dr. Frank Barry the obstetrician, settle down in front of the TV to watch the Red Sox play against a team on the West Coast.

You cannot give a laboring lady her anesthetic too early – it might slow the labor. At 3 a.m. Chuck gives her a caudal epidural anesthetic, her pain disappears and at 4.05 she delivers a little girl that everyone, including Chuck, agrees is the most beautiful baby ever born at the Union Hospital.

At 4.45 Chuck tries to settle down for a short sleep in the 'on call' bedroom before the next day's work begins. The traffic starts. He cannot sleep. He showers and then cajoles one of the early kitchen chefs to make breakfast for him. He drinks very strong coffee and pretends to himself he is not fatigued. We give him the easiest and quickest room of cases and he leaves for The State House at noon, exhausted.

That is why, in 1975, the Massachusetts Society of Anesthesiologists retained the services of Mr. Jack O'Leary an attorney, to represent us as its legal and legislative counsel.

Some of our members objected; they believed the purpose of the Society was solely educational and they did not want part of their annual dues used to pay his fees. The officers of the Society insisted and the rebellion was suppressed.

Two of the six insurance companies writing malpractice coverage policies planned to withdraw from the market on July 1 1975 and the other four would double their annual premium to $17,500 by July 1 1977. I remember well the feeling of helplessness we experienced.

We got lucky. Senator Foley was one of the few Massachusetts legislators who understood the implications. Senator Foley's reputation rested on his legislative drive to bring good health care to the poor and vulnerable. At various hearings on the malpractice coverage situation he repeatedly asked two critical question: What is the basis for these enormous increases in premiums? Are they justified by the number of bad outcomes from anesthesia in Massachusetts?

The answer to the first question soon became clear. The insurance companies admitted they were applying their *national* experience to Massachusetts. The answer to the second was that no one knew the answer. The subsequent negotiations are too complex to relate here but our sainted legislature got to grips with the problem in three ways.

First, it set up a quasi-independent insurance consortium they called the Joint Underwriters Association in which all Massachusetts insurance companies were obliged to share the risk. Second it set up a Board of Registration and Discipline made up of physicians, lawyers and legislators – to put it bluntly, to keep an eye on our behavior. Lastly it set up a panel that had to approve the merit of any malpractice suit brought by a patient and his lawyer against a physician.

Maybe you wonder what I think of malpractice suits against physicians. It's quite simple. If there is a clearly documented bad outcome the patient deserves financial compensation independent of whether or not the physician was negligent. The latter problem should be dealt with separately by his or her peers acting within the law.

One of the difficulties of writing history is that, concealed by the glow of large events, there are small but vital movements that remain undetected until later. In this case I am talking about the work of Jeffrey Cooper who is not a physician but an engineer with a PhD who came to work in the anesthesia department at the Massachusetts General Hospital (M.G.H.) in 1972. He had previously worked in industry where he became obsessed with safety measures to prevent industrial accidents. He wondered about the causes of anesthesia accidents and investigated the *human* in addition to the technical factors involved.

I worked on the anesthesia faculty at MGH for two years. At that time because of the shortage of American trained anesthesiologists,

Dr. Harry Beecher the Chairman, often traveled to Europe to recruit experienced additional faculty. One such was an Englishman, Dr. John Bland. As you know Englishmen mostly 'keep a stiff upper lip'; they do not express their feelings. One day John and I happened to bring our patients into the recovery room at the same moment and I heard him use some of the angriest language I had ever heard.

GLZ: "What's the matter John?"

JB: "I can't believe this ******* place is the famous MGH. The equipment stinks and no one seems to care. I nearly killed this patient. Twice the connection of the oxygen hose interlock came apart by itself. The patient turned black and I could not understand what the hell was happening until I happened to look under the surgeon's equipment table."

It took some time to calm him down.

In 1972 Jeff Cooper was hired to work in the Anesthesia Bioengineering Unit at MGH. Two years later he gave a lecture "The Anesthesia Machine: An Accident Waiting to Happen." I wonder if he ever heard of Dr. Bland's near-disaster.

In 1978 Dr. Cooper and three of his colleagues at M.G.H., published a paper in our journal 'Anesthesiology' titled 'Preventable Anesthesia Mishaps: a Study of Human Factors'.

In my opinion, and I'm far from alone in this belief, that paper is the seed from which a mighty tree named 'Patient Safety' has grown.

Chapter 21 COOPER'S TREE

The very title of Cooper's famous paper is revealing. Please note the words 'preventable' and 'human'. Cooper based the study on work done by the psychologist J.C. Flanagan on the study of critical incidents. Simply put these are incidents resulting from human error that might well or sometimes do, lead to harm. I doubt there are any anesthesiologists of any degree of experience who has never had a critical incident. Here is one of mine.

I was giving anesthesia for the excision and bypass of a man's femoral artery. It was blocked by atheroma and the patient could not walk more than 50 yards before he was stopped by pain in that leg. This occurred after I joined Chuck in private practice. All was going smoothly when the circulating nurse answered the phone and then read the results of some lab work that had been ordered for the patient by his cardiologist just before I anesthetized him. The serum potassium, a vital element that affects the function of the heart was too low. The surgeon asked me to give the patient an appropriate dose of potassium chloride intravenously. I should have given 30 mEq into the intravenous bag and dripped it in slowly. Instead I gave 300 mEq into the line. The patient's heart slowed and then nearly stopped. The surgeon was concerned and quite verbal about his concern. I gave the correct antidote. The heart resumed its usual boring rhythm. The patient did well and went home a week later in good spirits.

Do you know the childrens' nursery rhyme?

'I know an old lady who swallowed a fly.
I don't know why

*She swallowed that fly
Perhaps she'll die'*

Note the poet's use of the word 'perhaps'. That is the key to Dr. Cooper's study. He asked a number of anesthesiologists at M.G.H., ranging from experienced faculty to new residents to talk to him, under conditions of strict confidentiality about critical incidents they had had *whether or not* the patient was harmed. The point of course is that even if the patient was not harmed, they *might have been.*

He arrived at two key conclusions. First, only 14 percent of 359 incidents told to Dr. Cooper were due to equipment failure, as happened to Dr. Bland, whereas nearly all the rest were due to human error. Second, the interviewees had no difficulty in talking about their own errors. The purpose of the study as told by Dr. Cooper himself was to collect and analyze the events and seek to find patterns. Later, he told us the ultimate purpose was to expose human error in anesthesia and its underlying causes as problems that needed to be fixed.

That should be the obvious thing to do, you will say. It was, but *no one had ever done it before.* As you will have read in previous chapters all that had been done, other than John Snow and Goodman Levy's work was to add up the numbers of people who had died or been injured permanently as a result of anesthesia, so-called mortality and morbidity studies, lots of them. All those studies showed was that some agents, particularly chloroform, were more dangerous than others, and that anesthesia given by untrained non-specialists was a likely cause of the many deaths.

You know that in life its no use having regrets but I must here confess that I'm sorry I left MGH at the end of 1968 for private practice. What happened at MGH in those next two decades was exciting and original and out of it grew the first major branch of the tree planted by Jeff Cooper. But first another anecdote – I'm sorry, but it is completely true and very important.

Late one weary afternoon in 1983 at the Union Hospital, Chuck and Michael and I were finishing our cases. Michael was worried he'd be late for his tennis foursome, Chuck wondered if he would get a run in on Swampscott Beach before the rain began and I was dreaming of a pre-supper nap hoping the children would not need too much homework help. Our secretary called into the operating room to tell us she was going home but that there was a gentleman from a company called Nellcor who had a gadget to show us.

Ugh! Another gadget we did not really need.

Nevertheless we gathered in the office and with barely a word the salesman affixed a small clip to Chuck's finger, turned on a box of electronics and told Chuck to hold his breath as long as he could. The number on the screen started at 97 and slowly but surely fell until it reached 82. Chuck was in very good shape. Your body continues to use 250 to 300 cubic centimeters of oxygen at rest, much more if you are active, whether or not you are breathing. If you hold your breath that continues and the oxygen attached to your red blood cells becomes depleted. It reminds me of the anti-American joke we told when we first saw enormous American cars in London's West End after the war. The driver of a Hugemobile pulls into a gas station in Texas and tells the attendant,

"Fill her up, please."

He waits, with the engine idling. And waits. And waits.

The attendant reappears and says,

"Sir, please turn the engine off. You're getting ahead of me."

"Take three deep breaths," said the salesman. Chuck did and the number shot up to 98.

"It's measuring oxygen saturation," Michael and I exclaimed. Exclaimed is the right word because we immediately saw the value of a machine that *continuously* displayed the anesthetized patient's oxygen saturation. Prior to this invention we had used various methods and devices trying to prevent hypoxic, that is, lack of oxygen, injury to the patient. These instruments told us how much oxygen we were giving the patient but *none told us how well the patient was oxygenated.* This new machine would show us that something was occurring to the patient's level of oxygenation before actual harm occurred.

"Can we borrow it for a few days and try it out in the O.R.?" Chuck said.

"Only for twenty four hours," said the salesman. "All the other anesthesiologists are interested."

Next morning Chuck went to see the hospital's administrator Henry Moran and more or less forced him to make out a check for four thousand dollars to Nellcor, the manufacturer. When the salesman returned all he got was that check. The machine stayed with us; in fact until we were able to buy several more we used to compete for it.

"My patient is the sickest," we would say to each other.

As I said before, until this machine came along we were guessing whether the patient's oxygen level was adequate. In my case, 25 years of guessing. Guessing whether your patient is getting enough oxygen makes one anxious or, put another way, is stressful. After I had my first heart attack my wife used to say,

"I don't understand why you did not become a dermatologist."

Heart trouble is largely the result of the genes you got from your parents. Stress might exacerbate it. Paradoxically, the stress and the accompanying sense of responsibility is part of the excitement of anesthesiology. Soldiers go to war for the excitement and challenge. Many change their minds when they see one of their buddies disemboweled.

These digressions are as worrying to me as they are boring for you but I can think of no other way of getting you to understand what the practice of anesthesia is like *as seen from the inside.* In your every day life you see chaps and chapesses and their offspring walking down the High Street, painting their houses, digging their vegetable plots and climbing up the frames in the local playground. It never occurs to you to wonder if they are getting enough oxygen to do this stuff. Why? Because you know they are breathing air, which contains 21 percent oxygen.

On the other hand take the chap digging up his allotment, lay him down on an operating table, give him drugs that depress his ability to breathe, allow the surgeon to open his chest and compress one of his lungs so as to get at a tumor seen on an XRay. Now consider that *you* the anesthesiologist are completely in control and in charge of the atmosphere the patient is breathing. Put another way, under general anesthesia the patient breathes a completely artificial atmosphere with effects on his oxygenation that used to be unmeasurable and unpredictable.

Do you remember the word 'preventable' in the title of Dr. Cooper's paper? This machine, this oximeter, gave us hope in that regard.

What was going on at MGH during those years I spent in private practice? Probably the most important was that they realized that careful monitoring of the patient's condition was the key to safety. They *wrote and enforced* standards for the minimum degree of monitoring each and every time a patient was anesthetized in one of the nine Harvard Hospitals. Coincidentally, ideas being developed by the leaders of the Massachusetts Society of Anesthesiologists and its attorney, the legislature and the insurance consortium the Joint Underwriters Association to improve safety were derived from these monitoring standards.

The Harvard anesthesiologists got started on their project as a result of a kick in the ankle by an executive of Harvard's captive insurance company, the Risk Management Foundation. His name is Jim Holzer, and as Jeff Cooper wrote:

> *"Jim asked that something pro-active be done about the increasing (financial) losses from medical malpractice claims."*

One of the members of the committee then formed from the four main Harvard teaching hospitals, Dr. John Eichhorn analyzed the malpractice data and presented it to that committee. The committee *"came to the intuitive conclusion – the most critical feature common to the serious events was a lack of appropriate monitoring of the patient by the anesthetist"* (Cooper).

The Standards were published in the Journal of the American Medical Association in 1986. They were specific, and detailed and were mandatory at all the Harvard hospitals. The authors commented that such standards had not previously existed (for any medical specialty, author's comment) and resistance to the standards was anticipated but not seen: which is surprising since doctors as a whole think of themselves as independent professionals and do not want to follow rules, whether written by other physicians or for example, government bureaucrats. And, critically the final published standards required the use of pulse oximetry – the device we never gave back to the Nellcor salesman. Anesthesiologists introduced the use pulse oximeters into clinical medicine. Nowadays, measuring oxygen saturation with an oximeter has become a basic standard used by the nurse who undresses you and checks your weight, your pulse rate and your blood pressure in the your doctor's examination room.

When our son Jon married Lisa on top of Mount Baldy (9300 feet above sea level where the air is significantly thinner) four years ago I took a portable pulse oximeter with me on account of my bad heart: it only pumps out about half of the blood that it should at each heart beat. I took it very easy and felt fine. Interestingly, I previously had written to three of my colleagues who are experts in hearts and lungs and how they work. In essence they wrote back,

"Whatever happens, do not miss your son's wedding. If you die, you'll die happy."

As an afterthought they also said,

"If you feel unwell get on the chairlift and go down to the village."

None of them even considered oxygen or cardiopulmonary resuscitation as a precaution and no one had the gall to ask whether any of the guests had passed the Red Cross's Basic Life Support (BLS) test!

My story is like a braided cord. Each thread has to be considered and then carefully wound into the core.

Now we turn to Dr. Richard Ward, an anesthesiologist on the faculty of the University of Washington, Seattle, in the late 1970s. One of his residents (trainees) was Dr. Richard Solazzi whose wife was an attorney. As you have already seen this was a time of agonizing discussion of the damage that we anesthesiologists were inflicting on patients and the first serious attempts to ascertain its causes in detail. Although Dr. Davis of Duke University had already carried a similar but much more modest study it was Dr. Solazzi's wife, an attorney, who first instigated a large study by asking the question: are there clues in the history of anesthetic *malpractice* experience that might identify repetitively seen problems that can and should be avoided.

These two doctors, with the permission of the Aetna Life and Casualty Company, the University Hospital, the Health Cooperative in Seattle and the Medical Examiner of King County were allowed to review all their malpractice claim files from years 1971 to 1982. They reviewed 135 cases in which general anesthesia was used. In nearly all the cases the patient suffered harm. I am not going to tell you what they found – you'll soon see why! The important point is that the insurance company and the three other organizations actually allowed two doctors to look at their files. This is remarkable. Prior to this, bad results were kept as hidden as possible – an aspect of the practice of all of medicine going back into the Victorian era and in the case of anesthesia the innumerable disasters mostly but by no means exclusively resulting from chloroform use.

Chapter 22 JEEP

Do you remember Dr. Ellison (Jeep) Pierce, the chap who picked me up at Boston Harbor in 1965 and made me eat half a cow that evening at Ken's Steak House in Framingham?

He had left the Brigham and was appointed Chief of Anesthesia at the Deaconess Hospital in Boston. Around this time, the mid 1980s, he was appointed President of the American Society of Anesthesiologists. That year he reviewed the question of anesthesia safety and the mortality studies done in the 1950s through the 1970s. I sat in his audience at one of his lectures and vividly remember part of what he said about the harms some patients suffered from anesthesia:

We must stop blaming the surgeons, we must stop blaming the lawyers who sue us, we must stop blaming the hospitals for inadequate equipment, we must stop blaming the insurance companies for raising our premiums. We must look at ourselves and examine what we are doing.

One evening in 1985 I was sitting at a meeting of the Executive Committee of the Massachusetts Society of Anesthesiologists. Dr. Pierce was in attendance. He stood up and said, " I need someone to do closed claims reviews."

No further explanations. That is how he was. Everyone at the table had other responsibilities. I bowed my head and tried to hide behind my ice-cream slathered in chocolate sauce. That was before calories were invented. It was no good. Pierce pointed his Confederate finger at me.

"You, Gerry, will do Closed Claims reviews for Massachusetts," he said.

How could I deny him, he who had eased my almost subterfugious entry into American medicine? Unknown to me Dr. Ward and Dr. Pierce had got together and started the American Society of Anesthesiologists Closed Claims project, now a vast and totally accepted method of studying the complications of anesthesia. They realized the importance of Dr. Ward's work in Washington State and extended it to the whole country and because of Jeep's position were able to get the resources of the A.S.A. in support.

As a result of Jeep's command, on many Saturdays when I was not on call, I traveled into downtown Boston to the office of the Joint Underwriters Association. There, in a room exclusively provided by them for my use I would face fat files, the results of malpractice claims that were closed. Some had been won by the plaintiff, some had been dismissed but the majority were settled by negotiation involving the respective lawyers and the insurance companies. Some of these files were over two hundred pages thick. I had to find the essentials of what had happened and complete a questionnaire I received from Dr. Fred Cheney who now ran the project. Dr. Pierce had appointed him to head up the study together with Dr. Cheney's colleagues in Seattle who were appointed to analyze and draw conclusions from our findings out in the field.

I know this sounds gruesome but sometimes, on those lonely Saturdays I felt I was inspecting a Civil War battlefield gathering information about what caused these shredded men to be lying in agony or dying. Had they been hit be a Minie ball, a cannon ball or lanced by a bayonet? Having practiced anesthesia on a daily basis for 25 years and turning these dry pages I could visualize the terror and tragedy that lay behind these lawyers' bargaining letters and the analyses by physician experts of what was likely to have occurred in an operating room on a particular day. If you want to remind yourself what I'm talking about look at Chapter 11 again.

I have a copy of the questionnaire I used to complete for each case, sent to me by Professor Karen Posner, the chief coordinator of the Project. Even though each questionnaire had eight pages of detailed questions, just three questions will give you a better understanding of the philosophy behind the Project.

1. Would better monitoring have prevented the complication?
2. Was the (anesthesia) care less than appropriate? Appropriate? Clearly excellent? Impossible to judge?
3. Was the complication preventable? Non-preventable? Impossible to say?

Since that year the leaders of the Closed Claims Project have published more than thirty papers in the peer-reviewed anesthesia literature. Peer-reviewed simply means that selected experts tell a journal's editor whether the paper has value and conforms with established scientific principles. As you can imagine these papers at first caused some controversy because they relied on human judgment, that of reviewers like me. But new information, as it were, *inside* information about the mechanisms by which we were harming patients overwhelmed the objections. The findings over the last twenty years constitute a vast new body of knowledge – of course much too much to relate here.

One example will suffice. When they reviewed the first 1100 questionnaires Professors Cheney and Caplan judged that one-third of the negative outcomes (doctor-speak for damaged patients) could have been prevented if additional monitors such as pulse oximeters had been in use. That seemed self-evident to a lot of people at the time but medicine is littered with ideas to help patients that appeared obvious and turned out to be irrelevant or worse, misleading.

That is why Chuck never gave that oximeter back to the Nellcor representative. Our intuition told us its value. And that is why some organizations need dominating leaders like Jeep Pierce.

One further point is that the many insurances companies that opened their files to us were under no obligation to do so. It is my belief that when the need was explained to them they felt a civic responsibility. That is something we should not forget in these days of turmoil about the gambling activities of a few of these companies.

In recent years Jeep and I 'did lunch' together twice a year and told each other the same tales from the past, and we laughed. He died a few months ago. The memorial service was held in the Trinity Church, one of Boston's architectural glories. I hope our successors in anesthesia will never forget what he started.

Chapter 23 MY MISBEHAVIOR

I made my own notes from the files from the 150 or so Massachusetts cases I reviewed for the Closed Claims Project. A few had been reviewed by my Massachusetts' colleagues but I had copies of their questionnaires.

I like to browse junk, particularly old journals and newspapers. That is how I blundered across Dr. Memery's paper and that is how I got into a little academic trouble – may the Greek God of Sleep, Hypnos, forgive me.

In 1965, an anesthesiologist in private practice in Central Massachusetts published a paper in the Journal of the American Medical Association, titled 'Anesthesia Mortality in Private Practice.' That was the year we arrived in the USA. His name was Dr. Memery and he studied the records of 69291 anesthetics given in private practice and, using what were known as the Baltimore Anesthesia (Mortality) Study Committee criteria he asked,

"Did the anesthetic management contribute to the death of the patient?" and if the answer was 'yes', "Was it the principal cause?"

Memery reported 15 'anesthesia primary' deaths giving a rate of 2.16 per 10,000. This was a rough approximation to the rate (1 in 5000 anesthetics) that we had been led to believe was normal and acceptable for that era. When I was a resident in the United Kingdom, 20 years earlier, the rate was approximately 1 in 1500.

I found 31 deaths among the 150 Massachusetts 'malpractice' cases at the JUA, involving approximately 300 insured anesthesiologists over the eight year life of the JUA. These resulted from approximately 1,920,000 anesthetics giving a death rate of 0.16 per 10,000 or, a *thirteen-fold decrease.*

In 1988 I asked Dr. Cheney's permission to use these figures and publish a paper. In 1988 I was not an academic and thus was under no 'publish or perish' pressure. I just thought it was a suggestive tidbit. Dr. Cheney was firmly but rightly forbidding and indicated that if it would be over his dead body if I tried to get it published in an American journal – for which quite likely he would be the reviewer! Dr. Cheney is such a wonderful guy that we remain friends to this very day. Once he got me to fly all the way to St. Louis, Missouri to take a lady judge out to dinner who was booked to appear on one of his panels. I mean what's a slug of a Brit gasman doing in the Deep South trying to woo a lady judge?

Why was Dr. Cheney upset with me? Lots of good reasons: here is what I wrote when the paper was published in 'Anaesthesia' a *British* journal, subsequently:

Memery's study reported all deaths associated with anesthesia in one large hospital whereas the J.U.A. study only examines cases in which a malpractice case was started. All the anaesthetics were given by a single group of seven anesthesiologists in Memery's study. The JUA study pertains to 300 anesthesiologists working in a variety of hospital settings and who supervise nurse anesthetists and residents. Although it is likely that the majority of 'anesthesia' deaths would result in litigation there is no independent evidence for this. The denominators used in the JUA study are derived and are based on possible unwarranted assumptions.

I do not know how to explain why the Brits took it. How I got away with my concluding statement I'll never know.

... a comparison of the only two available series in Massachusetts, suggests, but does not prove there has been a substantial decline (in mortality) in the last 30 years.

Maybe even a thirteen-fold decline.

Now that you have struggled through this rigmarole you are entitled to ask the key question.

Is anesthesia less of a threat to life than it used to be?

I and thousands of my colleagues who practiced before 1980 are convinced it is. Can we prove this? Let us see.

In 2006 Dr. Cheney and his colleagues reviewed 26 years worth of data collection. They found a significant decrease in the proportion of claims for death or permanent brain damage resulting from anesthesia. Oddly enough this did not seem to be related to the use of the more sophisticated monitors that I discussed earlier. This same paradoxical-seeming observation was also made in a few other studies from other countries. Their methodology has come under attack for similar reasons to the weaknesses of my paper about Massachusetts' patients. And there is little question that other factors are helping the increase in safety, in particular the disappearance of the half-trained or part-time anesthesiologist and the growth of rigorous residency training programs with difficult exams to pass soon after the end of residency. This is not easy to say: the *quality* of people entering the specialty of anesthesiology has improved enormously.

Once, when I was still with Chuck I got tired of my long commute. I heard there was a vacancy for Chief of Anesthesia at a small hospital near my home. The Board members of that hospital interviewed me twice. Then they offered me the job at the end of the second interview. Just as I was leaving to go home and discuss it with my wife a member of the Board took me aside and said,

"You do know that when you start you will have to fire Dr. Smith (or Brown or Jones, I forget his name)."

"Who is Dr. Smith?" I asked.

"He is the current Chief of Anesthesia." came the answer. I was too bamboozled by this to say anything in response

As I got into my car another member of the Board tapped me on the arm.

"I just want you to know that Dr. Smith is a much loved family doctor here in Needham. Unfortunately he only ever took three months training in anesthesia and we have a bunch of thoracic and vascular surgeons who want to bring their patients here – they will not do so until we have a fully trained anesthesiologist."

I did not have the nerve to dismiss a well-loved family doctor. A large proportion of the anesthetics in the U.S.A. in that era were given by partially-trained physicians and nurse-anesthetists. The place of the latter group in the 21ˢᵗ century is a politically sensitive issue too complex to deal with here. Suffice it to say that of all the medically-sophisticated Western countries the U.S.A. is one of the very few that uses non-physician anesthesia providers. I should add that almost no published or significant advance in the theory or practice of anesthesiology has originated with a nurse-anesthetist. My experience of working with them has been most satisfactory. They are conscientious, knowledgeable and reliable and if I was young and in good health I would happily ask them to anesthetize me for say, a hernia repair.

Do the ASA Monitoring Standards actually benefit patients? The only way I can answer this is by asking you whether when you next go out and buy a new car you will buy one that is cheaper because it was manufactured without airbags or reinforcing steel bars in the frame or collapsing hoods. Five years ago my wife was driving slowly in a line of traffic when a flower delivery van pulled out suddenly from the sidewalk and completely smashed up the front 60 percent of our Lexus. All four airbags inflated and she just suffered some mild chest bruising. Just because you cannot prove that what intuitively seems to be an advance in safety in any aspect of modern life does not mean we should dismiss it.

There is another matter, rarely discussed. With all the oximeters and the many other monitors we have in daily use *we know from moment to moment* how the patient is doing. If I were still in practice that would give me confidence and serenity in taking care of a surgical patient. What would you rather have? The old 'guessing' Dr. Zeitlin or the new one who has the workings of your body completely under his control, with the ability to respond immediately to any adverse change?

Have you ever heard of an insurance company *reducing* its premiums for anything? Let us for a moment return to the malpractice crisis in Massachusetts I discussed a couple of chapters ago.

While the Harvard anesthesiologists and the leaders of the A.S.A. were pushing for the adoption of mandatory standards of monitoring our new attorney in Massachusetts Mr. Edward Brennan, who had taken over when Jack O'Leary died tragically and unexpectedly, together with the officials of the J.U.A. came up with a unique idea. Why not offer the members of the Massachusetts Society of Anesthesiologists a *prospective* discount of 20 percent on our premiums if we agreed in writing to abide by the monitoring standards of the A.S.A.?

The J.U.A. staff were all lay people and yet they were convinced that the incidence of bad things happening to patients and thus their payouts would decrease (and presumably they would still make a fair profit) if we all monitored patients with greater care. That is what happened.

This was the start of a dramatic change in the malpractice situation and now, approximately, all the anesthesiologists in the United States are paying about half the number of constant dollars than we were 25 years ago. I'll allow you to draw your own conclusion as to what that means about the incidence of injury to patients. Insurance companies are still in business to make a profit. One of the factors the J.U.A. took into account was the early findings of the Closed Claims Study of the 150 injured patients here in Massachusetts and the irresistible conclusion that better monitoring would at least have prevented a number of those injuries.

Chapter 24 THE END OF ME

For my last seven years in practice I went back to the Brigham and Women's Hospital. I loved the teaching and the intellectual challenges but I was not well. Every day I had abdominal pain. I worried that the pain would distract me from focusing on patients.

Then I had what we so politely call a 'near miss'. A non English-speaking Hispanic lady arrived at our Surgicentre for a laparoscopic abdominal procedure. When I interviewed her she kept pointing to her throat through an opened mouth and repeating the word "Brigham." This suggested to me, as it would have done to any anesthesiologist, that previously there been a problem passing the endotracheal tube. I examined her. I asked her to open her mouth wide and using the standard Mallampatti classification, she passed with flying colors; that is, I judged she would be easy to intubate. This is necessary for laparoscopic surgery because the surgeon distends the belly with carbon dioxide gas and the anesthesiologist therefore has to have control of the breathing because the diaphragm is pushed up into the chest. Marge Pothier, the most senior of our nurse anesthetists confirmed my opinion. The record of the patient's previous admission to the Brigham was not available at the Surgicentre that morning.

We anesthetized the patient and using the standard laryngoscope could not see the larynx at all. Even worse, her supply of oxygen was running out and I had that sickening, despairing feeling that accompanies an imminent cardiac arrest. I'm sure that Marge did, too. As Shakespeare wrote in Hamlet, Act 4, Scene 3,

"Diseases desperate grown by desperate appliance are relieved. Or not at all."

In this desperate situation one remedy is to push a needle directly into the trachea and insufflate oxygen until the muscle relaxant wears off and the patient regains normal muscle strength and can breathe on her own. This is called a cricothyrotomy: the patient goes to sleep for a minor procedure and wakes up with a hole in the front of her neck.

Fortunately we had a laryngeal mask airway (L.M.A.) to hand. Marge and I had read about this appliance and introduced its use to the Brigham a few months earlier. The L.M.A. is an airway management device that is passed blindly into the mouth and because of its ingenious structure almost always results in an open airway. Dr. Archie Brain, (a most appropriate name!) took many years to develop the L.M.A. but it is now used worldwide. Immediately we inserted it we could ventilate her. All was well. My blood pressure, I am sure, returned to normal.

Then I realized my error. I should have held up the operation and the surgeon and sent for her old records from the Brigham. I realized that my belly pain had influenced me to 'get on with it' and get home to bed earlier. When we looked at the Brigham record the next day we saw that our colleagues two years earlier had spent well over an hour passing an endotracheal tube and had needed sophisticated instruments and the help of E.N.T. surgeons to do so.

That afternoon, after thinking about this incident and a phone call to my wife I made an appointment to see my boss Dr. Simon Gelman, the brilliant Russian-born Professor of Anesthesia and Chairman at the Brigham. He told me he would wait in his office until I had finished the day's work.

He sat me down. I told him what had happened and that I was afraid of harming a patient because I was unwell.

"What do you want to do, Gerry?" he asked.

"I think I should retire," I said. The words came out just like that but truly I had not meant be so direct and final. I should have waffled and said something like,

"Well, Simon, I think I should think about retiring from clinical anesthesia."

"When do you want to retire?"

"Now. This evening," I said.

In his book 'Blink' the author Malcolm Gladwell hypothesizes and pretty much proves that we all make decisions at two levels. One is what may be called the Personal Committee level; your internal committee weighs all the pros and cons, and balancing them, comes to what we usually call a rational decision. The other is Gladwell's under-the-surface of consciousness decision; the instantaneous decision made without the clunky process of weighing a pound of potatoes on an old-fashioned balance. I imagine, that without being aware of it I had already made the decision to retire. You will of course point out that 40 years of giving anesthesia and the realization that at the end of that period I might harm a patient actually drove the decision.

Thirty years ago I saw a talented orthopedic surgeon go on too long. A subcapital fracture of the femur is common in the elderly. By using a fluoroscope, a continuous XRay, an orthopedic surgeon can stabilize it without an open cutting operation. Dr. Jim Halloran was an expert. We loved him because he was so quick and accurate. He was a whiz at driving nails along the neck of the femur and that would be that; he stabilized the fracture and allowed Nature to do the healing. The image on the fluoroscope screen was reversed but of course the surgeon always compensated for this. It's analogous to my training myself to read other people's newspapers upside down on the London Underground; for me, it saved money. I still do that even though I can now afford the New York Times.

Dr. Jim was in his seventies. On that worrying evening we watched him get confused and drive the nails *across* the neck of the femur. The radiographer working the fluoroscope was the first to speak up.

"Sir, would you mind checking the Xray plate when I have developed it?"

Jim went on operating for a year or two. I tried to avoid giving anesthesia for his patients but confess I did nothing to alert his

241

colleagues. That was the ethos of those days. You did not 'split' on your colleagues; but you knew that patients might be harmed.

"Gerald, there are two things only that you should consider. First is your health. Second is the safety of our patients. They go together," Dr. Gelman told me.

That was my last day at work.

If there is a quality that separates leaders from followers it is the ability to part the underbrush and find the well-lit open space where everything is clear. That was why within a few years of leaving Russia Dr. Gelman was appointed Full Professor and Chairman of an important department in Harvard Medical School. A year earlier, during the selection process Dr. Gelman came to Boston to give a lecture about his research concerning what happens when a surgeon releases the clamp after repairing an abdominal aortic aneurysm. These swellings in the great blood vessel that feeds most of the body are like a bike tire with a weakness in its wall. Eventually it will expand to the point of bursting. As we left the lecture hall I overheard one surgeon say to another,

"That was too simple. Does he have the intellectual capacity?"

I could not hear the reply but I thought,

"*I* understood what he was talking about."

Dr. Gelman was one of a number of Jewish 'refuseniks' sent to Siberia in the early 1970s. During the Yom Kippur war in 1973 the Israeli army captured a number of Russian rocket technicians assisting the Egyptian army. These men were most valuable to the Russian military. Dr. Gelman told me that the Russian Foreign Minister and Abba Eban the Israeli Foreign Minister probably were behind the next move. The evidence that they met to resolve this difficulty is scant. On the other hand, is it not curious that Eban and the Russian Foreign Minister both took a vacation in Budapest during the same week? The story continues. Eban told them that the price for the rocket technicians would be the release of many of the Jewish intellectuals imprisoned in Siberia. That is how the Gelman family got out of Russia.

These days people sometimes ask me,

"What do you think about retirement? I have a standard answer.

"I do not miss the stress. I do not miss getting up each morning at 5.30 a.m. I do not miss the frequent changes in the schedule and having to make correct decisions very quickly. I do not miss watching a new resident struggling to do an epidural in a nervous patient and restraining myself from taking over. I do miss the camaraderie. I miss making my colleagues laugh at my silly jokes. I miss the early morning case discussions and the intellectual challenge. I miss being a part of a team that brings a patient through what for most people is a critical event in their lives, smoothly, safely and with a gentle return to the conscious world.

But I am the most fortunate of men. I have a wife, three children, three in-laws, all unique and loving and seven grandchildren each in his or her own way a genius. I still love anesthesia and all it entails and will keep going to lectures and meetings when I'm in my wheelchair, even though I'll sleep most of the day, with my head fallen on my chest.

But on August 1 1998 I still had my undiagnosed bellyache. It was getting me down. It made me sad. There was no pleasure in anything and no cure in sight. Twice, before I retired and once after, I went through a gastro-intestinal work-up. In brief this means a doctor pushing his fingers into your belly or up into your rectum to see if he or she can find something nasty or hard, that is, cancer. My belly was soft as a down pillow and ticklish at the sides. Then those mystified doctors would order X-rays. In order to outline the inside of all twenty four feet of your gut you have to drink a white sludge that I suspect is dredged up from the bottom of the Bering Sea near what used to be called White Russia. Then came the oscopies: pharyngoscopy. laryngoscopy, esophagoscopy, gastroscopy, and duodenoscopy, Then the ground controller redirects the oscopist to land from the opposite direction.. There came anoscopy, rectoscopy, colonoscopy and appendicoscopy.

A couple of months after retirement my pain was so severe that Aideen took me to the Emergency Room at the Brigham.

My internist met me there, worried and puzzled. Two substantial doses of Demerol, meperidine, a powerful, synthetic narcotic, were needed to relieve the pain. He admitted me to the hospital for further study.

He brought Dr. Peter Banks the Chairman of the Gastroenterological department to see me. Dr. Banks was frank.

"I do not know what is causing your pain. But we'll get to the bottom of it. I have scheduled you on Monday for an endoscopic retrograde cholangiopancreatogram. I'm afraid it's not going to be very pleasant," he said in a kind, kind of voice.

That was enough for me. I called Aideen, my patient consort. Neither she nor our children could understand their husband and father. The father to whom they would all say,

"Dad, you are such an optimist, it's almost ridiculous. You always see the light in the darkest times."

Now I was a different Dad. I had changed or been changed into a different person. I became a person who was afraid to drive past a cemetery, in fact took alternative routes to avoid them; a person that hid away from company, that woke early every morning with the certainty that something bad would happen that day to himself or worse, his family. I became a person who lost interest in his grandchildren and avoided them and their noisy jollity.

I could not understand their joy in being alive.

I called Aideen on the phone next to my hospital bed.

"Come and get me after work. I'm discharging myself."

Amazingly, she did not even try to dissuade me.

"I'll be there after work. Tell the nurse what you are doing."

Aideen conducted the two beginners orchestras in the Extension Division of the New England Conservatory. I need say no more about her talent than to ask you to imagine putting a group of five to ten year olds together, and after a couple of months of once a week rehearsal starting at 8 a.m. on a Saturday morning, having them play a Haydn Symphony in Jordan Hall in front of a large audience.

I hid under my blanket, shaking and miserable. I must have drifted off because I was suddenly aware of voices and people in my room. I looked out. There stood Dr. James Michel, an internist and also the father of one of Aideen's students, with four medical students.

"Would you mind if these students asked you a few questions. They are learning how to take a medical history," Before I could say a word he took his glasses off and yelled,

"Gerald, what the hell are you doing in here?"

"I'm not well. Dr. Banks wants to … ," I was so frightened of what Dr. Banks had planned for me I could not even say the words.

"But I'm going home. I might as well suffer in my own bed rather than in this miserable dump. Do you know what it's like to be an in-patient on a Saturday afternoon. Unless you're dying or vomiting no one comes near you," I sounded angry. I felt furious, perhaps at my own weakness.

"Boys and girls. I want to talk to the doctor here. Privately. I'll meet you at the main door at 6.30 on Monday and we'll do it over," he told the students.

He went to the nurses station to get my chart, came back, closed the door, and we talked for an hour.

"I do not know what is the cause of your pain. We may never know. I suspect the abdominal pain is your body's manifestation of depression. But, in any case I am certain you are severely depressed," he said. Melancholic would have been a better word.

Without another word he picked up the phone at my bedside and spoke and listened. He hung up and held my hand. I was grateful but still could not understand why I, a strong, independent and by now rather senior physician, needed to have my hand held by another and younger physician.

"Go home, Gerald. Dr. Bernie will come to see you tomorrow morning. So far as I know he is the only psychiatrist in Boston who makes house calls," he told me.

That is how Dr. Bernie came into my life. Let us skip over the next four years. All that needs to be said is that finding the correct antidepressant drug is the most difficult part in treating this foul illness, this illness that turns you into someone you do not recognize. There were some partial successes but the side effects always overcame the benefits. Dr. Bernie retired. Dr. Michael took over and tried yet another drug. I developed an agitated depression. That is quite simple - you are both very depressed and very agitated. They alternate, sometimes within minutes of each other.

Dr. Michael saw me in the Emergency Room of the Beth Israel Hospital. I was so ill I *asked* for ECT treatment, electroconvulsive therapy.

That is why you should read what happened to me in my middle sixties. Thirteen ECT's means thirteen general anesthetics.

Here is what I turned over and over again in my head before the first one. My only comforting thought was that since I was now a certified lunatic some certified and desperate measures were needed to cure me. I worried that the anesthesiologist might not find a vein, and if he did get me off to sleep with the Propofol maybe he would lose my airway and not be able to ventilate me with the amount of oxygen my heart, my coronary-bypassed heart, needed. Maybe I would vomit or regurgitate my gastric content after losing consciousness, maybe the intravenous needle would clog before he could get the paralyzing agent into me and I would convulse wildly and break teeth or bones when the psychiatrist shocked my brain, maybe I had the gene for malignant hyperthermia and they did not have the antidote Dantrolene, in the ECT unit, this unit so far from the operating room where he could get help. Maybe they would send an inexperienced resident who would not know how to handle an anesthetized patient with a badly damaged heart. Maybe I would soil myself when I convulsed. I did once, one of the nurses told me after the last treatment. I knew for certain that if it were technically possible I would do a better job giving myself my own anesthetic.

Did the ECT help? It calmed me. I was much less agitated but remained melancholic. A few weeks later I was sitting in Dr. Michael's office still melancholic.

"We will find the right drug for you," he said with conviction. But because I was so ill I did not really believe him.

246

"Have you ever tried Prozac? It's the oldest and the original S.S.R.I antidepressant?" he asked.

He looked at his carefully kept notes on the computer.

"Nor you have. Let's give it a try."

For seven years I have taken 20 milligrams of Prozac every morning. My belly pain which had improved somewhat, disappeared completely and for seven years I have become again the optimistic, outgoing person I used to be. But the greatest single bonus is that I get *pleasure* from everything. The experience of thirteen successive general anesthetics within the space of four weeks taught me to have faith in my colleagues and in the success and safety of modern anesthesia.

There is a happier aspect to E.C.T. for me. Let us jump back in time – approximately 35 years.

You would not think that lunacy has anything to do with anesthesia, but you would be wrong. Some anesthesiologists might argue that they were lunatic to enter this strange specialty.

Here is a true story about lunacy and anesthesia. It's true because I experienced it. That is what historians call primary material, such as a box of the pills that George 111 took for his craziness, or the letters Napoleon smuggled out of Elba when he was locked up there for a few weeks. Secondary material is taking what other historians have written about these events and by chopping that material up, adding some garlic and onions and then presenting the resulting hamburger as *the* last word on the subject. For example if you put "Roosevelt, Theodore" into the Books search box on Amazon you will find well over 100 books, in print, about Teddy. My stories are the real deal.

When I was Senior Registrar at the Middlesex Hospital in London in 1963, ECT or, electroconvulsive therapy was already all the rage in the treatment of depression. At that time there were no good drugs for this devastating illness, an illness that steals who you are and what your ideals may be, away from you. The largest lunatic asylum (mental hospital) in England was called Colney Hatch, located in the North London suburb of

Friern Barnet. To show how attitudes have changed I'm embarrassed to tell you we called it a 'loony bin'

Every Monday, Wednesday and Friday morning the large oval dining room at Colney Hatch was taken over by the psychiatrist who administered ECT. The room was ringed with windows, twenty-four in all. Under each window a gurney was arranged radially, like the spokes of light in a drawing of the sun by an eight year old child. On each gurney lay a depressed patient, head toward the centre of the room.

The psychiatrist and his nurse with a mobile trolley carrying his 'shock' machine stood by Patient No. 1 when I arrived. I also had a mobile trolley on which 'my' nurse had arranged the same number of syringes of Sodium Pentothal and also syringes of succinyldicholine as there were depressed patients. I never saw anything about the patients' general health. Did they have lung disease? Had they had a heart attack? Were they in kidney failure? I never knew. Would they survive the anesthetic I was about to administer? I had no idea, and, no one seemed to care. That is how things stood in those days. Also, it was a part of the partially hidden idea at that time that anesthesiologists were considered expert technicians and hardly physicians.

Of course what we were doing for these patients was humanitarian, way ahead of what was done to poor Jack Nicholson in One Flew Over the Cuckoo's Nest: they just put the naked electrodes on his scalp and pressed the 'on' switch. He felt the terrible shock for an instant and then, unconscious, had a major convulsion.

We put the patient to 'sleep', that word we use so loosely to describe general anesthesia, and which it is not, with the Pentothal and then paralyze the patient briefly to modify, or damp-down, the convulsion, which sometimes are so violent, that if unmodified, bones break. I gave the patient some oxygen to breathe, put a wooden 'bite block' between the teeth so as to protect the tongue from its own teeth during the convulsion and nodded to the psychiatrist to go ahead. After the convulsion and making sure the patient was breathing, we would move on to the next patient like a honey bee in a sunlit ecstasy buzzing from one cornflower to the next. Or, if you prefer, because the room was almost a circle, the second hand on a very large clock; it pauses before moving on to the next piece of time. 'My' nurse stayed with the patient until he or she showed signs of consciousness.

At that that time a new intravenous anesthetic agent, metho-hexital, had appeared. Patients recovered consciousness much more quickly than with Pentothal. Because at that time I came from an important London teaching hospital, I felt it my duty to introduce my country bumpkin psychiatrist colleague to the very latest in anesthesia. We would get through the morning's work more quickly and enjoy a long leisurely lunch.

The next week, full of high pride, off I went with my new magic. After the third patient 'my' nurse came running up to me.

"Please, doctor, please stop using that stuff," she pleaded.

"Why, what's wrong?" I asked. I'm sure there was some huffi-ness in my voice. 46 years later I apologize to that nurse.

"They're waking up so quickly, they want to go to the toilet or go home – immediately. I can't help you and them at the same time. With the Pentothal they snooze until we've done the whole circle."

There was one consolation. The young psychiatrist and I became friends. I always warn my new friends to be wary of me because I tend to manipulate them. One day I said to Dr. Head, the psychiatrist,

"Do you mind slowing down?'

He looked at me curiously. One day fast, one day slow. Another madman, he must have thought, but then of course that *was* his business. When you are a psychiatrist you learn to humor people whether they are dangerous or not.

"Of course I don't mind. As long as you tell me why."

I swore him to silence.

"If we don't get to the last of your patients until 1 o'clock, I can phone my boss at the Middlesex and legally tell him I'm going to be late for my afternoon orthopedic list. He'll find someone else and I can go to the library and study for my exams."

He must also have had a little genetic criminality because he agreed.

Maybe Freud had something with his theories about the relationship of subconscious activities and mental illness but so far as depression/melancholia is concerned I am convinced it's a load of junk. Depression is a derangement of chemical activity in the brain analogous for example, to an overactive thyroid gland. The proof is that in accurately diagnosed cases of depression/melancholia one or other of the antidepressants nearly always work. The problems that remain are the side-effects of the drugs.

Dr. Bernie always told me that my experiences as a child growing up in England during the Second World War were the trigger for my late-in-life depression. The war in England for a child was a time of freedom and excitement. One of my most pleasurable memories is having seen the steeple of Llandaff Cathedral, in the middle of a German bombing raid on Cardiff in South Wales in 1941, catch fire, bend and crack and topple flaming to the ground. For me it was a spectacular thrilling fireworks show, the very stuff of risk and entertainment.

Chapter 25 A BUNCH OF FLOWERS

One day in the Spring of 2003 I returned to the Mount Auburn Cemetery in Cambridge. This was not my regular annual visit to and chat with William Thomas Green Morton (WTGM) (1809 – 1868). Instead I had come to study and photograph his son Dr. William James Morton's (WJM) headstone standing to the left of and slightly behind his Dad's monument.

Nevertheless I followed my usual ritual which is to walk round all four sides of Willie's monument in a clockwise direction and read the inscription aloud to the birds. I always hope none of the gravediggers and gardeners can hear me.

Front face:
W.T.G. Morton
Inventor and Revealer
Of
Anesthetic Inhalation
Born August 9 1819
Died July 15 1868
Left side:
Before whom
In all time
Surgery was Agony
Rear face:
By whom
Pain in Surgery
Was Averted and Annulled
Right Side:
Since whom

Science has control
Of Pain
Erected by Citizens of Boston

You can park your car quite legally on Spruce Avenue and as I got out at gravesite no. 1399, where WTGM has lived in the basement since 1868, I was surprised by what I saw. Surprise is an inadequate word for what I felt and thought when I saw a bunch of flowers, not a bouquet, that someone had placed upright against the pedestal of the monument. I stood in helpless thought. Who could possibly have done *that?* Why would someone do that? I walked closer. The flowers were not fresh nor were they stale. I estimated they had been placed within the last 48 hours. Fortunately I had my trusty digital camera with me. I have the proof.

In my historical research on the Morton family, as far as I had at that date pursued it, I had concluded that WTGM had no descendants alive today. Could it have been placed by someone grateful for the anesthesia care she or he had received for a recent operation?

I neglected my original purpose, drove back to the main gate and visited Meg Winslow in her office. She is the Archivist for Mount Auburn Cemetery. She had helped me in my research by unearthing old and relevant documents.

"What brings you here today? she said.

"A bunch of flowers," I said, and explained.

Without hesitation she called all the gardeners, maintenance men and gravediggers who were at work that day, on their cellphones. None had seen anyone placing those flowers. In fact none of them, having driven by Morton's monument in their trucks had even noticed the flowers.

Only one observation about this event remains. On October 16 1846 William Thomas Green Morton, in public, in front of the leading Boston surgeons "caused a deep sleep." Two and a half thousand years earlier, as I have previously explained, the Lord God did it. Unfortunately, He/She never explained how.

Chapter 26 SURGERY BEFORE ANESTHESIA

Dr. John George Metcalf of Mendon, Massachusetts attended Harvard Medical in 1825 and kept a notebook of the lectures given by the three leading surgeons in Boston, Drs. John Collins Warren, Jacob Bigelow and Walter Channing. The notebook also served as Dr. Metcalf's diary. His entry for December 11 1825 describes his attendance at an operation performed at the Massachusetts General Hospital 20 years before William T.G. Morton's demonstration of ether to remove the pain of surgery. Dr. Metcalf's grammar may be poor but his observations are clear.

> = *Boston Dec. 11. 1825* =
> *Visited the Massachusetts General Hospital yesterday to witness the operation for Hare-Lip; but as Dr. Warren had only* (sic) *Seventeen Assistants with him in the Area, you may well suppose that those in the Gallery could not have any very distinct views of the operation. In fact the poor fellow of a patient, was so surrounded with Doctors that we should not have know what was going on had we not been told beforehand. We could only discover the steps of the operation by the cries of the patient. The first incision was announced by an outcry, and the succeeding steps were traced by cries and now and then a kick (,) of the patient by the operator.*

In 1813 Fanny Burney, an author and playwright born in England but married to a French nobleman discovered she had a cancer in her breast. She consulted a surgeon M. Dubois, who told her only hope of survival was to remove the breast.

He would consult M. Larrey, probably the leading surgeon in France as to the correctness of the decision. M. Larrey agreed and said he would attend the operation. Here is part of Fanny Burney's description of the operation, *without anesthesia*, in a letter to her cousin Esther:

My distress was, I suppose, apparent, though not my Wishes, for M. Dubois himself now softened, & spoke soothingly. Can You, I cried, feel for an operation that, to You, must seem so trivial? - Trivial? he repeated - taking up a bit of paper, which he tore, unconsciously, into a million of pieces, oui - cest peu de chose - mais ("Yes, it is a little thing, but...") - 'he stammered, & could not go on. No one else attempted to speak, but I was softened myself, when I saw even M. Dubois grow agitated, while Dr Larrey kept always aloof, yet a glance showed me he was pale as ashes. I knew not, positively, then, the immediate danger, but every thing convinced me danger was hovering about me, & that this experiment could alone save me from its laws. I mounted, therefore, unbidden, the Bed stead - & M. Dubois placed me upon the mattress, & spread a cambric handkerchief upon my face.

It was transparent, however, & I saw, through it, that the Bedstead was instantly surrounded by the 7 men & my nurse.

Fanny Burney sees the glitter of polished steel. She also see M. Dubois indicating the whole breast will have to be removed. She continues:

My dearest Esther, - & all my dears to whom she communicates this doleful ditty, will rejoice to hear that this resolution once taken, was firmly adhered to, in defiance of a terror that surpasses all description, & the most torturing pain. Yet - when the dreadful steel was plunged into the breast - cutting through veins - arteries - flesh - nerves - I needed no injunctions not to restrain my cries. I began a scream that lasted unintermittingly during the whole time of the incision - & I almost marvel that it rings not in my Ears still! so excruciating was the agony. When the wound was made, & the instrument was withdrawn, the pain seemed undiminished, for the air that suddenly rushed into those delicate parts felt like a mass of minute but sharp & forked poniards, that were tearing the edges of the wound - but when again I felt the instrument - describing a curve - cutting against the grain, if I may so say, while the flesh resisted in a manner so forcible as to oppose & tire the hand of the operator, who was forced to change from the right to the left - then, indeed, I thought I must have expired.

In her last paragraph she describes how the surgeon scraped the last "attoms" of the cancer from her ribs.

Chapter 27 EMAIL ADDRESS

My Email address is: Zeitlin4@COMCAST.net

This memoir has several strongly expressed opinions. I would like to hear well-supported arguments contradicting those opinions.

This memoir has many historical vignettes. I would like to hear about those that are inaccurate or plain wrong.

This memoir interprets some of the incidents I saw. I would like to hear whether or not these are misinterpretations.

This memoir tries to show what it's like to be spend your life as an anesthesiologist. I would like to hear of the experience of others.

ACKNOWLEDGEMENTS

Many friends, colleagues, teachers and family members helped and advised me while I assembled this book. I list them here in reverse alphabetical order. All my life, ever since I was christened I have been placed at the end of alphabetical lists. Now I will copy the Australians who publish maps of the world with Australia and New Zealand at the top.

Dr. David Zuck, Prof. Harry Zeitlin, Jonathan Henry Zeitlin, David Michael Zeitlin, Louise Zeitlin, Dr. Robert Wise, Dr. Rod Westhorpe, A.J.Wright, MLS, Lisa Waltuch, Dr. David Wilkinson, Dr. Malcolm Veidenheimer, the late Dr. Leroy Vandam, Dr. John Severinghaus, Michelle Seaton, the late Patrick Sim MLS, Benjamin Nico Stever-Zeitlin, Jill Stever-Zeitlin, Richard Stever-Zeitlin, Jonathan Sheldon Esq., Dr. Alan Sessler, Dr. Abraham Szmukler, Dr. Oliver Sacks, Whitney Scharer, Dr. David Shephard, Dr. Eliot Slater, Dr. Daniel Sessler, Dan Raemer PhD, Dr. Robert Roth, Dr. Michael Rudin, Dr. Henry Rosenberg, Dr. Tim Quinn, Prof. Karen Posner, Dr. Jim Philip, Marge Pothier, CRNA, the late Dr. Ellison C. Pierce, Jr., Prof. Allon Pratt, Susan and Ted O'Brien, Dr. John McCarthy, Dr. Alasdair McKenzie, Dr. James Michel, Dr. Stanley LeeSon, Sonya Larson, Prof. Michell Lynn-Sachs, Prof. Amy Kalmanovsky, Dr. Michael Kahn, Dr. James Jovenich, Rachel Howsmon, Andrew Howsmon, Dr. Tom Hutchinson, Drs. Carol and Alex Hannenberg, Prof. James Howsmon, Prof. Simon Gelman, Dr. Bennie Geffin, Diane Griliches, Dr. Michael Goerig, Dr. Jim Gessner, Dr. Gabriel Gurman, Dr. David Filer, Dr. George Flesh, Richard Elliott Friedman, Prof. Freddy Frankel, Dr. Michael Edwards, Dr. Fred Davis, Governor Michael Dukakis, Dr. Robert Caplan, Prof. Fred Cheney, Jeffrey Cooper, PhD,

Dr. Donald Caton, Dr. Muqi Chaudhry, Dr. William Camann, Christopher Castellani, Eve Bridburg, Lisa Borders, Dr. John Bucchiere, Dr. George Battit, Edward Brennan Esq., Joel Babb, Dr. Thomas B. Boulton, Dr. Douglas Bacon, Debra Braitt, Dr. Richard Blacher, Dr. Israel Abroms, Dr. Ted Alston, Beth Arnold, Dr. Neil Adams, Dr. Sidney Alexander. And, all my fellow students at Grub Street Writers, Boston.

SELECTED BIBLIOGRAPHY

I find I have collected about 200 books on the history, the culture and the science of anesthesia over a 50 year period. If you travel to the Wood Library Museum of Anesthesiolology at the headquarters of the American Society of Anesthesiologists in Park Ridge, Illinois you will find many more. Here are a few of my favorites with brief comments.

Caton, D. *What a Blessing She had Chloroform,* New Haven & London: Yale University Press 1999

This fascinating book delves into the controversies surrounding the use of anesthesia for childbirth. The title quotes Queen Victoria when she heard that her daughter Vicky had delivered her first baby in 1857. Please read it, particularly if you or someone in your family is pregnant.

Duncum, BM. *The Development of Inhalation Anaesthesia, the special reference to the years 1846 to 1900,* London, New York: Oxford University Press; 1947

Freidman, R. Elliott. *Who Wrote the Bible?* New York, NY: Harper 1987

I read a few books on the authorship of the Old Testament. I found this one the most convincing.

Eliot, TS. The Love Song of J. Alfred Prufrock. *Prufrock and Other Observations. In, Collected Poems,* London: Faber and Faber; 1917

I know almost nothing about the evolution of poetic style but it I have read that this poem changed it dramatically, perhaps analogous to Picasso's work in art - both of them somewhat mysterious. In my enthusiastic but amateurish way I try to solve the problems raised by the (famous) third line of 'Prufrock'.

Keys, TE, *The History of Surgical Anesthesia,* New York: Schuman's; 1946

This volume and the one by Barbara Duncum (above) are the classics of our history, both published immediately after the Second World War. Duncum's story ends in 1900 and Keys' book celebrates the first centennial of anesthesia, 1946.

Maltby, JR (Editor). *Notable Names in Anesthesia.* London, Royal Society of Medicne Press, 2002

An illuminating book about many of the great figures in our specialty. I mention some of them in my stories but Maltby and his Co-Editors bring them to life. It resembles a 'tasting' menu in a great restaurant!

Shephard, D. *From Craft to Specialty: A Medical and Social History and Its Changing Role in Health Care.* Thunder Bay, Ontario; York Point Publishing, 2009

This is the book I would have liked to have written. All I can do is tell stories.

Dr. Shephard has here written the very best book ever on what anesthesia is all about, its evolution to a sophisticated science, its place in the wider field of medicine and its role in society. For any researcher, whether medical or historical or just curious this book has the best Glossary of Terms, the best Bibliography and the most complete and relevant list of References.

Sykes, WS. *Essays on the First Hundred Years of Anaesthesia, Volumes 1, 2 and 3. Park Ridge, Il:* (reprinted by) Wood Library Museum of Anesthesiology; 1982

If some of the chapters in my book have not succeeded in scaring you about our past, just dip into any of Sykes's terrifying material; a tale of ignorance, sheer obstinacy and horror that surrounded the development of our specialty.

Thomas, KB. *The Development of Anaesthetic Apparatus,* Oxford and London; Blackwell Scientific, 1975

Sounds dreary but has fascinating illustrations and diagrams of what our predecessors struggled with and the patients had to tolerate.

Wolfe, RJ. *Tarnished Idol, William T.G. Morton and the Introduction of Surgical Anesthesia.* San Anselmo, California, Norman Publishing, 2001

As you know William T.G. Morton first publicly and successfully demonstrated ether's use as a surgical anesthetic in 1846. You would think he should be revered as an icon by us. In this book Wolfe conclusively shows us that Morton was a petty criminal and thief and his sole aim in demonstrating ether was to make more money – he spent the rest of his life trying to exploit it for gain.

Made in the USA
Charleston, SC
03 June 2012